OBSCURE SCRIBBLERS

OBSCURE SCRIBBLERS

A History of Parliamentary Journalism

ANDREW SPARROW

POLITICO'S

First published in Great Britain 2003 by
Politico's Publishing, an imprint of
Methuen Publishing Limited
215 Vauxhall Bridge Road
London SW1V 1EJ

1 3 5 7 9 10 8 6 4 2

A CIP catalogue record for this book is available from the British Library

ISBN 1 84275 061 5

Printed and bound in Great Britain by
St Edmundsbury Press

What we certainly know to have been done by him in this way was the Debates in both Houses of Parliament, under the name of 'The Senate of Lilliput', sometimes with feigned denominations of the several speakers, sometimes with denominations formed of the letters of their real names, in the manner of what is called anagram, so that they might easily be deciphered. Parliament then kept the press in a kind of mysterious awe, which made it necessary to have recourse to such devices. In our time it has acquired an unrestrained freedom, so that the people in all parts of the kingdom have a fair, open and exact report of the actual proceedings of their representatives and legislators, which in our constitution is highly to be valued; though, unquestionably, there has of late been too much reason to complain of the petulance with which obscure scribblers have presumed to treat men of the most respectable character and situation.

James Boswell, Life of Johnson, *1791*

To Anna

CONTENTS

Acknowledgements   ix
A Note to Readers   xi

Introduction: The First Press Corps   1
Chapter 1:   Printers Defy the Ban   7
Chapter 2:   The Gallery Becomes the Fourth Estate of the Realm   24
Chapter 3:   The Lobby Starts to Dominate   57
Chapter 4:   War, Deference and Responsibility   83
Chapter 5:   Secrecy and Openness: The 1960s and 1970s   120
Chapter 6:   Secrecy and Openness: The 1980s   151
Chapter 7:   Sleaze, Spin and Cynicism   178
Conclusion: 'Mutual Suspicion and Constant Hostility'   198

Notes   207
Bibliography   225
Index   229

ACKNOWLEDGEMENTS

This is *a* history of parliamentary journalism, not *the* history. I have been allowed to consult the records kept by the press gallery committee and the lobby committee but this is not an authorised book and I have been free to draw my own conclusions. I am grateful to all concerned for being so cooperative, particularly Ben Brogan and James Hardy, the press gallery secretary and lobby chairman respectively at the time I was doing my research. I would also like to thank Stella Thomas, the gallery's administrator until 2002, for letting me set up camp in her office for a while.

I also carried out research in the House of Lords Record Office, the Public Record Office, the British Library Newspaper Library, the London Library, the St Bride Printing Library, the Westminster Reference Library and the Telegraph reference library. I would like to record my thanks to the many helpful members of staff in these places who dealt with my enquiries.

I am particularly grateful to those people who agreed to be interviewed. They include: Ian Aitken, Adam Boulton, Colin Brown, David Butler, John Deans, Bill Deedes (Lord Deedes), Richard Evans, Joe Haines, David Hencke, Professor Peter Hennessy, David Holmes, Anthony Howard, David Hughes, Sir Bernard Ingham, Gordon Jackson, Frank Johnson, Sir Donald Maitland, Lord Marlesford (Mark Shreiber), Glyn Mathias, Sir Tom McCaffrey, Andy McSmith, Chris Moncrieff, Charles Moore, Ivor Owen and Michael White. Some of these people kindly lent me books or documents and I am especially grateful to them.

Among the other people who helped I would like to thank: Sir Nicolas Bevan, the Speaker's Secretary, and Mary Healey, in the Serjeant at Arms' office, for arranging permission for me to see some papers in the House of Lords Record Office; Professor Bob Franklin and Philip Cowley for sending me some of their academic articles; the Hansard Society and the Fabian Society for providing certain reports; the BBC and Sky for supplying cuttings, tapes and transcripts; and the various clerks and officials in the Commons and the Lords who answered my questions.

I owe a big debt to my fellow journalists. Since I joined the press gallery in 1994 I have spent many hours arguing, gossiping and moaning about parliamentary journalism and this book could not have been written if I had not had that background. I started in the lobby working for Thomson Regional Newspapers and then the *Western Mail*, but I have spent most of my time working for the *Daily Mail*, with David Hughes as political editor, and the *Daily Telegraph*, with George Jones as political editor. I have learnt a huge amount about politics and journalism on both papers and I would like to record my gratitude to my various colleagues over the years. At the *Telegraph* I would also like to thank everyone who has been tolerant and encouraging while I have been busy with the book.

Writing for Politico's has been a pleasure and I am grateful to Iain Dale for backing the idea with enthusiasm right from the start and to Sean Magee, the book's editor, for his endless wise counsel along the way. I was particularly pleased that Peter Riddell, Professor Colin Seymour-Ure, Robert Shrimsley and Christopher Silvester agreed to read the manuscript, either in whole or in part. They identified errors and suggested additions and as a result they improved the book. Needless to say, any mistakes that have crept through are entirely my own responsibility. Anyone who would like to take up any of the issues in the following pages can contact me at: andrewsparrow@rozelroad.freeserve.co.uk

Finally, I must thank my family. I would not have been able to finish on time had it not been for the willingness of Kate's grandparents, Roger and Daphne, and Eddie and Yvonne, to do more than their fair share of childminding. But it was my wife, Anna, who had to put up with the real burden. She remained thoroughly supportive, even though the project distracted me for the best part of a year. My book is dedicated to her with love.

A NOTE TO READERS

My approach is broadly chronological. As a rough guide, Chapter 1 runs from the 1600s to 1771, Chapter 2 from 1771 to the 1890s, Chapter 3 from the 1870s to 1939, Chapter 4 from 1939 to 1964, Chapter 5 from 1964 to 1979, Chapter 6 from 1979 to 1990 and Chapter 7 from 1990 to the present day. But where it has made sense to tackle subjects thematically, I have done so, and as a result some events crop up out of sequence. The section headings within chapters should make it clear where this happens. In quoted material, spellings and occasionally punctuation have been modernised. For the sake of simplicity, I have referred to individuals throughout by the names and titles they had at the point where they first appeared in the narrative. This means that various knighthoods and peerages have gone unrecognised. If anyone minds, I'm sorry.

INTRODUCTION

The First Press Corps

I think that those who report politics, and by and large that's members of that parliamentary group of journalists called the lobby, I think they are a very inward-looking, very incestuous bunch of people, who are overly preoccupied with process rather than policies.

Peter Mandelson, 9 April 2002

On 31 December 1798 William Windham delivered one of the most reactionary attacks on the press ever made by a member of a British Cabinet. The House of Commons was sitting, the country was fighting France, and Windham, a brilliant, waspish orator, was Secretary at War. Parliamentary reporting, he said, was 'an evil in its nature'. It was to blame for the naval mutiny in 1797, and in other countries newspapers had contributed to the overthrow of governments. 'That newspaper writers were not the best judges of political affairs he considered as an undisputed point.' Yet Parliament had now got itself into a position where views that were not supposed to be heard outside its doors were being circulated among the lower orders. 'For the great mass of the readers of newspapers were not the most discerning class of society . . . [Newspapers] were carried everywhere, read everywhere, by persons of very inferior capacities, and in common alehouses and places frequented chiefly by those who were least of all accustomed to reflection, to any great mental efforts.' As a result, 'the most rank sedition that was ever yet thought of' was being spread across the country. Then Windham invited his fellow Members, when considering whether parliamentary reporting should continue, to ask themselves the following question:

How much of the talents of those who wrote for newspapers had been employed in scattering poison wherever they could; in bringing virtue into discredit, by telling the people everywhere that those who professed it, and who ought to possess it, and who in general did possess virtue, had no virtue whatever, by teaching the ignorant and the credulous to despise every man and every measure that was respectable. Such were the efforts, generally speaking, of those who wrote for newspapers.

Windham said that he could not look at a man 'of a low condition with a newspaper in his hand' without comparing him to 'a man who was swallowing poison under the hope of improving his health'.[1]

As Windham spoke, there were reporters in the public gallery straining to hear what he said. Within the previous thirty years the Commons had given up trying to ban newspapers from covering its debates and at the time there was a small, but competitive, pool of men who specialised in parliamentary reporting. Windham's attempts to persuade the House to bring back censorship failed (although the newspapers later succeeded in censoring Windham, by not reporting him) and over the following years the reporters established themselves as a permanent fixture at Westminster. Most politicians since Windham have been more accommodating , but the practice of regarding reporters with disdain – as 'obscure scribblers', or whatever – has persisted.

This was apparent two hundred years later, when a Labour government was in power, Parliament and the media had changed enormously – and MPs were still complaining about the attitude of the political reporters. Peter Mandelson, for example, (like Windham, a press gallery bogeyman) spoke about relations with the press in a long television interview in April 2002. 'I think that those who report politics, and by and large that's members of that parliamentary group of journalists called the lobby, I think they are a very inward-looking, very inces-tuous bunch of people, who are overly preoccupied with process rather than policies.' As a result, he said, 'we're not getting the coverage of politics that the voters deserve.'[2] At the time the Government was going through one of its periodic crises in relations with the media, and it was common to hear Labour politicians complain about the alleged inadequacies of the lobby. In the eigh-teenth century political reporters were accused of spreading sedition; by the beginning of the twenty-first, press responsibility was still an issue, but now they were accused of spreading cynicism.

This book is about the reporters who are supposedly at the root of all this trouble, the ones who have covered politics from Parliament. It is not a comprehensive guide to relations between politicians and the press. It is not even a history of all political journalism; some, perhaps most, of the best journalism about politics has been produced by people who have had very little contact with the Houses of Parliament. This is a book about the people who have worked in the press gallery. They have not necessarily been as powerful as their editors and proprietors, but for more than two centuries they have been the people who, day in, day out, have had the job of telling the public what Parliament and the Government have been doing.

I am a political correspondent myself and, in writing a history of this kind, I suppose I am behaving in exactly the kind of inward-looking way that Mandelson deplores. At any one time the number of political journalists working in Parliament has been relatively small, and most of them have known one another. But their story is an important one, politically and journalistically. Parliamentary reporting contributed to the democratisation of Britain. The House of Commons tried to stop the publication of debate reports for more than a hundred years not because Members were shy about having their names in the papers, but because they realised that being reported would make them accountable. This was understood very clearly at the time. Windham, indeed, explained in his 1798 speech that debate reporting would transform the system of government from a representative one into something more sinister. 'What was the natural effect of such publication?' he asked.

> It must be that of changing the present form of government, and of making it democratical; for it was calling every day on the public to judge of the proceedings of Parliament. By these daily publications the people were taught to look upon themselves as present at the discussion of Parliament, and sitting in judgment on them.

Or, to put it another way, publishing debates was 'an appeal from the representative body, to the people at large out of doors, of all orders, from the highest to the lowest'.[3]

The early parliamentary correspondents were just as significant in the history of journalism. According to one academic, the men who started turning up at the Commons in the reign of George III to cover the debates were perhaps the first full-time newspaper reporters, and collectively they may have formed the world's first press corps.[4] At the end of the eighteenth century, several British newspapers were launched largely in response to the public demand for reports from Parliament. In the nineteenth century, covering debates was one of the main functions of a newspaper and, when Parliament was sitting, the gallery reporters were expected to fill the paper; in recess, they were required to use their reporting skills elsewhere. Then, in the twentieth century, gallery reporting (taking an accurate shorthand note of a speech and writing it up almost verbatim) largely died out. Instead, most political reporters concentrated on lobby journalism, so-called because it involves gathering political news by talking to MPs in the Members' lobby in the Commons. This book is largely about those two traditions. But there are other forms of political journalism practised at Westminster – sketch writing, Whitehall investigative reporting and column writing – and they are included too. Broadcasting is also covered, not least because it has had a huge effect on the way newspaper journalism operates.

Given that gallery reporting and lobby journalism are so different, it is easy to see why people have treated the two activities quite separately. In 1913, when Michael MacDonagh wrote *The Reporters' Gallery* (the last full-length history of the press gallery), he devoted just one of fifty chapters to the lobby. More recently the lobby has grabbed almost all the attention. For a long time the lobby journalists themselves upheld this rigid demarcation. In a prototype rulebook drawn up in 1945, Guy Eden, the lobby secretary, said that members should not use quotes in their stories because that would reduce lobbying to 'mere reporting'.[5] That is the point at which the lobby probably started to go wrong.

When I began researching the subject, I was slightly worried that I would end up with half a book about the gallery, half a book about the lobby and an uneasy join somewhere *circa* 1930. To some extent I have. But the two forms of journalism have more in common than one might assume. In the eighteenth century, reporters often could not get into the public gallery and, to find out what was said in a debate, they had to work their contacts just like a modern lobby correspondent. Even when the gallery reporters were formally admitted, they had no right to hear what was happening in the chamber and were liable to be excluded if a Member objected. Journalists given permission to be in the lobby were made to feel that they, too, had been granted a privilege rather than a right. This partly explains why the lobby correspondents became so secretive. The reporters had to conceal the source of their stories because MPs could not stomach the idea that the press was getting information from the Government before them.

In other words, what the gallery reporters and the lobby correspondents have had in common is that they have both had difficult relations with

Parliament. One of the oddities of British politics is that while the political parties have been quite sophisticated in their approach to the media, Parliament (which is full of party politicians) has been conservative and cack-handed. The key event was supposed to have taken place in 1771, when the Commons gave up trying to stop the publication of debates, but in fact that was only an admission of defeat, rather than an acceptance that proceedings should be reported. 'The press, constitutionally and historically, is here on suffer-ance,' Sir Barnett Cocks, Clerk of the House, told journalists in the early 1960s, and he was right.[6] Accommodation problems have illustrated this; to secure more space, the reporters had to rely on some dimwit labourers burning the place down in 1834 and the *Luftwaffe* carrying out its own remodelling work in 1941. But accommodation is largely irrelevant. The real issue is whether Parliament accepts that journalists have a right to report what MPs are doing. In theory the answer is yes, but as recently as 1986 the Commons came close to voting to ban a journalist from the premises for six months for publishing a story based on a select committee leak. The proposal was supported by otherwise sensible people like John Biffen and Peter Shore, and defeated by only thirty-four votes. More recently, the House voted to exclude the press and sit in private for nearly an hour in December 2001. It is hard to get indignant about an event that took place after midnight during a debate that would never have been reported anyway. Nevertheless, the fact that the rules allowed it to happen suggests that the conflicts of the eighteenth century have not been entirely resolved.

Although 1771 is a key date in the history of the press gallery, it is not the only one. This book was written to coincide with the bicentenary events taking place in 2003. The press gallery is fond of centenaries; it celebrates one roughly every twenty years. In April 1932 it held a dinner to celebrate the hundredth anniver-sary of the opening of the reporters' gallery in the House of Lords (in December 1831). That was the first gallery constructed for the benefit of the press. In 1952 the press gallery's annual dinner was used to celebrate the centenary of Charles Barry's new House of Commons, including the facilities for reporters incorpo-rated as part of the design. In 1981 there was another event to commemorate the creation of the press gallery committee a hundred years earlier. And in 1984 the lobby held its own centenary lunch, even though the anniversary was bogus because the lobby list originated in the 1870s. The 2003 bicentenary relates to the moment when the Speaker first ruled that seats in the public gallery should be reserved for reporters. It is easy to mock this anniversaryitis, which could be held up as evidence that political correspondents have short memories (some of them do). But it is also a tribute to journalism's genius for manufacturing significance. And, in this case, it has inspired a book which otherwise would probably not have been written.

ONE

Printers Defy the Ban

I agree with the gentleman ... a stop should be put to the practice which has been so justly complained of. I think no appeals should be made to the public with regard to what is said in this assembly, and to print or publish the speeches of gentlemen in this House, even though they were not misrepresented, looks very like making them accountable without doors for what they say within.

William Pulteney, House of Commons, 13 April 1738

Johnson told me that as soon as he found that the speeches were thought genuine, he determined that he would write no more of them; for 'he would not be accessory to the propagation of falsehood'.

James Boswell, Life of Johnson, *1791*

For this purpose they employed one Wall, who went down to the House of Commons every evening, to pick up what he could in the lobby, in the coffee houses etc. It was impossible he should be accurate; however by perseverance and habit, and sometimes by getting admission into the gallery, he improved.

John Almon, Memoirs of John Almon, *1790*

High Indignities: To 1738

Parliament has existed for at least seven hundred years and for the first half of its life it was in the happy position of not having to worry about the press. The House of Commons had a Speaker, a Serjeant at Arms and other paraphernalia that survive today before the printing press had even been invented. That is not to say that those ruling through Parliament did not have to worry about being held to account. There were people in the system who were variously critical, sycophantic, abusive, gullible or unforgiving, sometimes well-informed and sometimes woefully ignorant, but nevertheless pumping out a running commentary on the affairs of the state and claiming (on fairly dubious grounds) to be representing the population at large as they did so. They were, of, course, the Members.

Print journalism did not start to evolve until the early seventeenth century, and its arrival broadly coincided with Parliament consolidating its position as a political force in its own right. The oldest surviving 'newspaper' printed in England was produced in 1621. It was a newsbook, or coranto, published weekly and modelled on similar publications being produced in Amsterdam, where the news industry was more advanced. Printers needed a licence and they were allowed to publish only news from abroad. But that did not mean that Parliament went totally unreported. In 1625 Charles I took the throne and relations between the monarch and the legislature, which were not exactly smooth under his predecessor, grew ever more rancorous. There was considerable interest in what was happening in both the Commons and the Lords, and in the late 1620s enterprising news merchants began to sell accounts of parliamentary proceedings. Their reports were copied by hand by commercial scriveners and sent to private subscribers. The numbers involved were relatively small, but, in the words of Simon Schama, the writers were responsible for something quite profound: 'the creation of a public sphere of politics, the birth, in fact, of English public opinion'.[1] For the first time, unofficial, written news about political events in the capital was being systematically dispersed across the country.

It was a subversive operation. The newsletters may have read like a seventeenth-century *Hansard*, but there was a long-established convention that parliamentary proceedings should be kept secret, and the reports were more a form of Stuart samizdat. Writing about procedure in the Commons around 1560, John Hooker said: 'Every person of the Parliament ought to keep secret, and not to disclose the secrets and things done and spoken in the Parliament House, to any manner [of] person, unless he be one of the same House, upon pain to be sequestered out of the House, or otherwise punished.'[2] Members enforced the ruled to stop the Sovereign from finding out what they were saying, which they were keen to do because Members could be, and were, arrested for seditious language. At around the same time as the first parliamentary newsletters were being written, the Commons started to take action against unauthorised disclosure of its proceedings. The first case mentioned in the

Commons Journals relates to 1626 when a scrivener, 'one Turnor, dwelling without Westminster door', sold a copy of the Remonstrance from the Commons before it had been presented to the King. 'The Serjeant sent for him, but answer brought he was not within.'[3] Two years later the Commons launched an (apparently unsuccessful) investigation into 'a book in print concerning some proceedings in Parliament'.[4] It was the first recorded attempt to take action against a publication for reporting debates.

Charles I ruled without Parliament in the 1630s, but he summoned it again in 1640 and, with the Civil War looming, the Commons became the focus for a flurry of journalistic activity. The abolition of the Star Chamber in 1641 put an end to press licensing, and printers were quick to exploit their new freedom. Newsbooks with reports relating to domestic affairs started appearing on the streets regularly for the first time. Ignoring its own rules, the Long Parliament allowed the publication of accounts of its own activities as a propaganda exercise in its struggle against the King. But the Commons was highly selective with regard to press freedom and in 1641 it resolved that 'no Member of the House shall either give a copy, or publish in print, anything that he shall speak here, without leave of the House.' This was in response to Lord Digby, who had printed a copy of a speech he had delivered in the chamber; fellow parliamentarians did not approve, and the Commons resolved that Digby's speech should be 'burnt publicly by the hands of the common hangman'.[5] In 1642, when Sir Edward Dering published a collection of his parliamentary speeches, the hangman was ordered to arrange another bonfire. Dering was also expelled from the House and imprisoned in the Tower for acting 'against the honour and privilege of the House'.[6]

After the Restoration in 1660, strict controls were again imposed on the press. The Licensing Act was passed in 1662 'for preventing the frequent abuses in printing seditious, treasonable, and unlicensed books and pamphlets, and for regulating of printing and printing presses',[7] and for the next thirty years newspapers were subject to pre-publication censorship. Debate reporting was not allowed and Parliament's relations with the Sovereign were still characterised by mutual mistrust. The Commons took a small step towards openness in 1680 when it decided to print the *Votes* of the House. The following year the order was amended so that the *Votes and Proceedings* were published. But these reports listed only the motions carried, not the arguments used or individual votes cast on either side. Secrecy was still paramount.

In theory, the Glorious Revolution and the Bill of Rights should have made a difference. After William and Mary agreed a settlement that emphasised the primacy of Parliament, there was no longer any need for the Commons to keep them out of earshot. At around the same time, in 1695, the licensing system collapsed because it was becoming impossible for the censors to cope with the large volume of material going into print. This led to rapid expansion in the newspaper industry, with more than twenty titles on sale in London at the start of the eighteenth century. Parliament should have been an obvious source of material. But after years of trying so hard to avoid sharing its thoughts with the Crown, Parliament was not minded to start revealing them to the press. There was no actual change in policy. The rule against disclosing what was said in the chamber had been in force for years, and the Commons was only doing what it had always done. But the context was changing, and a rule that had been consistent with Parliament being on the side of the people (against the King) was starting to look as if it had been dreamed up because Parliament was against them.

One of the first reporters to get into trouble with the Commons after 1688 was John Dyer, the author of a newsletter that covered events in Parliament. Dyer was perceived as a Jacobite propagandist and 1693 he was accused of writing 'false news' and 'seditious news against the Government'.[8] In December 1694 there was a complaint in the Commons that Dyer had 'presumed in his newsletter to take notice of the proceedings in the House'.[9] He was seized by the Serjeant at Arms, summoned to the Bar of the House, required to apologise and fined (or, technically, made to pay the Serjeant a fee for detaining him). This happened to him several more times, and on other occasions, when the Serjeant was ordered to seize him, Dyer absconded. He was not alone; other contemporary newsletter writers were summoned to the Bar for similar offences. The situation was sufficiently serious for the House to pass a resolution specifically banning newsletter writers from 'intermeddling' with the affairs of the Commons.[10]

The parliamentary coverage in newsletters was sporadic; for the first regular coverage of events in the Commons and the Lords, eighteenth-century readers had to turn to monthly magazines . The pioneer was a French author and pamphleteer called Abel Boyer, who in January 1711 started publishing the *Political State of Great Britain*, a periodical that reported parliamentary debates and other current affairs in the form of a pretend letter to a friend in Holland. He was cautious about identifying speakers, and his reports used formulae like Mr P—y, or Lord H—x. Two months after the *Political State* was launched, the Lords ruled that its publication was contrary to a standing order of the House. Boyer was gaoled for six days, forced to apologise and fined. But thereafter both the Commons and the Lords left Boyer alone and he was allowed to carry on publishing unhindered. Writing in 1729, he said that he had not received complaints because he had always proceeded with 'caution and circumspection'.[11] Boyer prided himself on his impartiality, and this may have protected him. Members did not seem to object to his reportage, and indeed many supplied him with copies of their speeches.

The *Political State* carried on for some years after Boyer's death in 1729 and in the following decade two important rival magazines were founded. The most influential was the *Gentleman's Magazine, or Monthly Intelligencer*, launched by Edward Cave. A cobbler's son, Cave had a senior job in the Post Office and his work brought him into contact with Parliament. He was able to find out what was being said in the chamber and in 1725 he started sending out a Dyer-style newsletter to subscribers. The *Gloucester Journal* was one recipient and in 1728 its printer, Robert Raikes, was summoned to the Bar of the Commons to explain why he had ignored the ban on parliamentary reporting. (His offence was to publish a short paragraph about a debate on the national debt.) When he appeared before the House, Raikes said his information was supplied by Cave, and Cave was subsequently called to the Bar as well. He was held in custody for nearly two weeks and released only after apologising and paying his fine. The experience did not put him off journalism and in 1731 he started the *Gentleman's Magazine*. A year later Thomas Astley set up the *London Magazine* in competition. Both publications reported debates, but they did so tentatively. 'We don't pretend to give the very words of every speech, but we hope we have done justice to the arguments on each side,' said an early edition of the *Gentleman's Magazine*.[12] Sometimes the names of speakers were not given at all; sometimes they were disguised with dashes being used instead of middle letters, as Boyer had done. Both magazines lifted speeches from the *Political State*, but they also engaged in their own newsgathering. This became essential after the *Political State* folded in 1737. Members of the public could get into the Commons and the Lords to listen to debates and, according to one account, Cave would do much of the reporting himself.

> His method of proceeding is variously reported, but I have been informed by some who were much about him that, taking with him a friend or two, he found means to procure for them and himself admission into the gallery of the House of Commons, or to some concealed station in the other, and that then they privately took down notes of the several speeches, and the general tendency and substance of the arguments. Thus furnished, Cave and his associates would adjourn to a neighbouring tavern and compare and adjust their notes, by means whereof, and the help of their memories, they became

enabled at least to fix the substance of what they had lately heard and remarked.[13]

The *London Magazine* often reported debates before Cave did, and it sometimes complained that he lifted his material straight from its pages. But the *Gentleman's Magazine* sold more and, with its circulation rising to fifteen thousand copies a month, Cave became a wealthy man.

The two magazines were able to get away with their reporting activities because the Commons was wary about enforcing its own rules. They also benefited from the fact that they tended to report speeches in the recess, long after they were delivered in the House, and there was some uncertainty as to whether the ban on reporting debates still applied at that stage. But in 1738 the Commons struck back, declaring that printing speeches was outlawed even in the recess and that offenders could expect a severe punishment. The debate, which took place on 13 April, was provoked by Cave's publishing a speech before it had been delivered (in modern terms, breaking an embargo). It was an important occasion, because it required Members to explain and justify a reporting ban that was starting to look anachronistic. At least one contemporary was prepared to take no notice of the Commons' resolution and an account of what was said survives in a collection of debates compiled by Richard Chandler.

The Speaker, Arthur Onslow, opened the debate holding a newspaper in his hands, which, he complained, contained 'his Majesty's answer to their late address, before it had been reported from the chair'. He wanted to bring the matter to the attention of the House because the newspapers had 'of late . . . run into very great abuses' and he hoped the Commons would find some way of dealing with the matter.[14] Sir William Yonge followed, and he too had observed that accounts of debates were regularly printed and circulated through the town and the country. 'At the same time there are often gross misrepresentations, both of the sense and language of gentlemen. This is very liable to give the public false impressions both of gentlemen's conduct and abilities.'[15] Thomas Winnington said that the House of Lords had recently punished printers, 'not because their words or meaning were misrepresented, but because they conceived it to be an indignity done to them as a House of Parliament', and that the Commons should do the same.

> If we do not put a speedy stop to this practice, it will be looked upon without doors that we have no power to do it, for the public will justly think that if we had such a power, we would exercise it. And then, Sir, what will be the conse-

quence? Why, Sir, you will have every word that is spoken here by gentlemen misrepresented by fellows who thrust themselves into our gallery. You will have the speeches of this House every day printed, even during your session. And we shall be looked upon as the most contemptible assembly on the face of the earth.[16]

William Pulteney, the leader of the Tory opposition, spoke next and articulated particularly clearly the case against disclosure.

I think no appeals should be made to the public with regard to what is said in this assembly, and to print or publish the speeches of gentlemen in this House, even though they were not misrepresented, looks very like making them accountable without doors for what they say within. Besides, Sir, we know very well that no man can be so guarded in his expressions as to wish to see everything he says in this House in print. I remember the time when this House was so jealous, so cautious of doing anything that might look like an appeal to their constituents, that not even the *Votes* were printed without leave.[17]

The debate was wound up by Sir Robert Walpole, the Prime Minister. He described the press reporting of debates as 'a forgery of the worst kind' because the newspapers misrepresented the work of Parliament to the nation as a whole.

I have read some debates of this House, Sir, in which I have been made to speak the very reverse of what I meant. I have read others of them wherein all the wit, the learning, and the argument has been thrown on one side, and on the other nothing but what was low, mean, and ridiculous. And yet when it comes to the question, the division has gone against the side which upon the face of the debate had reason and justice to support it. So that, Sir, had I been a stranger to the proceedings and to the nature of the arguments themselves, I must have thought this to have been one of the most contemptible assemblies on the face of the earth.

He claimed that he 'very seldom' read the offending magazines. But that did not stop him confidently asserting that he had particular cause to feel hard done by. 'No Government, I will venture to say, ever punished so few libels, and no Government ever had provocation to punish so many.'[18]

There is a familiar ring to all this: the press 'getting worse', the minister saying he doesn't take much notice, but still (not surprisingly) having read enough to know that it is all grossly unfair, etc. It is impossible to know how reliable Chandler's ten-page account of the debate is. But assuming it is at least broadly accurate, three features stand out. First, Members did not see the issue as one of press freedom. Most of them claimed they were in favour of the idea. 'Not that I should be attacking the liberty of the press; that is a point I would be as tender of as any gentlemen in this House,' said Yonge.[19] 'I hope we never shall stretch our privilege so as to cramp the freedom of writing on public affairs,' said Pulteney.[20]

Second, they tended to think that if the House was to be reported, it would inevitably be misreported. According to Chandler, there were five main speakers. Only one, Sir William Wyndham, seriously advanced the argument that the Commons should punish newspapers for publishing reports that were misleading, but not ones that were accurate. 'I have indeed seen many speeches of gentlemen in this House that were fairly and accurately taken, and no gentleman, when that is the case, ought to be ashamed that the world should know every word he speaks in this House,' he said. Wyndham went further, and offered Members a novel constitutional proposition.

> The other consideration that weighs very much, Sir, with me upon this occasion is the prejudice which the public will think they sustain by being deprived of all knowledge of what passes in this House, otherwise than by the printed *Votes*, which are very lame and imperfect for satisfying their curiosity of knowing in what manner their representatives act within doors . . . Nay, Sir, I must go further: I don't know but they may have a right to know somewhat more of the proceedings of this House than what appears upon your *Votes*. And if I were sure that the sentiments of gentlemen were not misrepresented, I should be against our coming to any resolution that could deprive them of a knowledge that is so necessary for their being able to judge the merits of their representatives within doors.[21]

Wyndham was not persuasive. According to Chandler's account, none of the other speakers was interested in discussing the idea that there might be a 'right to know'. The House sided with Walpole and Pulteney, and it passed the following resolution:

> That it is a high indignity to, and a notorious breach of the privilege of this House for any news-writer, in letters or other papers, (as minutes or under any other denomination) or for any printer or publisher, of any printed newspaper

of any denomination, to presume to insert in the said letters or papers, or to give therein any account of the debates, or other proceedings of this House, or any committee thereof, as well during the recess as the sitting of Parliament; and that this House will proceed with the utmost severity against such offenders.[22]

This resolution was enforced for another thirty-three years. As a statement of institutional prejudice, it was even more potent because Parliament's gut suspicion of and hostility towards the press (and, from the twentieth century, the broadcast media too) was to last much longer. Members strongly objected to the idea of being reported.

And the third point to make is that it was the opponents of parliamentary reporting who seemed to have the clearest understanding of the issues at stake. 'To print or publish the speeches of gentlemen in this House, even though they were not misrepresented, looks very like making them accountable without doors for what they say within'. Pulteney realised that it was not just a question of embarrassment or inconvenience; if parliamentarians were reported, they would become accountable, and if they became accountable, the balance of power between Parliament and the public would shift. No wonder most of them seemed to think 'utmost severity' appropriate.

Samuel Johnson and Having to Make it Up

In 1770 or thereabouts, Samuel Johnson attended a dinner party. The host was Samuel Foote, a playwright and society wit, and he had assembled around his table some of the celebrity conversationalists of the time: Arthur Murphy, another playwright and actor; Alexander Wedderburn, a lawyer, politician and future Lord Chancellor; Dr Philip Francis, a renowned classical scholar; and Dr Johnson himself, who, as 'Dictionary' Johnson, was at the height of his fame as a literary sage. The talk turned to politics, and a debate that had taken place at the end of Sir Robert Walpole's administration; Dr Francis said that the speech delivered on that occasion by William Pitt (the Elder) was the best he had ever read. He had spent eight years studying Demosthenes, but the Greek orator was no match for Pitt.

Many of the company remembered the debate; and some passages were cited, with the approbation and applause of all present. During the ardour of conversation, Johnson remained silent. As soon as the warmth of praise subsided, he opened with these words: 'That speech I wrote in a garret in Exeter Street.'[23]

Johnson explained that, when he was working for Edward Cave on the *Gentleman's Magazine*, he wrote up the debates having been told just a few details about who spoke and what their main arguments were. Those around the table praised his eloquence and impartiality. 'That is not quite true,' said Johnson. 'I saved appearances tolerably well, but I took care that the Whig dogs should not have the best of it.'[24]

Johnson had evidently managed to conceal his short career as a parliamentary reporter very effectively. His first work for the *Gentleman's Magazine*, some Latin poetry, was published in the issue for March 1738. He appears to have contributed to the debates from that year, but he was the sole author of them for less than three years, writing up the speeches delivered between November 1740 and February 1743. Consequently he was working at a time when Cave and his rival publisher were working under the threat of the Commons resolution to punish reporters with 'the utmost severity' – which explains at least in part why that facet of his career was kept secret.

Parliament did not stop the *London Magazine* and the *Gentleman's Magazine* reporting debates, but it forced them to adopt camouflage. The *London Magazine* was the first to unveil its solution. After Parliament was prorogued in the spring of 1738, its May edition came out with a new feature, the 'Proceedings of a Political Club'. It was introduced in the form of a letter from the secretary of the club, who wrote: 'As it is now rendered unsafe for you to entertain the public with any account of the proceedings or debates of those who rule over us, it may be thought not altogether improper to substitute in its stead the journals of a political and learned club of young noblemen and gentlemen established some time ago here in London.'[25] The speakers were given classical names, like M Tullius Cicero (Walpole) and M Cato (Pulteney), although no explanation as to who was who was given until four years later. Readers had to guess, or rely on word of mouth.

When the *Gentleman's Magazine* started its reports, it disguised them as Debates in the Senate of Magna Lilliputia (pretending that they came from Gulliver's grandson after a return voyage to Lilliput). The code here was easier to follow: the House of Clinab was the Commons, Sir Rubs Waleup was Walpole and so on. But neither system was ideal. Writing in 1790, John Almon, a printer and pioneering parliamentary reporter in his own right, complained that the disguises used in the Johnson era rendered the debate reports 'almost unintelligible to everybody, but those persons who were conversant in this kind of writing'.[26] To reduce the chance of causing offence, the two magazines continued to publish their proceedings only in the recess, as they had done before the 1738 clampdown. The strategy seemed to work, because the reports were tolerated by Parliament.

Originally William Guthrie, a talented critic and historian, wrote the *Gentleman's Magazine* reports, using information that either he or someone else had picked up around the Commons and the Lords. When Johnson started working for Cave, his first job was just to polish Guthrie's prose. Later he took complete charge of the writing. Cave tried to get Members to cooperate, and would write asking them to correct mistakes in his draft debate reports, or urging them to send him a copy of a speech to allow the *Gentleman's Magazine* to correct a false account appearing somewhere else. But sometimes Johnson had nothing more to go on than a list of who the speakers were on each side during a debate. This seems to have been the case with the Pitt speech. Pitt, who was speaking against a Bill extending the powers of press gangs, was at the time just thirty-three. Taunted by Horatio Walpole, the Prime Minister's brother, about his youth and inexperience, Pitt (thanks to Johnson's imagination) hit back with a speech that subsequently made it into anthologies of great oratory. It began:

> The atrocious crime of being a young man, with which the honourable gentleman has with such spirit and decency charged upon me, I shall neither attempt to palliate or deny, but content myself with wishing that I may be one of those whose follies may cease with their youth, and not of the number who are ignorant in spite of experience.[27]

Johnson was able to churn this kind of material out – longhand, of course – at the rate of three columns, or around a thousand words, an hour: faster than any other element of his literary output. Some of Johnson's reports did broadly reproduce the arguments made by individual speakers. But others, like that of Pitt's speech, were entirely made up; or were true only in the sense that they reflected what Pitt, or someone else, might like to have said. Readers had no way of telling the difference. Interestingly, in the light of Johnson's jibe about the 'Whig dogs', bias was not one of his main faults. In his writing he explored the arguments on both sides of an issue.[28] That made him exemplary as an essayist. But even-handedness is not the same as veracity, and as a reporter he was entirely unreliable.

Johnson himself never claimed otherwise. In its February 1743 edition, the *Gentleman's Magazine* announced that one of its debate reports was deemed to be so important that it had been translated into French, Spanish and Dutch. The author was mortified. 'Johnson told me that as soon as he found that the speeches were thought genuine, he determined that he would write no more of

them; for "he would not be accessory to the propagation of falsehood",' Boswell
wrote.[29] Later, Johnson expressed regret for what he had done. When he learned
that Tobias Smollett was writing a history of England, he warned him not to use
the reports in the *Gentleman's Magazine* because they could not be believed; and,
shortly before dying, he discussed the matter with his friend, John Nichols. 'He
said that the parliamentary debates were the only part of his writings which then
gave him any compunction: but that at the time he wrote them, he had no
conception that he was imposing upon the world . . . the mere coinage of his own
imagination,' Nichols recalled.[30] Among his other distinctions, Johnson deserves
to be singled out as one of the few writers in the history of British journalism to
have been embarrassed by the fact that people actually believed what he wrote.

'Little Cocking George' and his Battle with the Printers: To 1771

Samuel Johnson may have contributed to the history of debate reporting, but it
is hard to see him as a true prototype for the parliamentary or political correspondent. According to contemporaries, he never even visited the House of
Commons, or if he did go, it was only once.[31] He was not employed as a news-
gatherer. If one had to identify the first recognisable member of the press gallery,
someone who was reporting contemporary debates for a newspaper, and doing
so in a way that would be familiar to journalists two hundred years later, an
obvious candidate would be the bookseller and printer John Almon. Certainly, in
his memoirs (written in the third person), he claims the credit for inventing
parliamentary reporting. He says he was inspired by two events of 1768: the
election of the radical John Wilkes in Middlesex, which the Commons refused
to recognise; and a riot which ended with several of Wilkes's supporters being
shot dead by soldiers.

> When the spirit of the nation was raised high by the massacre in St George's
> Fields, the unjust decision upon the Middlesex election etc, Mr Almon
> resolved to make the nation acquainted with the proceedings of Parliament:
> for this purpose, he employed himself sedulously, in obtaining from different
> gentlemen, by conversation at his own house, and sometimes at their houses,
> sufficient information to write a sketch of every day's debate, on the most
> important and interesting questions; which he printed three times a week
> regularly in the *London Evening Post* . . . During two sessions, this practice of
> printing sketches of the debates continued, without any notice being taken;
> and Mr Almon furnished them constantly, from the best information he could

obtain. Though they were short, they were in general pretty accurate; and their accuracy was perhaps the cause of the printer's security.

Almon then goes on to explain how the owners of the *St James's Chronicle*, another thrice-weekly, 'observing the impunity with which these accounts of the proceedings of Parliament were printed', decided to copy him.

> And for this purpose they employed one Wall, who went down to the House of Commons every evening, to pick up what he could in the lobby, in the coffee houses etc. It was impossible he should be accurate; however by perseverance and habit, and sometimes by getting admission into the gallery, he improved; and judging, in a little time, that he could supply two newspapers as well as one, he amplified his accounts for the *Gazetteer*, after having published the heads in the *St James's Chronicle*. This encouraged the printers of other papers to follow the example.[32]

On the basis of this account, Wall has an even better claim to be regarded as the first political correspondent: he was a genuine hired hand. Lobby journalism was at least another hundred years away, but with his late-night loitering, guile, story recycling (and accuracy record), Wall was obviously an early practitioner.[33]

Almon and Wall were in the Commons when parliamentary reporting became firmly established as a newspaper activity rather than a magazine activity. Following Johnson's departure, the *Gentleman's Magazine* carried on reporting its Lilliputian debates until 1746. The *London Magazine* also continued its 'political club'. In 1747 both magazines published an account of Lord Lovat's trial in the House of Lords. This was a breach of privilege, and Cave and Astley were arrested by Black Rod and held in custody for several days. Afterwards both were much more wary about publishing debates. The *Gentleman's Magazine* did not start printing reports again until 1752, and then it did so with the utmost caution. The *London Magazine* was also more circumspect than it had been, and after 1757 the 'political club' was discontinued. Newspapers had, until then, made little attempt to report debates, but around this time they were starting to take more of an interest. In February 1760 there was a complaint about four titles that published accounts of Commons proceedings: the *London Chronicle*, the *Gazetteer*, the *Public Advertiser* and the *Daily Advertiser*, and the printers were summoned to the Bar and reprimanded. Two years later there was another complaint about the *London Chronicle*, and this time the printer was ordered into the custody of the Serjeant. For the rest of the decade the papers were no keener than the magazines to take risks.

Almon's decision to start publishing debate reports in 1768 coincided with the launch of several new titles. The *North Briton* was revived that year, the *Middlesex Journal or Chronicle of Liberty* was first published in April 1769, and a few weeks later William Woodfall set up the *Morning Chronicle*. By the middle of 1770 there were at least five daily newspapers being published in London, eight thrice-weeklies and four weeklies – and all of them were interested in politics. At that stage it was normal to publish only the general outline of a parliamentary debate. But from the start of the new session in November, under the influence of Almon, newspapers began to publish full reports. It was common for an account in one newspaper to be widely copied elsewhere, and some papers made no effort to gather original material. (Since newspapers were not supposed to cover Parliament anyway, there was no form of redress against the plagiarisers.) Other newspapers did try to obtain their own accounts, and at any one time several different versions of a debate might be in circulation.[34]

The 1738 resolution was still technically in force and, as the newspapers grew increasingly bold, it was inevitable that Parliament would react. The initiative was taken by Colonel George Onslow, nephew of Arthur Onslow (Speaker from 1728 to 1761), a lieutenant-colonel in the 1st Foot Guards, the Member for Guildford and a full-bloodied reactionary. Onslow was, according to one contemporary, 'one of those burlesque orators who are favoured in all public assemblies, and to whom one or two happy sallies of impudence secure a constant attention, though their voice and manner are often their only patents, and who, being laughed at for absurdity as frequently as for humour, obtain a licence for what they please.'[35] He had already been responsible for having the author of an anti-Parliament placard dispatched to Newgate. On Tuesday 5 February 1771 he complained in the Commons about misrepresentation by newspapers and, at his instigation, the House reaffirmed its ban on reporting. The *Middlesex Journal*, a thrice-weekly, was not exactly deferential when it covered his initiative two days later.

> It was reported that a scheme was at last hit upon by the ministry to prevent the public being informed of their iniquity; accordingly on Tuesday last little Cocking George Onslow made a motion, 'That the order against printing the debates should be read, and entered on the minutes of the day.'
> Mr Charles Turner opposed the motion with great spirit: he said that not only the debates ought to be published but a list of the divisions likewise; and

he affirmed that no man would object to it unless he was ashamed of the vote
he gave.

Mr Edmund Burke supported Mr Turner's opinion; he said that so far
from it being proper to conceal their debates, he wished they would follow the
ancient rule, which was to record them in the Journals.

The following day the *Gazetteer*, a daily, also reported Onslow's move, in almost
identical language. (It probably lifted the account straight from the *Middlesex
Journal.*) Within hours of the second report appearing, Onslow was on his feet
in the Commons, protesting vehemently. 'Sometimes I am held up as a villain;
sometimes I am held up as an idiot; and sometimes as both.'[36] He said the
printers of the two papers, John Wheble (the *Middlesex Journal*) and Roger
Thompson (the *Gazetteer*), should be summoned to the Bar for punishment.
Some Members tried to persuade him to desist. 'By agreeing to this motion you
will only make their papers sell better. They will be read with avidity, and
believed with credulity,' Captain Constantine Phipps argued.[37] But, by ninety
votes to fifty-five, the House voted with Onslow.

The printers were summoned to appear on the following Monday, 11
February. They did not show up. Another summons was sent out, and again it
was ignored. On Onslow's insistence, the Commons passed a motion ordering
the Serjeant to arrest them. He tried, but whenever his deputy went to their
homes, he could not find them. A reward of £50 each was offered for their
capture at the beginning of March, but even that did not bring them to the Bar.
With the Commons looking increasingly impotent, Onslow dramatically upped
the stakes on 12 March by calling for six more printers to be reprimanded for
reporting debates. There seems to have been a general feeling that, having
started a battle, the House should see it through. Onslow had the support of
Lord North, the Prime Minister, and a majority of the House, and all six were
summoned to appear on 14 March. On the day, four of them made an appearance at Westminster: Thomas Evans of the *London Packet*; Henry Baldwin of the
St James's Chronicle; S. Bladon of the *General Evening Post*; and T. Wright of the
Whitehall Evening Post. By the time the Commons got round to dealing with
them, Evans had gone home. Baldwin and Wright were summoned to the Bar
and reprimanded by the Speaker. Bladon was also summoned, but he got away
without a reprimand because Members were impressed by his apology. Of the
other two printers on Onslow's original list of six, William Woodfall of the
Morning Chronicle could not attend because he was already in the custody of
Black Rod for a reporting offence in the Lords. The other, John Miller of the

London Evening Post, decided to follow Wheble and Thompson and just ignore the House.

The three recalcitrant printers were at large within the City of London. In defying the House of Commons, they were not on their own; they were acting in alliance with John Wilkes. Wilkes was an accomplished political troublemaker who was noted for his charm, his ugliness and his libertine lifestyle. He was originally elected to represent Aylesbury and in 1762 he launched the *North Briton,* a paper published anonymously that specialised in anti-Government scandal. Issue 45 was particularly offensive and Wilkes was arrested. He was released on the grounds that, as a Member of Parliament, he was protected by privilege. But eventually the Commons branded his publication a seditious libel and he was expelled. After a period in exile, he returned to London and stood for Parliament as a champion of liberty. He repeatedly topped the poll in Middlesex and, when the Commons refused to accept the result (on the grounds of his earlier expulsion), he became more popular than ever as a figurehead for radical, anti-Parliament sentiment. A group called the Society for the Supporters of the Bill of Rights campaigned on his behalf and, as part of its drive for parliamentary reform, it had been encouraging the printers to defy the reporting ban before the Onslow affair actually started.[38] In 1771 Wilkes was an alderman in the City, and he was able to turn Onslow's attack on the printers into a constitutional showdown between the Commons and the Corporation of London. On 15 March Wheble was 'arrested' by a fellow printer and taken to court in the City where, conveniently, the sitting magistrate was Wilkes. Wilkes ruled that Wheble had not committed a crime and immediately set him free. Another magistrate did the same with Thompson. A day later a messenger from the Commons arrested Miller. But the messenger was himself arrested and three City magistrates (including Wilkes) sent him for trial. The Commons had effectively been told to get lost.

Parliament was incensed. The two magistrates sitting with Wilkes were also Members (Brass Crosby, the Lord Mayor, and Richard Oliver), and the House decided to punish them for undermining its authority; but in doing so, it turned them into popular heroes. A large crowd gathered outside the Commons on 25 March when Crosby and Oliver arrived to hear what action would be taken against them. Oliver was found guilty of a breach of privilege and, by 170 votes to 38, he was committed to the Tower. Two days later Crosby returned to the House to learn his fate, and this time his supporters staged a riot. Coaches driving into the Commons were stopped and they were mobbed if they were carrying anti-Crosby Members. North was even pulled out of his carriage; his

hat was torn to shreds and he was apparently hit on the head with a baton. Later
he was seen weeping. The debate did not start until 8.00 p.m. and it ended with
Crosby following Oliver to the Tower.

Technically, the Commons had won. It enforced its will and Crosby and
Oliver were detained for about six weeks, until the prorogation of Parliament.
But the price for such a victory was too high, and the episode established parliamentary reporting as a permanent feature of the Westminster landscape. Never
again did the House of Commons try to punish newspapers for reporting
debates. In 1775 the House of Lords came close to a confrontation with the press
when Lord Lyttelton complained that a debate report had appeared in the *Public
Ledger*. Black Rod was ordered to arrest the City-based printer, but when Wilkes,
who was by now Lord Mayor, let it be known quietly that he was looking forward
to gaoling Black Rod, peers let the matter drop. After that, proceedings in the
Lords were also freely reported.

Yet the 1771 settlement was significant in another way too. It may have been
less than a triumph for the Commons, but the outcome was not an unqualified
endorsement of press freedom either. The old rules banning reporting were still
in place, and although it was generally accepted that they could not be used,
their spirit was to permeate parliamentary life into the nineteenth century and
beyond. The Commons had really accepted that debate reporting should be
allowed only on the basis that it was impossible to do otherwise. The argument
that Wyndham had advanced in 1738, that the public had a 'right to know', was
still attractive only to a minority. Onslow's battle with the printers ended in a
draw, and the result was that relations between Parliament and the press were
left in a state of ambiguity. The consequences of that were to be felt for years.

TWO

The Gallery Becomes
the Fourth Estate of the Realm

The gallery in which the reporters sit has become a fourth estate of the realm. The publication of the debates, a practice which seemed to the most liberal statesman of the old school full of danger to the great safeguards of public liberty, is now regarded by many persons as a safeguard, tantamount, and more than tantamount, to all the rest together.

Thomas Babington Macaulay, Edinburgh Review, *September 1828*

I have worn my knees by writing on them on the old back row of the old gallery of the House of Commons; and I have worn my feet by standing to write in a preposterous pen in the old House of Lords, where we used to be huddled together like so many sheep.

Charles Dickens, speech to the Newspaper Press Fund, May 1865

Shorthand writing has become the accomplishment of thousands of young men who have no other. There are abundant proofs in the parliamentary reports day by day that the reporters are, as a rule, commonplace men.

Anonymous writer in Contemporary Review, *June 1877*

Getting Established: The 1770s to around 1800

Parliamentary reporting in the eighteenth century was an arduous job. The House of Commons sat in the dark and dingy St Stephen's Chapel, where the gallery was likely to be crowded and uncomfortable and the acoustics were poor. 'Sir William [Meredith] spoke a great deal, but a loud snoring in the gallery prevented much of what he said from reaching the ears of the strangers in the gallery,' one reporter wrote near the top of a debate report in the *Morning Post* in 1779. 'Whether the snoring arose from the want of taste in the persons who slept so soundly, or from any soporiferous effluvia from the Hon Baronet, it is not our province to decide.'[1] There were no special facilities for reporters, who had to queue to get in alongside interested members of the public. Sometimes this would take hours. Once inside, a correspondent would have to sit through the whole debate before returning to his newspaper, late at night or in the early hours of the morning, to write up his report. Originally reporters were not even supposed to take notes, and they had to reconstruct long debates from memory. (This ban was lifted in the Commons, apparently in 1783, but in the Lords pencil and paper were outlawed for much longer.) Among the reporters who experienced conditions in the gallery at the time was Samuel Taylor Coleridge. 'I shall give up this newspaper business; it is too, too fatiguing,' he wrote to a friend early in 1800, after visiting the Commons on behalf of the *Morning Post*. 'I have attended the debates twice, and the first time I was twenty-five hours in activity, and that of a very unpleasant kind; and the second time from ten in the morning till four o'clock the next morning.' A few weeks later, after reporting another debate, he was complaining again. 'I have not a moment's time, and my head aches. I was up till five o'clock this morning. My brain is so overworked that I could doze troublously and with cold limbs, so affected was my circulation.'[2]

On many occasions the reporters were spared Coleridge's problems because they were not even allowed in. Strangers (parliamentary jargon for non-Members) had no right to be in the Commons while it was sitting, and the standing orders of the House included a rule saying that the Serjeant at Arms should take into custody 'any stranger or strangers that he shall see, or be informed of to be in the House or gallery, while the House, or any committee of the whole House, is sitting'.[3] Any Member could activate the ban simply by drawing attention to the presence of strangers (a procedure that came to be known as 'I spy strangers'); there was no need for a vote, and an individual determined to clear the gallery could override the wishes of the majority. The rule was used frequently during the 1770s, particularly when Parliament was debating its humiliation at the hands of the American colonists, and newspapers that wanted to report what was said had to fall back on the old methods, gleaning their accounts second-hand. Gradually Members became more reluctant to use the standing order, but the Commons continued to allow the use of the one-man veto until 1875. It was a stark illustration of the fact that although the reporters were tolerated, they had no intrinsic right to do their job.

The most prominent parliamentary reporter in the 1770s was William Woodfall. Born into a family of printers, with a brother, Henry, who ran the *Public Advertiser*, Woodfall entered the family trade in 1769, at the age of twenty-four, when he launched a new Whig newspaper, the *Morning Chronicle*. As was common at the time, he combined editing with printing and reporting. Woodfall served as theatre critic as well as parliamentary reporter, but his fame rested principally on his ability to 'remember' vast chunks of a debate and serve it up for readers the following day. With note-taking still banned this was a valuable talent, and 'Memory' Woodfall's paper established a reputation for publishing the longest reports. At the time the public demand for information about what was said in Parliament was, according to one historian, 'insatiable'.[4] In a typical four-page newspaper of the day, the debate reports, when available, were the main items of domestic news, and success in competing for readers depended mainly upon their quality. Woodfall's talents in this field brought him a measure of fame, and when he went to Dublin, by invitation, to report two important debates in the Irish Parliament, he was mobbed by crowds of well-wishers.

However impressive his mental faculties were, Woodfall's technique had considerable disadvantages. He wrote his reports in the third person and did not pretend to be offering his readers word-for-word accuracy. 'The public are requested to read the above not as an exact account of the debate on the subject, but as a mere skeleton of the arguments urged upon the occasion,' he wrote at the bottom of one of his reports in 1774.[5] According to one academic, who compared Woodfall's reports of certain debates with the records taken by Sir Henry Cavendish, Woodfall did not remember any of the actual phrases used by speakers. 'At best only the general pattern of the speeches are the same; the wording is entirely different.'[6] Some of his contemporaries in the press gallery were also sceptical about his abilities. Woodfall was 'a bad reporter', according to Lord Campbell, a member of the press gallery who went on to become Lord Chancellor.[7] James Stephen, another reporter who became a lawyer and politician, paid tribute to Woodfall's 'extraordinary talents' in his memoirs. But he went on:

> We his contemporary fellow labourers well knew the advantages he possessed, and which reduced the apparently preternatural talent to intelligible, though certainly more than ordinary, dimensions. Being absolute master of his own paper, and being inclined from vanity or mistaken self interest to sacrifice all

other considerations to its reputation for parliamentary reports, he used to publish the day after an important or long debate in either House several hours later than any other morning paper, and never sent his paper to press, or went himself to bed on such occasions till he had read all the other reports and supplied from them as far as he thought fit the omissions of his own.[8]

In other words, prodigy though he may have been, Woodfall was not ashamed to supplement his efforts using the oldest technique in journalism – copying from someone else.

Woodfall was pre-eminent for some years, but by the end of the 1780s he could no longer claim to be producing the fullest parliamentary coverage. The decision of the Commons to allow note-taking may have made conditions easier for his competitors, but the main problem for the man who liked being 'master of his own paper' came when a rival editor decided that it would be better to have a team covering debates instead of a single individual. James Perry, the son of an Aberdonian carpenter and builder, came up with the idea when he became editor of the *Gazetteer* in 1783. Blindingly obvious as it seems now, it was an important innovation in terms of the development of collective reporting, and ultimately it meant that one-man, Woodfall-style newspaper operations were doomed. Announcing his intentions in an address to the readers, Perry said that the 'parliamentary intelligence' in his paper would be his priority and that he had employed 'two gentlemen of literary character' to provide it. 'They will make it their study to seize, as much as possible, on the manner of the speaker as well as on the words, and to give a picture of his eloquence along with the report of his argument,' Perry added.[9]

It seems that Perry's staff comprised just himself and his two recruits. But, covering debates in relays, they were able to provide fuller reports than other papers. Woodfall suffered a further blow when the *Morning Chronicle* was taken over in 1789 by a set of new owners that included Perry. One of Perry's co-investors was John Bellamy, the parliamentary caterer and doorkeeper to the Commons. Perry became editor (a position he was to hold for more than thirty years) and brought team reporting with him; the connection with Bellamy apparently helped him to get his staff in and out of the gallery. Woodfall set up another one-man paper, the *Diary*, but this was unsuccessful and it folded in 1793. Eventually he rejoined the *Morning Chronicle*, as a reporter covering the Lords; he died in 1803.

Perry 'was a man of strong natural sense, some acquired knowledge, a quick tact; prudent, plausible, and with great heartiness and warmth of feeling,' according to William Hazlitt, who was taken on as a parliamentary reporter on the paper in 1813. Like Woodfall, Perry appeared to enjoy the kudos that went with running a newspaper. 'The editor of the *Morning Chronicle* wrote up his own paper, and he had an ambition to have it thought that every good thing in it, unless it came from a lord, or an acknowledged wit, was his own. If he paid for the article itself, he thought he paid for the credit of it also,' said Hazlitt.[10] Rightly or wrongly, the credit did head his way. The *Morning Chronicle* was seen by many during this period as the most influential paper in London and, in a Commons debate in 1810, Stephen, the reporter-turned-parliamentarian, described Perry as a man 'esteemed by many Members of [the] House, and reckoned among his friends one of the finest characters of the country'.[11]

As debate reporting became more elaborate, other readers were not so supportive. Newspapers did not try to compartmentalise their coverage in the way that they did later in the nineteenth century (starting with the publication of a summary alongside the main debate report), and the sketch, as a separate feature, had yet to be invented. But the reporters were already introducing comment into the long accounts of who said what, and doing so in such a way as to invite complaint. In a letter to the *Gazetteer* in 1777, a writer complained that the adjectives used in reports exposed the paper's anti-ministerial bias.

> Your very candid correspondent who favours you with the parliamentary debates is desired for the future to amend . . . the title which he generally prefixes thereto: and instead of 'A short account of the debate in the House, on, etc' to introduce his parliamentary memoirs by calling them, according to their true appellation, 'Strictures on the debate, etc.' He will then be justified in puffing the harangues of every minority declaimer by the side-wind epithets of 'ably, pointed, pertinently, usual ability,' and innumerable others.[12]

For James Boswell, the problem was lack of respect on the part of the reporters. In his *Life of Johnson*, he welcomed the fact that parliamentary reporting was more open than it was in the 1740s. But, mindful, perhaps, of remarks like that made about Sir William Meredith, he included the following rider: 'Unquestionably, there has of late been too much reason to complain of the petulance with which obscure scribblers have presumed to treat men of the most respectable character and situation.'[13] At the end of the century, William Windham, the Secretary at War, was to cite the inclusion of pejorative and extraneous comment in the debate coverage as one of his main reasons for believing that the House had made a mistake in letting the reporters in.

What was to be the character of that House in the eye of the public if what passed in it was not only to be reported in the newspapers, but a description was to be given also of the tone, manner and action of each member, like that of a criticism upon another description of persons, of whom he had not disposition to speak contumeliously, but of whom it was no disparagement to say they were more adapted than the senate for public entertainment – he meant persons who were called actors. What was to become of the dignity of the House, he would ask, if the manners and gestures and tone and action of each Member were to be subject to the licence, the abuse, the ribaldry of newspapers?[14]

Windham's views on the press were not necessarily representative, but his comments show that at least some Members could see where opinionated reporting was heading. Speaking at least 150 years before MPs had to worry about the consequences of television, Windham already had a clear sense of the way the media engenders celebrity. He also realised that this process was not necessarily flattering. In appealing not to be judged by his manners and gestures, Windham was rehearsing an argument that was to be heard repeatedly when the Commons debated televising its proceedings in the 1960s, 1970s and 1980s.

Official Recognition: 1803

One consequence of the fact that reporters had no special status in Parliament was that they had to turn up very early if they wanted to be sure of getting a seat in the gallery. Around the beginning of the nineteenth century the Commons did not start sitting until 4.00 p.m. The public gallery was open from noon, but the writers who wanted to be sure of getting a place turned up much earlier. When Coleridge was covering debates for the *Morning Post*, he once had to be at Westminster at 7.00 a.m. There was always a danger that a reporter would be unable to get in at all; this happened to Woodfall more than once, as he described after one such failure.

Feeling it to be a day of great public curiosity and expectation, the printer made it a point to attend Parliament House at an hour more than usually early; but unfortunately for him, such was the eagerness of the crowd (who had obtained admission into the lobby) to make sure of hearing what might pass, that they suddenly overpowered the doorkeepers and, pressing onward through the front door of the House, filled the gallery in a second.

Woodfall then faced the 'very irksome task' of waiting around all day to find out what had happened from a friend.[15]

The same thing happened again in 1803, but this time it led to what Michael MacDonagh describes as 'the first slight official recognition of the existence of the reporters' by the parliamentary authorities.[16] Britain was at war with Napoleon, and on Monday 23 May William Pitt was due to speak at the beginning of a two-day debate on the hostilities. There was bound to be a rush for seats. To make matters worse, Charles Abbot, the Speaker, decided that the gallery would stay closed until business started after prayers, instead of opening at noon. 'This will be peculiarly severe on those who attend to take the debates,' the *Morning Chronicle* said two days beforehand. 'It would be much better if the House would forbid the publishing of debates altogether than to render it impossible to report them as they might be. How is it to be expected that persons obliged to struggle in a crowd the whole day should be able to go through the fatigue of writing the debate?'[17]

On the Monday the reporters found it impossible to get in, and the newspapers the following morning did not carry the debate. *The Times* explained why its reporters, 'in common with those of the other papers', were excluded:

> From the hour of eight in the morning till nearly half after three o'clock, the doors of the House of Commons were surrounded, and the avenues filled with a considerable number of strangers who were desirous to attend a discussion of such importance. When the doors were opened, their disappointment was extreme at finding the gallery nearly filled with the friends of Members, or persons smuggled into the gallery through the body of the House. Of the whole number outside, many of whom had remained there for seven hours, very few, not more than four or five, gained admission, and those succeeded after suffering a most severe pressure in the passage to the gallery, and being in constant danger of having a leg or an arm broken.[18]

The *Morning Chronicle* made a similar complaint. 'No paper had a single reporter in the House of Commons, so that the debate, we believe, is entirely lost,' it said.[19]

Some Members were unhappy that Pitt's speech was not reported, and Abbot decided to issue instructions designed to stop the same thing happening again. On Tuesday 24 May he wrote in his diary: 'Settled with the Serjeant at Arms . . . that the gallery door should be opened every day, as required, at twelve; and the Serjeant would let the housekeeper understand that the "newswriters" might be let in in their usual places (the back row of the gallery), as being understood to have the order of particular Members.'[20] It was only a tentative step forward, and Abbot's ruling did not guarantee that the reporters were always able to get into the gallery in the future. In April 1804 they complained again when they turned up for an important debate to find most of the seats in the gallery taken by the friends of Members. Nevertheless, the Abbot decision marked the first time that Parliament, in any formal sense, acknowledged that reporters performed a positive function and deserved some assistance.

'Give Me but the Liberty of the Press': 1800 to the 1830s

At some point in the history of journalism, reporters started to acquire a collective identity. There must have been a stage when they stopped thinking of themselves just as individual gossip merchants and started to view themselves as members of a trade – the press, or Fleet Street – with its own traditions, values and intrinsic self-worth. When this happened is another matter. Mitchell Stephens, an academic, says journalists began to think of themselves as 'professionals' at the end of the nineteenth century.[21] As the Commons debate in 1738 showed, the idea that there was something called the 'liberty of the press', which people were supposed to be in favour of, was around much earlier. If Woodfall and his rivals were the world's first press corps, they must have had their own collegiate spirit. But equally one could pick the early nineteenth century as the moment when the press, as an institution, became a force in its own right. 'The gallery in which the reporters sit has become a fourth estate of the realm,' wrote Thomas Babington Macaulay in 1828. 'The publication of the debates, a practice which seemed to the most liberal statesman of the old school full of danger to the great safeguards of public liberty, is now regarded by many persons as a safeguard, tantamount, and more than tantamount, to all the rest together.'[22] Macaulay was probably the first person to put the press on a par with the Lords spiritual, Lords temporal and Commons. Effectively, he gave the parliamentary reporters a constitutional role.

They were already familiar with the idea that they were there to provide some kind of public safeguard. In February 1810, in a debate in the Commons, Richard Sheridan, the playwright and Whig politician, articulated the value of a free press in terms that still resonate. He wanted to change the standing order for the exclusion of strangers, the rule that allowed any Member to clear the public gallery on a whim. His main opponent was William Windham, whose opinion of the press had if anything gone down since 1798, and the debate allowed both sides to rehearse the arguments for and against the fourth estate.

Windham wanted to know 'how much the country had gained in the improvement of its affairs' from debate reporting. He could not see any advantages at all. Again he set out his belief that debate reporting would turn a representative government into a democracy, and he claimed that the same practice had 'led directly to that despotism which had so lately desolated other countries'. Windham was particularly offhand about the reporters themselves, 'amongst which persons were to be found men of all descriptions: bankrupts, lottery-office keepers, footmen and decayed tradesmen'. At the time it was common for newspapers to receive secret government subsidies,[23] and Windham cited this as evidence that the newspapers were corrupt.

> What did this prove – not the value or actual importance of papers – but it clearly showed that if government could have them in their pay, then papers were liable to be let for hire – to be bought and sold – and that the press, which had been thought in this country the palladium of its liberty, was always to be purchased by the highest bidder . . . He did not know any of the conductors of the press; but he understood them to be a set of men who would give into the corrupt misrepresentation of opposite sides.

He therefore had no intention of supporting Sheridan's move to change a standing order designed to correct such abuses.[24]

Sheridan dismissed the idea that the press was biased. In publishing debates the newspapers were guided by the principle of 'strictest impartiality', he said. 'Were even the editors inclined from motives of their own, or corrupt views of self interest, to excite any improper prejudice by mutilated or unjustifiable statements, he was confident that not one of the gentlemen who were in the habit of taking the reports of that House would lend himself to such an improper service.' In his winding-up speech, Sheridan sought to explain why the freedom of the press was so important with this battle cry.

> Give me but the liberty of the press, and I will give the minister a venal House of peers, I will give him a corrupt and servile House of Commons, I will give him the full swing of the patronage of office, I will give him the whole host of ministerial influence, I will give him all the power that place can confer upon him to purchase up submission and overawe resistance. And yet, armed with the liberty of the press, I will go forth to meet him undismayed, I will attack

the mighty fabric he has reared with that mightier engine, I will shake down from its height corruption, and bury it beneath the ruins of the abuses it was meant to shelter.

Sheridan insisted that freedom of the press and debate reporting were not to blame for the situation in France, as Windham implied. 'Was it not, on the contrary, the suppression of all liberty of discussion, the prohibition of all publications not sanctioned by the permission of authority, the prevention of that rational and temperate consideration of public interests and measures, which alone could excite and nourish patriotic feelings and public spirit, that had caused all the mischiefs which had attended that Revolution?' Sheridan also sought to answer perhaps the hardest question that Windham had posed: What good had the reporters done? Sheridan cited the war against Napoleon, and income tax, introduced by Pitt in 1798 to pay for it. Britain was able to bid defiance to the powerful enemy across the channel, he said.

> All this he could attribute to the effect of liberty of the press alone, and most particularly and emphatically to the unrestrained publication of the debates and proceedings of Parliament . . . He would tell the right honourable gentleman that the publicity given to all public measures, and especially to great measures of finance in modern times, had been the principal, if not the sole, means of reconciling the nation to a weight of taxes which in these boasted periods of former excellence would neither have been thought of, nor supposed likely to be borne or endured by the country.[25]

The Commons did not accept Sheridan's arguments. Members voted 166 to 80 against a review of the standing order relating to strangers. But a few weeks later the champion of the reporters did secure them a concession of sorts. The benchers at Lincoln's Inn had started operating a by-law that prevented anyone who had ever written for a newspaper studying at the Bar. At the time many of the parliamentary reporters were doing just that, and the ban (which was introduced on the grounds that newspapermen were not respectable enough to become lawyers) was perceived as grossly unfair. George Farquharson, a reporter and a law student, petitioned the Commons about the matter and Sheridan took up the case. In doing so, he challenged the idea that the reporters were all bankrupts and decayed tradesmen. 'Of about 23 gentlemen who were now employed in reporting parliamentary debates for the newspapers, no less than 18 were men regularly educated at the Universities of Oxford or

Cambridge, Edinburgh or Dublin, most of them graduates at those universities, and several of them had gained prizes and other distinctions there by their literary attainments,' according to Sheridan.[26] James Stephen, a distinguished barrister, said that in his youth he had reported debates from the gallery himself. 'It is an incident of my life which I am much more disposed to be proud of, or let me rather say to be grateful for to a kind disposing providence, than to blush for,' he said.[27] Members agreed that working for a newspaper should not be a cause of lifelong disgrace and those who were benchers at Lincoln's Inn said the rule would be withdrawn, which it was. Even Windham did not try to defend the status quo. But at the start of the debate he did use the standing order for the exclusion of strangers to clear the gallery, on the grounds that Sheridan was going to use the occasion to praise the reporters and 'it was not the custom to drink the chairman's health until he had withdrawn.'[28] The next day the *Morning Post* carried the exchanges that took place before the reporters were sent out, but just eight lines on what happened afterwards. *The Times* managed a column and a half. Clearing the gallery did not always stop the newspapers reporting debates, but it made it much harder for them.

Windham's comments about the integrity and respectability of the parliamentary reporters went down badly. One of them sought to refute the charge that they were all corrupt by writing to the *Morning Post* saying that he had once been offered a bribe by a Member to pay particular attention to a speech, and that he had ignored the offer. He just gave the speech what he thought it deserved. 'The next day the honourable Member enclosed to me a cheque upon his banker. This I instantly returned, accompanied by a few lines in which I observed that he had entirely mistaken my character, and, I firmly believed, the character of all my coadjutors, if he imagined that we were to be influenced in the performance of that which we conceived to be a public duty by any private consideration.'[29] Windham was also accused of hypocrisy. Although he criticised the publication of debate reports, it turned that he was very keen to have his own speeches recorded for posterity in *Hansard*, which at the time was an independent publication compiling debate reports from the best accounts available in newspapers. According to William Cobbett, *Hansard*'s owner, Windham sent in two hundred notes and letters designed to ensure that *Hansard* did him justice. The journalists took their revenge and, after the debate of February 1810, gave up reporting his speeches. The boycott lasted until Windham's death in May that year. Another Member was also targeted. In the February debate George Tierney complained about being misrepresented in the newspapers. 'He himself seldom, if ever, looked into reports . . . but when he did, he remembered to have felt considerable pain, that sentiments should be put into his mouth, and should go down to his constituents, one syllable of which he had never uttered.'[30] Tierney was in favour of Sheridan's proposal to review the standing order. But that was not enough to redeem him in the eyes of the reporters, and he too was blacklisted for a time.

As John Payne Collier discovered in June 1819, the House of Commons could deploy sanctions of its own. Collier was a reporter on *The Times* and, in the course of covering a speech by Joseph Hume, he depicted Hume making a bitter personal attack on George Canning. Canning and Hume both complained, and, even though *The Times* published an apology, Collier was summoned to the Bar of the Commons to explain what went wrong. He said that the mistake was an innocent one, and that it happened because he had missed what was said during one particularly noisy debate. 'Anxious to collect what had occurred during the confusion . . . I asked a stranger who was placed before me, and from him I received, if not the exact words, at least the point which I afterwards embodied in my report.'[31] Members were not impressed. They passed a resolution denouncing Collier for 'a scandalous misrepresentation of the debates and proceedings of the House',[32] and decided to place him in the custody of the Serjeant at Arms. After spending the night locked up, Collier was summoned to the Bar again and reprimanded by the Speaker, Charles Manners-Sutton. 'Let this be a public warning that the repetition of this offence . . . will assuredly be visited with the utmost rigour and the severest punishment,' the Speaker said.[33] Collier was then ordered to pay around £15 (at least £500 today) to secure his release.

He was not the only reporter to get in trouble on that occasion. As the House considered what to do with Collier, Peter Finnerty, an Irish adventurer, sometime war correspondent and parliamentary reporter on the *Morning Chronicle*, staged a protest in the public gallery in solidarity with his colleague. Rather than sit in his customary place in the back row, he sat at the front, waved his notebook conspicuously and swore at the attendants. He too was detained by the Serjeant, reprimanded at the Bar and ordered to pay for his release. Writing his memoirs between 1819 and 1832, James Stephen complained that the reporters in the gallery were 'very inferior . . . in moral character as well as general talents' to the men he worked with in the 1780s.[34] Stephen, a devout man and a leader of the anti-slavery movement, may well have been thinking of Finnerty at the time.

A more serious confrontation between the press and the House took place a few years later, in 1832, when the Irish nationalist Daniel O'Connell accused *The Times* of misrepresenting one of his speeches. Thomas Barnes, the paper's editor, wrote back saying that he took the matter even more seriously than O'Connell and that the reporter, one E. Nugent, would be sacked if he could not explain the mistake.[35] Nugent, a fellow Irish Catholic, met O'Connell and managed to pacify him with an explanation involving poor accoustics and a notebook getting soaked in the rain. O'Connell accepted that the paper had not intended to get its report wrong. But a year later, in a speech to a meeting of radicals, he renewed his campaign aggressively.

> But why did he talk of newspapers? It was all vain for the public to expect from newspapers, as they were then constituted and managed, anything like honesty. No; they would have nothing but the distillation of individual malignity and the concentration of private hate through those foul mediums. What did the newspapers do but evil? People might talk of them as they liked; but he maintained that, constituted and managed as they were, they did nothing but evil.[36]

O'Connell was used to his speeches being covered at great length in the Irish papers, and the failure of the London press to give him quite so much space seems to have been one of the factors that angered him most. For whatever reason, he continued to make sweeping and public attacks on the honesty and competence of reporters in general. *The Times* was the worst, he said, and the *Morning Chronicle* was just as bad. The *Morning Post* was the most impartial, he said, 'a circumstance which probably arose from the reporters being generally Scotchmen.'[37] In July 1833 O'Connell raised his complaints in the Commons and said that if the papers did not improve, he would try to have the owners summoned to the Bar.

The following day *The Times* came back with what must have seemed like a safe act of retaliation. Eleven members of the parliamentary staff published a letter to the editor in their paper telling him that they had resolved not to report any of O'Connell's speeches until he had withdrawn his allegations. The editorial supported them. O'Connell deserved to be reported if he acted like an MP, it said.

> But do not let him entertain the monstrous supposition that, whenever he chooses to pour forth the most unprovoked and unmeasured abuse, and in the coarsest language, on men of honour and education, such persons can so far throw off the common feelings of human nature as to quietly and deliberately record the calumnious charge and the foul expressions in which it is couched.[38]

The *Morning Chronicle* parliamentary staff published a similar letter in their own paper a day later.

As soon as *The Times* announced its boycott, O'Connell tabled a motion in the Commons summoning the owner and the printer to the Bar to answer the charge that they had infringed the privileges of the House. But when his proposal was debated, MPs supported the press. Sir Robert Peel, the Tory opposition leader, said there were up to fifty reporters in the gallery, 'some of them holding commissions in the Army and Navy, several at the Bar, most of them having received an academical education and occupying, therefore, the situation of gentlemen'.[39] He said that he had always found them impartial and that it was not surprising that they objected to being depicted as liars. O'Connell's motion was defeated.

At that point O'Connell had the reporters expelled from the gallery. Using the standing order for the exclusion of strangers which had been popular in the 1770s, he could clear everyone from the gallery just by asking the Speaker. O'Connell also made it clear that he would use the 'I spy strangers' mechanism every day until the reporters abandoned their boycott. With all the London newspapers heavily dependent on parliamentary reports (when available) to pad out their news coverage, it was not surprising that the reporters backed down immediately. The next day, 30 July, *The Times* announced that their reporters would deal with O'Connell normally. O'Connell spoke in a debate that evening (on slavery) and was reported at length in the papers the following morning. The episode was instructive. Whatever Macaulay said about the 'fourth estate', O'Connell had demonstrated that the reporters had no clout within Parliament. They were admitted entirely at the discretion of Members. So much for the 'liberty of the press'.

Dickens in the Press Gallery: The 1830s

Charles Dickens was not a bankrupt or a decayed tradesman when he became a parliamentary correspondent, but he was not a graduate of Oxford or Cambridge either. He moved into reporting as an escape route from a clerkship with a firm of solicitors, the job he did after leaving school (which itself was a step up from his boyhood stint in a blacking factory). After spending eighteen months teaching himself shorthand, Dickens started as a reporter at Doctors' Commons, an association of civil and ecclesiastical lawyers. His father, John, worked for a time as a reporter in Parliament and Dickens soon followed in his footsteps, probably in 1830 or 1831.[40]

He seems to have started on the *Mirror of Parliament*, a publication which was owned and edited by his uncle, John Henry Barrow, and which, like *Hansard*, specialised in debate transcripts. He then joined the *True Sun*, an evening paper, at its launch in March 1832. He remained there for only a few months, but he was on the paper when the third Reform Bill was going through its Commons committee stage. In the autumn he transferred back to the *Mirror of Parliament*. While he was on the staff Dickens made a particular impression on Lord Stanley, the Irish Secretary. At the second reading of the Bill for the Suppression of Disturbances in Ireland, Stanley made a speech that he wanted to print and circulate in Ireland. The version that appeared in the *Mirror of Parliament* was full of mistakes – except for the beginning and the end, which were accurately reported. Stanley asked the editor to get the man responsible for those sections to report the speech in full. It was Dickens, who was then summoned to see Stanley in Carlton House Terrace, where the minister delivered the whole speech again. Stanley was not the only person to be impressed by Dickens's abilities. According to James Grant of the *Morning Advertiser*, who worked alongside him (and later wrote a three-volume history of the British press), 'a more talented reporter never occupied a seat in the gallery of either House of Parliament.'[41] Tom Beard, another contemporary, described him as 'the fastest and most accurate man in the gallery'.[42] Barrow wanted to get his nephew a job on *The Times*. There were no vacancies, but instead he was able to get Dickens a post on the parliamentary staff of one its principal rivals, the liberal *Morning Chronicle*.

Many reporters at the time were employed on a sessional basis and paid only when Parliament was sitting. Dickens, however, had a permanent job, and, like others in his position, he was expected to report speaking engagements outside London when the House was in recess. Parliamentary reporting is a relatively non-peripatetic form of journalism, but the Dickens literature makes it clear that the press gallery was doing 'trips' (and racking up extravagant expenses) long before the start of party conferences and prime ministerial overseas diplomacy. In a letter to his friend John Forster, Dickens looked back on his life on the road.

> There never was anybody connected with newspapers who, in the same space of time, had so much express and post-chaise experience as I. And what gentlemen they were to serve, in such things, at the old *Morning Chronicle*! Great or small, it did not matter. I have had to charge for half-a-dozen break-downs in half-a-dozen times as many miles. I have had to charge for the damage of a great coat from the drippings of a blazing wax candle, in writing through the smallest hours of the night in a swift-flying carriage and pair. I have had to charge for all sorts of breakages fifty times in a journey without

question, such being the ordinary results of the pace which we went at. I have charged for broken hats, broken luggage, broken chaises, broken harness – everything but a broken head, which is the only thing they would have grumbled to pay for.[43]

Dickens carried on working for the *Morning Chronicle* until the end of 1836. He may have found his late-night deadline-chasing exhilarating, but he did not enjoy covering debates, and during his time in the gallery he developed a lifelong aversion to parliamentary pomposity. In *David Copperfield*, his autobiographical novel, his hero becomes a parliamentary reporter. 'Night after night, I record predictions that never come to pass, professions that are never fulfilled, explanations that are only meant to mystify,' says David. 'I am sufficiently behind the scenes to know the worth of political life. I am quite an Infidel about it, and shall never be converted.'[44] Dickens felt the same way and, after leaving the Commons, he said he would never return because he could not bear to listen to another worthless speech.

The 1834 Fire and the Opening of the Reporters' Gallery

When Dickens started as a reporter in Parliament, the facilities for note-taking were still rudimentary. 'I have worn my knees by writing on them on the old back row of the old gallery of the House of Commons; and I have worn my feet by standing to write in a preposterous pen in the old House of Lords, where we used to be huddled together like so many sheep,' he recalled many years later.[45] The Lords did not provide seating for strangers and originally the reporters had to stand below the Bar, alongside anyone else who turned up to listen. But in 1828, in an Upper House equivalent of the Abbot ruling, the Lords set aside some floor space for the exclusive use of reporters. They were granted their 'preposterous pen' because the debates on the Catholic Emancipation Bill were attracting huge public interest and the peers did not want to go unreported.

Three years later the same problem occurred on an even grander scale when the second Reform Bill reached the Lords. Peers rejected the Bill at its second reading in October 1831. This triggered a general election. But before Parliament was dissolved, the Lords set up a committee to consider what additional accommodation should be provided for strangers. It reported very quickly and recommended the installation of a gallery. The committee did not make any reference to the press (reporting Lords debates was still theoretically banned), but it was understood that the reporters would be accommodated, and when the gallery opened at the start of the new Parliament in December, the newspaper writers were allowed to take over the front row.

On 16 October 1834 the Houses of Parliament were largely burned down in the worst fire seen in London since 1666. The blaze started because workmen were burning tally sticks, blocks of wood with notches in them, which, amazingly, had been used for government accounting until 1826 and which were still being stored at Westminster. The House of Commons chamber in St Stephen's Chapel was completely destroyed and the Lords premises, in the Court of Requests, were gutted. The fire was seen at the time as a divine contribution to the parliamentary reform process, an architectural amendment to the Bill passed two years earlier. In the short term the two Houses moved into temporary accommodation and there were special facilities for reporters in both. The Commons sat in the refurbished Court of Requests, where a gallery was set aside for the exclusive use of the press. Peers met in the Painted Chamber and, as in their old chamber, the front row of the strangers' gallery was reserved for the reporters. The renovation work was carried out quickly and the two Houses settled in at the start of the new session in February 1835.

Charles Barry won the architectural competition to rebuild Westminster, and embarked on the project in collaboration with the designer Augustus Pugin. For the parliamentary reporters, the fire and its aftermath offered the prospect of a permanent improvement in the facilities available to them. In the new Lords building, which was used for the first time in April 1847, the reporters had their own gallery, with twelve boxes at the front where writers could take notes, and fourteen seats behind for the people waiting to replace them. There was also a reporters' gallery in the Commons, with some space behind it set aside for the press. Barry's Palace of Westminster is now revered as a masterpiece, but at the time the project attracted the kind of press that would make the Millennium Dome look like a triumph. Countless problems emerged, including one that became apparent when the new Commons chamber was first used in 1850: the reporters in the new gallery could not hear. Lord John Russell, the Prime Minister, came up to investigate; Thomas Clarkson, a reporter who was there, later recalled the conversation.

> I said to him that we could not hear at all . . . though in the temporary House I always heard him very well. He said: 'What's to be done? The House has been built.' I ventured to suggest that the best thing to be done was to erect a dome roof of wood under the ceiling. He pointed to the beautifully decorated ceiling, and said it would be a pity to hide it.[46]

The acoustics were not the only issue. As MPs discovered in 1850, the heating and ventilation were awful too. Barry, to his considerable annoyance, had to make major alterations. For the benefit of the reporters, the roof was lowered. The new chamber, and its press gallery, did not start being used on a permanent basis until 1852.

The Importance of Shorthand

By the time the new gallery opened, parliamentary reporting was increasingly reliant on an important development – shorthand. It was not a new invention. Timothy Bright had published a book outlining what is said to be Britain's first system of shorthand in 1588. Thomas Gurney, who developed his own method, was appointed shorthand writer at the Old Bailey in 1738. He sought to popularise the technique with a book called *Brachygraphy, or an Easy and Compendious System of Shorthand* (1750), and one of the people who took it up was Sir Henry Cavendish, who used it to keep his own, very thorough, record of debates when he was in the Commons. Gurney's son, Joseph, took notes on behalf of the House of Commons during the Warren Hastings trial of the 1780s, and his successor, W. B. Gurney, was made official shorthand writer to both Houses of Parliament in 1813. The family firm went on to take notes during Lords and Commons committee hearings for more than a century. But even though shorthand was available when the newspapers started reporting debates, and when note-taking was allowed, it was not seen as a requirement. Charles Ross, the *Times* reporter whose career in the gallery spanned more than half a century, told MPs in 1878 that when he started in 1820 the shorthand writers were 'very few'. Most men in the gallery used longhand. 'But they were able men as a rule, chiefly barristers,' Ross recalled. 'And they wrote a good style and took pains. They were indifferent to the words, but they wrote accurately the substance of the speaker's remarks.'[47]

Ross wrote shorthand himself, but he did not necessarily think that gave him an advantage over his colleagues. That was because he did not equate reporting with the exact reproduction of what a Member said. 'You want a man's opinions, not his words,' he asserted.[48] One of the longhand writers from around this time went even further. Lord Campbell, who worked for the *Morning Chronicle* in his youth, said that shorthand writers were good at taking down evidence in a court but 'wholly incompetent to report a good speech'. Why? 'They attend to words without entering into the thoughts of the speaker. They cannot by any means take down at full length all that is uttered by a speaker of ordinary rapidity, and, if they did, they would convey a very imperfect notion of the spirit and effect of the speech.' In the gallery, he said, his job was to prepare an edited version, true to the spirit of what the speaker meant.

> To have a good report of a speech, the reporter must thoroughly understand the subject discussed, and be qualified to follow the reasoning, to feel the pathos, to relish the wit, and to be warmed by the eloquence of the speaker. He must apprehend the whole scope of the speech, as well as attend to the happy phraseology in which the ideas of the speaker are expressed. He should take down notes in an abbreviated longhand as rapidly as he can for aids to his memory. He must then retire to his room and, looking at these, recollect the speech as it was delivered, and give it with all fidelity, point and spirit, as the speaker would write it out if preparing it for the press.

Campbell said that 'fidelity' was indispensable, but that did not mean the reporter had to repeat 'inaccuracies and repetitions'.[49]

Campbell was in the press gallery at the start of the nineteenth century, when debates were normally written up in the third person. Shorthand allowed newspapers to provide long, accurate reports in the first person and as the century went on they came to prefer this form of truthfulness (factual precision) to the Ross/Campbell one (fidelity to the spirit of a speech). But it was a hard skill to acquire. Dickens taught himself shorthand between 1827 and 1828, using Gurney's *Brachygraphy*, and in *David Copperfield* he described the process vividly. Not put off by being told that 'a perfect and entire command of the mystery of shorthand was about equal in difficulty to the mastery of six languages',[50] David decided to persevere because he wanted to work in the Commons.

> I bought an approved scheme of the noble art and mystery of stenography (which cost me ten and sixpence) and plunged into a sea of perplexity that brought me, in a few weeks, to the confines of distraction. The changes that were rung upon dots, which in such a position meant such a thing, and in such another position something else, entirely different; the wonderful vagaries that were played by circles; the unaccountable consequences that resulted from marks like flies' legs; the tremendous effects of a curve in the wrong place; not only troubled my waking hours, but reappeared before me in my sleep.[51]

Eventually David 'tamed that savage stenographic mystery' and went on to earn a respectable living in the gallery.[52] By the 1870s, apparently, all debate reporters in the gallery had tamed the mystery too, and longhand was no longer being used.[53]

The arrival of shorthand as an essential job qualification did not mean that newspapers started reporting speeches word for word. A verbatim report, as Ross said in 1878, was 'a horrible thing'.[54] Reporters were expected to 'tidy up', and MacDonagh explains why. 'In first-person reports by even the leading parliamentarians it is sometimes necessary to smooth out intricacies, to suppress a trite or aimless phrase, to omit purposeless repetition, to make the halting sentence march in due line with its companions, and to emphasise the main point by careful adjustment and proportion.'[55] He is describing what is essentially copy-editing, which was a skill that the reporters were expected to master alongside shorthand. Politicians accepted that their speeches were often improved as a result. 'We all of us owe to the kind attention of the reporter the excision of many superfluities, not always, perhaps, regarded as superfluities by the orator, the correction of many gross errors of grammar, and an improvement of our oratory which we may be reluctant to admit, but which is nevertheless there,' Arthur Balfour, the former Prime Minister, told a press gallery dinner in 1908.[56] 'Tidying up' has remained a legitimate newspaper practice, but in the twentieth century broadcasting has made it much more problematic. It is not feasible to reword an important extract from a speech if the reader is likely to have heard the original version on the television news or *Yesterday in Parliament*.

As well as influencing the content of newspapers, the development of shorthand affected their staffing. In the days of John Campbell and James Stephen, reporting was an activity that required a flair for writing and the ability to marshal an argument, the sort of skills associated (rightly or wrongly) with a university education. By the end of the century these were becoming more of a bonus, and what really mattered for a reporting job was Pitman's, not a specialism that has ever featured on the Oxbridge curriculum. 'Shorthand writing has become the accomplishment of thousands of young men who have no other,' an anonymous writer said in 1877, in an article on parliamentary reporting. 'There are abundant proofs in the parliamentary reports day by day that the reporters are, as a rule, commonplace men.'[57] Parliamentary journalism, like other branches of journalism, was widening its class intake, and for this shorthand was partly responsible. Recruitment did not start shifting back towards graduates until after the Second World War.

Life in the Gallery: The 1850s to the 1890s

Debate reporting of the kind that flourished in the second half of the nineteenth century is one of the most anonymous forms of journalism. Using shorthand, the reporters were able to record what MPs and peers said in a relatively 'pure' form. With no description, no value judgements and no narrative, it is virtually impossible for a reader to infer anything about the person doing the writing. On the page, the men reporting debates throughout this period were more or less identical. Off the page, outside the chamber and in the press gallery, a different picture emerges. The gallery was occupied by people like 'General' O'Hennessy, 'a typical fine old Irish gentleman, the pink of politeness and suavity . . . [whose] work was largely done for him by colleagues on the *Advertiser*'. And White and R. Kisbey, who 'were unfortunately for themselves to over-indulge in beverage'. And Henry Dunphy, 'for many years leader of the *Post* corps . . . a well-favoured man of somewhat cynical style'. And Kerr, who 'became a dangerous lunatic, and ought to have been removed from the gallery long before Mr Bussy administered to him the richly deserved punishment which brought him under the notice of the Serjeant at Arms'. And Mr Fleming, 'a stout, florid person, said to have been a Chartist . . . [who] latterly was fond of impressing on young men . . . that he had a place down at Hastings'.[58] It is a cast list that would not be unfamiliar to anyone who has worked for a newspaper.

By the time these pen portraits were written in 1890, the press gallery was not just the place where the reporters sat. It was an institution in its own right, with its own committee, its own set of premises and its own social life. Its members had more in common with one another than with the other journalists on their own papers. This happened because the men who were covering Parliament started to spend more and more time actually working there.

The method used to cover debates, the 'turn' system, had not changed much since James Perry first had the idea of hiring more than one reporter to cover a day's worth of proceedings. A team of reporters for each paper would divide up the debate, and when one man's turn was over, another would take his place in the gallery. In the early nineteenth century it was normal for a turn to last three-quarters of an hour, or even longer if the Lords was sitting and resources were stretched. At the end of his shift, the reporter would then have to walk back to the office of his paper to write up his copy. 'When I mention that some of the offices – those of *The Times*, the *Morning Herald*, the *Morning Advertiser* and the *Daily News* – were more than a mile and a half away from the House of Commons, and that the *Morning Chronicle* and *Morning Post* were considerably more than a mile distant, it can be easily imagined how fatiguing this was for the reporters, even where they had not to return to the House after they had finished their first "turn" to take a second,' James Grant wrote in his 1871 history of journalism.[59] The reporters used to swap information about what was going on as they walked to and fro, and, according to Thomas Clarkson's memoir, 'the most cheering intelligence they ever had was that instead of some Member, or perhaps some minister, being "up", the House itself was up, thereby liberating them for the evening.'[60] Cabs were allowed if someone had to get back to the office in a hurry, with the result that parliamentary reporters with a turn of speed were able to pioneer one of Fleet Street's earlier expenses fiddles.[61]

The reporters were encouraged to head back to their offices because the facilities available for them in the Commons were meagre. After 1852 they improved: two rooms behind the gallery were set aside for the press. At first the reporters continued to leave the Commons after each turn and write up their notes on their own premises. But the Commons authorities opened another room for the reporters, committee room 18, and soon the parliamentary correspondents on all the main papers were compiling their reports together, more or less around the one table. Messengers were used to take copy back to newspaper offices, although later the job was done by telephone and telegraph. With reporters staying on the premises, turns could be made shorter, too. On a paper like *The Times*, with a large parliamentary staff, turns lasted fifteen minutes for most of the evening, and for shorter periods of time later on, as printing deadlines got closer. At the end of a night the reporters could be changing shifts every two and a half minutes.

Writing out in committee room 18 had one considerable advantage for the reporters: it meant they could compare notes. In *The Reporters' Gallery*, MacDonagh explains how this worked and why it was necessary.

> One of the group, who has possibly a better note than the others, reads aloud as he transcribes, and all the others as they write, practically from his dictation, follow the speech on their own notes, so that if he is stopped by a gap, or a doubtful phrase, someone else in the combination is usually able to come to the rescue . . . Though each of the reporters may not have succeeded in transferring to his notebook every sentence of the speech, five or six are almost certain to have between them a fairly complete record.[62]

This is a ritual that is still performed by hacks with notebooks today, in Parliament and elsewhere, and, given the limitations of shorthand, it is a fairly sensible one. In the spirit of Labour's new Clause Four, shorthand writers achieve more by common endeavour than they do alone. Yet, in the press gallery, collective 'writing out' was more than just a matter of fact-checking. It meant that collaboration between supposed rivals became routine. When sketch-writers appeared towards the end of the nineteenth century, they were just as willing to help each other out. John Foster Fraser described the frustration of sitting through a boring debate for three hours and going off to get a cup of tea, only for someone to come in 'and carelessly remark there has been no end of a shindy between Mr Chamberlain and Mr Lloyd George'. In those circumstances, one could rely on the 'comradeship of the gallery', he said. 'You soon hunt up a friend who has seen it all, and he describes the scene to you, knowing you will do the same for him should occasion arise. It is only by this means a parliamentary descriptive writer can be omnipresent.'[63] As news reporting and lobby journalism came to dominate the press gallery's output in the twentieth century, the habit persevered. One of the charges levelled against the lobby has been that its members act as a cartel, fixing a collective 'line' to take with the news events of the day. This would probably happen anyway, but agreeing stories must come more easily to reporters who are used to agreeing quotes. Arguably, you could trace it all back to committee room 18.

Even in the nineteenth century, some of the reporters appear to have had their doubts about all this. Charles Cooper became editor of the *Scotsman*, but before he did so, in 1861, he did a stint in the press gallery as a parliamentary reporter on the *Morning Star*. While he was there he took part in the note-comparing workshops in committee room 18 and concluded that the system was unfair on MPs who were misreported and anxious to set the record straight.

> All the reports or almost all were the same, and the public naturally thought that where there was such general agreement in them, they must be right and the Member wrong. Experience has convinced me that nothing is more hurtful to the public, so far as reporting is concerned, than the collaboration of the representatives of different newspapers in the production of a report. Any report appearing in a score or a hundred newspapers, if it has a common origin, may and often does lead to mischief. Independent reports correct each other. They can be compared, and errors in one can be shown by reference to another.[64]

Cooper had a point. But it does not seem that his concerns were widely shared.

Collaboration was necessary because the acoustics were terrible. Even after the adjustments to the roof of the chamber, it really was very difficult for the reporters to hear what was being said. The position was even worse in the House of Lords, where Lord Salisbury told a committee in 1880 that defective reporting was a 'very serious evil'. When he was Foreign Secretary, inaccurate reporting had sometimes damaged Britain's diplomatic interests. 'Statements of mine, misreported, either to India or foreign courts, have produced considerable misconception. And it has more than once happened, though not frequently, that that misconception, before it could be corrected, has produced results which I regretted.'[65] Salisbury did not blame the reporters for the fact they could not always make out what was being said and the committee, in its report, agreed with him. 'So bad are the acoustic properties of the House . . . that it often takes a reporter three to three and a half hours to write out his notes in the House of Lords, as compared with two hours in the Commons, because of the necessity, if the speech is an important one, to "cobble and tinker" it up, and that very often is a mere matter of guesswork, only broken sentences being heard.'.[66] The Lords did try to improve matters that year by allowing reporters to sit in the side galleries, which were normally used by the wives and daughters of peers, instead of the gallery at the end of the chamber. But this was not popular with the women who were excluded, and the reporters, who had to rush from one gallery to another to be in the best position to hear successive speakers, were not keen either. The experiment was swiftly abandoned.

Most parliamentary reporters did not fraternise with MPs and peers during this period. Wemyss Reid started in Parliament in 1867 as London correspondent of the *Leeds Mercury*. Provincial papers were not entitled to a seat in the gallery and, to cover debates in the Commons, he had to arrange to do occasional reporting for the *Morning Star*. On his first night in the Commons he was seen talking to Edward Baines, who was owner and editor of the *Leeds Mercury* – and thus his boss – and also an MP. 'I little knew what offence I was unconsciously giving to my colleagues,' he recalled later in his autobiography. 'In those days a gulf that was regarded as impassable divided the members of the press from the Members of the House . . . The overwhelming majority of the reporters had never exchanged a word with a Member of Parliament in their lives, and, to do them justice, they evidently had no desire to do so.'[67]

The reporters were able to keep their distance from the Members because, although they were spending all their working hours at Westminster, they had their own separate facilities. When the new chamber opened, the reporters were apparently quite pleased with the accommodation available. Within a decade, it had become something to complain about. 'All the rooms were low-ceilinged, dark and dismal. If you remained in them for half an hour you were tortured with a headache,' recalled Cooper.[68] Some writers working for Sunday newspapers had tickets allowing them into the gallery on Thursdays and Fridays, and it was claimed that this caused particular overcrowding. The doorkeeper, a man called Wright, sold food and drink, but in none of the accounts of the period are his wares made to sound appetising. 'He always had a bottle of whisky on tap, a loaf or two of stale bread, and a most nauseous-looking ham,' Reid wrote in his memoirs. 'The tradition was that every night, when Mr Wright, at the close of his duties, retired to his modest abode in Lambeth, he took with him the ham, wrapped in a large red bandana which he had been flourishing, and using, during the evening, and for greater security placed it under his bed at night.' Reid said he did not know whether that story was true, but that it was 'universally believed by the gallery men of my day.'[69]

In 1881 the reporters decided to set up an organisation to represent their own interests. At a meeting on 17 February to which everyone holding a gallery ticket was invited, it was agreed that a committee should be empowered 'to make arrangements for the supply of refreshments and for the general comfort and convenience of gentlemen using the gallery'.[70] One hundred and twenty-four members voted in the subsequent election, and fifty-four of them put their names forward as candidates for the twelve vacancies on the committee. Thompson Cooper was elected the first chairman, and Herbert Wright the first secretary. The committee's priorities were administrative rather than political and, in the light of the experience with (the other) Wright's ham, it is not surprising that in its first year it 'devoted a good deal of attention to the catering arrangements'.[71]

Some Modest Reforms

Although the reporters were by now well established, they still had no actual right to operate within Parliament. The theoretical ban on reporting was still in place (the resolution of 1738 had never been cancelled) and it was still possible for a single MP to clear the galleries. The full absurdity of the rules was high-lighted in 1875 by an incident that prompted a small piece of 'modernisation'.

The ban on debate reporting also covered select committee evidence and in April Charles Lewis, a Tory, used this to argue that *The Times* and the *Daily News* were in breach of privilege because they had reported evidence given to the select committee on foreign loans. The evidence in question was a letter to the committee chairman casting aspersions on another MP. It had been read out loud in a hearing with reporters present, and the chairman had even shown them a copy so that they could transcribe it accurately. In spite of all this, the Commons agreed with Lewis and a motion was passed summoning the printers of the two newspapers to the Bar. But on the day in question Benjamin Disraeli, the Prime Minister, proposed the matter should be dropped. The Commons accepted.

At the time the Irish MPs had taken to disrupting Commons business to advance the cause of Home Rule and, after the foreign loans committee affair, some of them decided that press freedom was a good issue to exploit. Perversely, they maintained that the way to help the reporters was to kick them out. Alexander Sullivan (who was also editor of the *Nation* in Dublin) announced on 22 April that he would clear the galleries every day until the Commons decided to introduce some reforms to benefit the newspapers. Lord Hartington, the Liberal opposition leader, agreed to move a resolution addressing the grievances of the press and Sullivan said that, in the light of that commitment, he would abandon his protest. But a few days later Joseph Biggar, another Irish Member, did make the press and the public leave during a debate. The House was discussing stud horses and among those watching from the public gallery was the Prince of Wales. Biggar spied strangers, claiming that he was doing so because he wanted to draw attention to the problems the parliamentary authorities were causing the press. MPs generally were horrified at the snub to the heir to the throne and Disraeli called for the rule about the removal of strangers to be suspended for the night. The Commons supported him unanimously and, having waited outside the chamber for about twenty minutes, the Prince and other strangers were allowed back in.

After that, MPs accepted the rules had to change and, on 4 May, they debated two proposals from Hartington. The first would remove the theoretical ban on reporting. Hartington's resolution said the House would not 'entertain any complaint, in respect of the publication of the debates or proceedings of the House, or of any committee thereof,' unless the relevant debate took place in private or the newspaper was guilty of misrepresentation.[72] The second would allow strangers to be removed from the gallery only if the Speaker decided it was necessary to prevent disorder. During the debate Sullivan exercised his right to have the public and the press kicked out (again, the stunt was supposed to be in support of press freedom), and the debate was adjourned until 31 May. Hartington failed to get his first reform through. Disraeli said the House should 'pause before assenting to a proposal which would add to our restrictions',[73] and MPs voted along party lines. But the House agreed that something had to be done to stop individual Members being able to exclude the press, and the Commons passed a revised version of Hartington's motion on the exclusion of strangers. An MP could still call for the galleries to be cleared, but it would happen only if the House voted in favour.

Although the Commons refused to lift the notional ban on reporting, a case in 1868 confirmed that debate coverage had acquired legal status. The hearing, in *Wason* v. *Walter*, established the principle that the publication of parliamentary debates is covered by qualified privilege. The case arose out of a petition presented to the Lords by Rigby Wason alleging that a newly appointed judge had lied in the past before a Commons election committee. In the debate Wason was accused of making up the allegation. When *The Times* reported the claims, Wason brought a libel case against its owner, John Walter. The case was heard before Lord Chief Justice Cockburn, who instructed the jury that an accurate report of a parliamentary debate was privileged. *The Times* won. Wason tried to argue that privilege could not apply because debate reporting was still technically banned, but Cockburn rejected this notion. 'Practically, such publication is sanctioned by Parliament,' he said. 'It is essential to the working of our parliamentary system, and to the welfare of the nation.'[74]

One group had particular difficulties with the Commons authorities during this period: the provincial reporters. There were only nineteen front-row seats, or boxes, in the reporters' gallery at the time; fifteen were reserved for the London papers, three for news agencies, and one for the *Hansard* service, which was still an independent operation. There were another nineteen seats behind, but the acoustics made them unsuitable for debate reporting. They were normally used by leader-writers, or reporters awaiting their turn. Tickets for the press gallery were issued only to the organisations entitled to a seat, and as a result the provincial papers were excluded. Some of them came to arrangements with the London papers, like the *Leeds Mercury*, where Wemyss Reid doubled up as a reporter on the *Morning Star*; others relied on the news agencies or used established parliamentary reporters who worked for them freelance; sometimes they could arrange to get a reporter in for a special occasion. At the start of the nineteenth century the problem was not particularly acute as the papers outside London had no means of getting reports from Parliament into print quickly; they had to rely on surface transport if they wanted to use copy from Westminster. But the invention of the telegraph in 1844 opened up the possibilities for next-day debate reporting outside the capital. The real breakthrough came in 1870, when the Post Office took control of the telegraph system in Britain and cut the rates for transmitting news. Two news agencies, the Press Association and Central News, were set up as a consequence. With technology making it easier for the provincial papers to cover Parliament, they were increasingly keen to get their own press gallery tickets.

The Commons authorities argued that there was not enough space. Ralph Allen Gosset, the Serjeant at Arms, told a select committee in 1878 that provincial reporters had been banned from the press gallery ever since the new building opened. 'That has been the rule . . . because there are 134 daily provincial newspapers in England, Scotland and Ireland, and they would all be entitled to the same privilege if one were admitted,' he said.[75] At the time 123 people held press gallery tickets already.[76] Metropolitan bias may have been a factor too. Lord Charles James Fox Russell said when he was Serjeant in 1867 that he had been pressed 'very strongly' by MPs to let Scottish and Irish reporters into the gallery, and that he had always fought the idea. 'I considered that the best way to serve the interests of the public in the reporters' gallery was to give every accommodation to the London press, and to restrict it entirely to the London press.'[77] But the editors from outside London kept the pressure up. In his memoirs, Charles Cooper describes spending twelve years as editor of the *Scotsman* trying to get a reporter into Parliament.

> Shall I ever forget the interviews I had, the talking I had to do, the dead weight of uninformed obstruction with which I was met! Of course I gave prominent politicians a bad time of it; I was ever worrying them on the subject. Then it was that a great truth dawned on me: the House of Commons – I do not mean the building, but the members – is the most hidebound Chinese-like institution in the world . . . I should not be surprised to learn that it required reams of paper and bottles of ink to get a door opened if it had once been shut by order.[78]

Cooper even raised the matter with William Gladstone when he was Prime Minister, only for Gladstone to suggest that extra reporters could be accommodated under the floor of the chamber. Cooper inspected the basement and found that the ventilation passages made it easy to hear what was being said in the chamber but that not being able to see anything was something of a disadvantage.

The 1878 select committee came up with a preferable alternative. Although it was set up mainly to look into the case for having an official report of parliamentary proceedings, it also considered the needs of the provincial press and recommended extending the reporters' gallery by taking seats from the adjacent, sidelong galleries used by Members. The work was carried out in 1881 and the press gallery got five boxes on each side. The *Scotsman* got its seat. The London reporters at first resented the arrival of the newcomers because previously they had been able to earn vast sums freelancing for the provincial papers.[79] But 'ultimately the change had a good effect', according to one contemporary, because the big national titles gave up recruiting sessional staff, who were paid only when the House was sitting on the assumption that they could make up their earnings elsewhere, and instead hired more reporters full-time.[80]

'Sensational Reporting': The Rise of the Sketch

On 1 July 1878 the same select committee took evidence from Charles Ross. By this time almost eighty, 'an imposing figure with a shaggy head of snow-white hair',[81] he had been working in the Commons for more than half a century and for about twenty-five years or so had been head of the parliamentary corps on *The Times*. There were fifteen reporters in his team, and they were renowned for producing the fullest debate reports. Every day Parliament was sitting they would produce at least two pages of copy, and often three or four (without advertisements). There were six columns on a page, and around two thousand words a column. The speeches from the Commons and Lords took precedence over everything else, and the paper regularly left out other material to create space for them. In terms of thoroughness, debate reporting on *The Times*, while Ross was in charge in the Commons, had become as good as it had ever been in Britain, and probably anywhere in the world. Doubtless the MPs expected him to view the whole enterprise with some pride and satisfaction. If they did, they were in for a surprise.

Shortly after the hearing started, when Ross was asked if he thought the Commons should publish its own official report of its debates, he said nobody would read it. Then he went on to make the same point about his own publication. 'Few persons read the debates in *The Times*, they are so long; for one who reads a debate in *The Times*, I should think there would be 20 who will read the summary.' Ross predicted that members of the public would turn away from an official report of parliamentary proceedings 'with feelings of extreme distaste', and he suggested that they reacted in the same way to the debate reports in his paper. '*The Times* does it as a point of honour, I suppose, but if I could control it, I would give half the quantity; it would be more read, and I dare say *The Times* would save £20,000 or £30,000 a year; but it is not my business, and I never interfere.' In another answer he speculated further on the advantages of a different approach.

> They would get more interesting matter, and matter that is paid for and kept out by the debates. Matter from various parts of the country is sent up and

paid for; then there comes a debate of 12 columns (I have seen 16, I think, this session, or 18); and that matter from the country is all put on one side; it is all lost. Not only that, there are advertisements; they must be worth, I take it at a rough guess . . . at least £20 a column; say that upon the average you keep out six columns of advertisements, that is £120 a day; and there are five days a week.

Ross said he had never met anyone who had read a long debate in full. So, he was asked, was *The Times* sacrificing itself when it published debate reports? 'I think so. I have thought so for years. I have never expressed the opinion till now, publicly, or to any person connected with the paper till the other day, about three days ago; but I have long felt it.'[82]

Ross was obviously interested in news as well as reporting; not just in the recording-what-happened aspect of journalism, but in the here's-what-you-want-to-know side of it too. When parliamentary reporting started in the seventeenth and eighteenth centuries, the printers and writers did not have to worry about this distinction. An account of what was said in the House of Commons was news, partly because it was secret, or semi-secret, but largely because there was little else in the public sphere clamouring for attention. By the time Ross gave evidence to the committee, the market was changing. Adult literacy was increasing, and the same telegraph that was bringing *Scotsman* readers speeches from Parliament was also providing the newspaper with a rich array of dispatches from home and abroad, any of which might prove to be more interesting than some of the waffle coming from the House of Commons. Some newspapers were becoming more sensational, and the term 'new journalism' was coined to describe the trend. At the end of the century this process was accelerated by the launch of three new titles, the *Daily Mail* (founded in 1896), the *Daily Express* (1900) and the *Daily Mirror* (1903). This did not automatically mean the end of old-fashioned debate reporting. But by the end of the nineteenth century it was already in decline as the newspapers began to develop more reader-friendly ways of writing about Parliament.

At the time Ross was giving evidence to the committee, newspapers normally presented political information in one of three guises. There was the debate report, probably carried under the title 'Imperial Parliament' and recounting at great length what was said in the chamber, with little or no extraneous comment. This was the job that most press gallery members did. Then there was the summary, a self-contained article setting out, in the space of a column or so, the main events in Parliament the previous day. It was produced by an individual and not by a team, and the summary writer often doubled up as manager of the parliamentary corps. Finally there were the editorials, or leaders. Modern parliamentary journalism developed out of these three sections of the newspaper.

Leaders in the nineteenth century performed the same function they do today: they articulated the considered view of the newspaper on a particular matter. In doing so, they anticipated the development of the opinion column. More importantly, the leader was also a vehicle for news. When Thomas Barnes and John Delane were editing *The Times* and they had an important story to break, they printed it at the top of the leader column. (Delane also had a habit of 'disguising' confidential revelations by writing about them in a leader as if they were common knowledge.) Other editors took a similar approach, and the practice also reflected the fact that nineteenth-century papers had no equivalent of the modern front page on which to display their best stories.

The reporters in the press gallery who were covering debates produced the vast majority of the political output and in that respect they were the early political reporters. But the debate reports were not really news. The correspondents wrote up the most interesting speeches, and ignored the boring ones, but beyond that there was no attempt to identify a story and give it precedence. The nearest thing to a modern news story was probably the summary. It was self-contained (unlike the snippets of news that appeared in the leader columns, where a paragraph on one subject might be followed by another on something quite different) and the writer had to exercise editorial judgement in deciding what mattered and what didn't. The skill was different from that required for straight reporting and it was helpful not to write too much down. 'Many reporters who feverishly take a shorthand note of nearly every word are hopeless at writing summaries,' recalled one journalist.[83] Summaries did not start with arresting intros, and they were written as narratives rather than news. But for the reader who wanted to find out the key facts, they were a starting point.

While it is arguable that the summary evolved into the news story, it is clear that it evolved into the sketch. There had been witty writing about Parliament in the past, but it was not until the late nineteenth century that newspapers started carrying sketches on a daily basis. This development is sometimes attributed to Henry Lucy, a dapper, ultra-prolific smoothie who became the most prominent political hack of his generation. Born in Crosby in 1844 or 1845, the son of an engraver, Lucy joined the *Shrewsbury Chronicle* after school, headed for London and by 1873 had become manager of the parliamentary corps on the *Daily News* and the writer of its summary. For more than thirty years he continued to operate from the gallery (apart from a brief stint as editor of the *News*), writing for a bewildering array of titles and doing as much as any of his contemporaries to popularise political journalism. In the 1870s the summary was just that: a summary of what happened. Lucy filled in some colour; he told readers about the expressions and gestures he could see from the gallery, hyped up the drama and wrote it all up with wry, affectionate humour. Eventually the *Daily News* published his column under the title 'Pictures in Parliament', with HWL at the bottom, the contemporary equivalent of a byline. It would typically run to two thousand words a night. A separate, more conventional summary would appear elsewhere in the paper. Lucy also wrote a weekly 'London letter' that was syndicated to several papers outside the capital. Part sketch, part column, the London letter was a standard feature in the provincial press and it combined parliamentary news with metropolitan gossip. Although Lucy was a pioneer, he was by no means the only person writing about politics in a lighter manner. When the *Scotsman* gained admittance to the gallery, Cooper decided that he wanted someone to write a summary that conveyed 'the tone and feeling' of the House, as well as what was said. He hired a writer called Spellan for the task, 'an educated man' with 'a ready pen', and in his memoirs Cooper claimed that Spellan's summary, 'brightly descriptive', was the model that was widely copied.[84]

The development of the descriptive sketch was not popular with colleagues left performing the more mundane reporting duties. 'Descriptive writers naturally make the most of every detail and give it a colour not always its own; and nothing is more easy than to convey an erroneous impression without laying oneself open to the charge of altering or suppressing facts,' wrote William Maxwell in 1889. Maxwell was a reporting purist who said that anyone who wanted the 'unsullied truth about a "scene"' (nineteenth-century euphemism for a parliamentary shouting match, or worse) should read the report.[85] John Fisher McCullum, who headed the Press Association's parliamentary team, was more blunt. 'We are simply crowded out by sketch writers, and these gentlemen who are rather lofty, some of them thinking they are a cut above the ordinary reporter, have very little regard to his convenience; they will chatter when he is busily engaged taking notes, and make his task sometimes excessively difficult,' he said in 1907.[86] Lucy admitted that he was 'something of a fraud in the important matter of shorthand writing',[87] and it is probably fair to assume that this was added to the list of grievances held against him by the reporters who had tamed the 'savage stenographic mystery'.

MPs were also wary about the emergence of the sketch-writers. In May 1875, the day before the Commons was due to debate the Hartington reforms relating to the press, the *Daily News* tackled the subject in a leader. 'No London paper could exist which inflicted upon its readers a full report every morning of the proceedings of Parliament to the exclusion of other matter,' it said. 'The public finds it often more interesting and more profitable to read the criticism of a journal upon a long debate, or a summary of it, than to attempt to read the long debate itself . . . The idea that the press gallery is only or even especially a gallery where persons are to sit who are to report the debates ought to be frankly given up in our days.'[88] The editorial was quoted in the House as MPs reflected regretfully on the fact that they were not getting as much space in the newspapers as they used to. Mitchell Henry, a Liberal, told the House that while the leading journal, *The Times*, gave very full reports, and so did one other morning paper,

> the other papers, however, rightly considered that they ought not to occupy space, which to them was money, with matter which would not be generally interesting to the public, [and] cut down the debates to the smallest dimensions. Moreover, there had crept into the House of Commons the practice of sensational reporting. Sketches of what occurred, or of what was supposed to have occurred, were given to the public. The appearance of Members and their manner was described, although, God knew, gentlemen who worked till 2 or 3 o'clock in the morning might be excused if sometimes they were ungainly in their manners.[89]

Within a period of around a century, Parliament had gone from trying to stop its proceedings being reported to moaning rather pitifully that it was not getting enough attention. It was a complaint that was to be heard repeatedly in the years to come.

THREE

The Lobby Starts to Dominate

It is to be feared . . . that much of the gossip of the lobby is fiction, or at any rate supposition and exaggeration. The London newspapers attach little importance to the paragraphs as news and make a sparing use of them as hints to the leader writers.

William Maxwell, parliamentary correspondent on the Standard, *1889*

I feel myself that the House of Commons is losing by the fact that the reporting is less good of its proceedings in the papers, and I do not believe that these sketch accounts of what goes on within our walls, even if they were impartial (which they rarely or never are), are in any sense a substitute for reasoned argument.

Arthur Balfour, evidence to a Commons select committee, 4 June 1907

The year has been important in the history of the lobby and precedents have been made which your committee trust may be of future use. During the General Strike the committee ensured that the Government's official informant saw lobby correspondents separately from the rest of the press.

Lobby journalists' committee annual report, 1926/7

The Start of 'Lobbying': The 1870s Onwards

In January 1984, as the lobby celebrated its centenary with a lunch at the Savoy, a brief pamphlet was published to commemorate the event. On the back, a piece by Ian Waller of the *Sunday Telegraph* began: 'The Commons resolution in 1884, admitting "a gentleman of the press" to the Member's Lobby, was a historic step . . . ' But on the inside, the *Guardian*'s Michael White declared that, actually, there was no resolution of the House in 1884.[1] Readers were left wondering whether there even was an anniversary to celebrate. Elegant as the booklet looked, it was hardly a good advertisement for the reliability of lobby journalism.

Almost all the early lobby files were destroyed when the Commons was bombed in 1941, with the result that there is no authoritative record of how it all started. Some accounts mention 1884, and the supposed 'gentleman of the press' resolution. Others insist that the first lobby list (the list held by the Serjeant at Arms naming reporters entitled to use the Members' lobby) was drawn up in 1885. James Margach, in his chapter on the lobby in *The Anatomy of Power*, offered 1881 as a key year, largely, it seemed, because he remembered two journalists celebrating fifty years in the lobby in 1931.[2] In fact, none of these dates marks the starting point. Lobby journalism goes back to the 1870s.

For years the Members' lobby at the House of Commons was open to anyone. Just as strangers had ready access to MPs in the old building, in the new one they could walk into the lobby and accost a Member going into or coming out of the chamber. Reporters went there to meet MPs, and members of the public sometimes wandered in just to gawp. This lasted until 1870 when John Evelyn Denison, the Speaker, changed the rules. Writing in his diary, he complained that the lobby was so crowded that 'Members could not get to the Vote Office, or to the refreshment room, or to and from the House, without being pressed upon and thronged, not only by constituents, but by members of deputations and other strangers, to their excessive inconvenience.'[3] Denison ordered the Serjeant at Arms to make sure that the Members' lobby was reserved exclusively for the use of MPs, and to keep everyone else in Parliament's Central Hall. But exceptions were allowed, and at some point afterwards a list was drawn up of strangers, including reporters, who were allowed into the lobby. This was when lobby journalism began; a select group of reporters being granted access to MPs that was not available to others.

In 1878 Ralph Allen Gosset, the Serjeant, explained the system to MPs. 'Strangers were all admitted some years ago, and it was found so inconvenient to Members that an order was given that no stranger was to be admitted except he had an order from me, and his name was on the list.' Gosset was asked what reporters had to do to get on the list. 'They apply to me, and I always grant leave for one from each paper to be admitted to the lobby,' he replied. At the time provincial reporters were not allowed into the gallery because there were not enough seats. But Gosset told the MPs that his one-reporter-per-paper rule applied to the provincial press as well.⁴ For all the mystique it later acquired, the lobby in its early days was, in some respects, less exclusive than the gallery.

There were important developments in the 1880s. The 'gentleman of the press' resolution said to have been passed in 1884 is apocryphal; there appears to be no reference to any resolution of that kind in the *Commons Journals*. But in 1885, following a dynamite attack at Westminster, Arthur Peel, the Speaker, revised the rules governing admission to the lobby. Peel is sometimes associated with the creation of the lobby. In fact, like Joe Haines and Alastair Campbell, he was seen at the time (for a few days, at least) as someone more interested in closing it down. He supposedly proposed abolishing the lobby list and was forced to change his mind. The episode did not have much practical effect on the reporters because the new, post-1885 lobby rules were much the same as the old ones. But it was significant. Throughout its history the lobby has been involved in a series of overblown confrontations with the authorities, revolving around access, and with the grievances on each occasion combining high principle with factors like how far the hacks might have to walk. The 1885 row with Peel launched this tradition, and it encouraged the lobby correspondents to act collectively in a way that they had not done before. In that sense it was a defining moment.

The attack happened on Saturday 24 January. The Commons was open to the public at the time, and just after 2.00 p.m. a black bag containing dynamite exploded in Westminster Hall, near the entrance to the Crypt. Shortly after-wards, there was another explosion in the chamber itself. There was a third at around the same time at the Tower of London. Fenian terrorists were respon-sible. No one was killed, but the incident encouraged officials at the Commons to reconsider their security arrangements and Peel issued a series of new rules. These were published in February. The existing lobby list was cancelled, and the Members' lobby was reserved for MPs, peers and various others. Strangers were ordered to stay away from the committee rooms when committees were not sitting, with the result, the reporters assumed, that they would not be allowed to use committee room 18 for writing out their notes and that at certain times they would not be able to use the corridor connecting the Lords with the Commons. Non-MPs were also told they were not permitted to use the subway under Bridge Street connecting Parliament with the underground after 4.00 p.m.

The press reaction was very hostile. 'The absurdity of the whole business is demonstrated by allusion to the fact . . . that no one is admitted to the press gallery without the special authorisation of the Serjeant at Arms,' said the *Daily*

News. 'If there be any who under the guileless appearance of a reporter conceal the purposes of a dynamitard, it will not be difficult to trace him.'[5] One correspondent described the rules as 'a gratuitous offence'. Another argued: 'The loss to the public would be immense if the press lost touch of each political situation as it arose.'[6] The *Dundee Advertiser* said that excluding journalists from the lobby was intolerable because 'their presence there has become a necessity of political life.'[7] The newspapers clearly believed that there was a public interest case to be made against the Peel rules. But the men writing the protest articles seemed to be more concerned with the practicalities. One unnamed parliamentary reporter wrote to the *Observer* to explain how he would be affected by the new regime. Without committee room 18, 'we shall have to sit on the stairs, or elbow each other out of rooms crowded to suffocation, and the result will be – to us general hindrance and injury to health, and to the public inferior reports.' The writer also complained about the reporters not being allowed to take the quick route from the Commons to the Lords. 'To close this corridor to us will simply mean an utter disorganisation of our work, and incalculable inconvenience to every individual concerned.'[8] The situation was so serious that some journalists suggested effectively going on strike and not reporting Parliament. A similar tactic had recently been tried in Austria. 'The country would probably manage to exist even if for a night or two there were no reports in the newspapers of parliamentary debates,' said the *Daily News.*[9]

In the event, the journalists managed to solve their problems in a more straightforward manner, with meetings and delegations to the Speaker. Interestingly, the two groups of reporters met separately. The lobby correspondents, known as 'lobbyists', convened on Monday 16 February, at Anderton's Hotel in Fleet Street. The following day the National Association of Journalists, which had only been formed the previous year, organised a meeting for parliamentary correspondents in the same hotel. Both groups sent representatives to see the Speaker. On the Tuesday afternoon the two delegations returned with the news that Peel was giving them everything they wanted: tickets for the lobby (one per paper, except for London morning papers, which were entitled to two), the use of committee room 18, free passage down the corridor to the Lords and even access to the subway. The reporters were particularly glad to hear that the lobby list was becoming more selective, and that some non-journalists who had been allowed on in the past would in future be excluded. 'Of late the list has grown out of all reason and proportion,' said the *Manchester Examiner.*[10] 'None will be more pleased than those who have real work to do in the lobby to find it closed in future against the *soi-disant* leaders of opinion, the miscellaneous button-holers and the propagandist idlers who haunt the House on important occasions and pester Members with their trivialities,' said the *Standard*.[11] Peel claimed that he had never intended to ban the reporters from the lobby, and he was probably telling the truth. The original rules issued the previous weekend said that 'others, as the Speaker may think fit' would be allowed into the lobby. It seems that either Peel failed to tell the reporters that this was referring to them, or the newspapers wilfully assumed the worst, or both. To that extent the 1885 crisis was manufactured. But at the time it was seen as having served 'a useful purpose in having obtained a practical recognition for the first time of the rights of the press to be adequately represented at Westminster'.[12]

Who were the lobby correspondents who started operating in the 1870s? One of them was Henry Lucy, the journalist also associated with the creation of the modern sketch. 'In the old days journalists engaged in Parliament had very little personal contact with Members in the lobby,' he said in later years. 'I happened to know a number of Members, and I contributed political paragraphs to the *Daily News*. Of course, everybody was much shocked at this journalistic innovation, but it was a decided success. I found plenty of information coming to hand, and as time went on I paid more and more attention to the lobby.'[13] Lucy was a consummate networker and he was not intimidated by the 'impassable gulf' that divided reporters from MPs when Wemyss Reid started in Parliament. The most famous of Lucy's many journalistic achievements was not 'Pictures in Parliament' but 'the Diary of Toby, MP', a column that appeared in *Punch* from 1881 until 1916. It was a spoof Westminster diary, written as if by Toby, Mr Punch's dog (as featured on the magazine's title page) and, for the purposes of Lucy's conceit, a Member of Parliament. It was much more anodyne than the equivalent parodies that appear today in *Private Eye*, but at the time the device was relatively novel. Lucy used the lobby to gather material and, as a result, was able to present himself as a fictional MP with a measure of authority.

Having access to the Members' lobby was important because it was – and remains – the best place to go for a reporter wanting to see a large number of MPs quickly.[14] Ernest Pitt was the first full-time lobby correspondent on *The Times* and, like other successful exponents of this form of journalism, he had a flair for handling politicians. According to Spencer Leigh Hughes, a lobby correspondent who became a Liberal MP, Pitt's technique was as follows.

> He said very little indeed, but he was what may be called a voracious listener, and he could listen in such a way as to encourage the other man to talk. I have often watched him when some Member has been eagerly confiding some

information. At stated intervals Mr Pitt would give a solemn nod, and you would think from his serious demeanour that the Member was uttering the last word of wisdom about something or other. But afterwards, if I alluded to the incident, he would sometimes say, as I enjoyed his friendship, 'Ah, poor fellow! He thinks he knows all about it, but he knows nothing.' For it was not easy to tell Mr Pitt some move in the game of which he had not heard – but he never discouraged men by showing this previous knowledge, for he knew well enough that every one may be useful some time or other. Thus he endured what may be called the 'chestnuts' of political information with an equanimity and a complacence worthy of a martyr.[15]

But not all MPs could be found in the lobby. In the nineteenth century, just as in the twenty-first, there were complaints that ministers stayed away. 'The moment a man is in office, he becomes as close as an oyster, and avoids the lobby to communicate his information to favoured journals in a more private way,' wrote William Maxwell in 1889.[16]

The lobby correspondents of the 1870s were involved in a fairly haphazard form of journalism and it was common for political 'stories' to appear as isolated sentences or paragraphs in the space where the editorials went. Gradually, as lobby journalism became more established, so it found a more stable place in print. In 1885, after Gladstone resigned the premiership, *The Times* started running paragraphs of news under the headline 'Political Situation', and eventually this led to the regular publication of lobby news under the heading 'Political Notes'. Other papers adopted a similar approach. The reporters tried to find out what was going on behind the scenes and, as Frederick Higginbottom, a lobby correspondent in the 1890s, explained, their work involved the production of intelligent guesswork.

> While the practitioners in the gallery are limited to writing about the daily debates, the lobby men must be forever looking for the events that are to come, anticipating and foreshadowing developments in policy and parliamentary tactics. The faculty of anticipation is cultivated by constant contact with members of all shades of opinion and every degree of influence: by conversation, observation and questioning, deduction and speculation. Ingenuity on this field of enterprise has to be tempered by extreme caution and a sort of instinctive estimate of probabilities, and these qualities guide the practised lobby journalist to a remarkable approximation to the facts in many cases where he does not hit the nail squarely on the head.[17]

As they cultivated the faculty of anticipation, the lobby correspondents received little help from ministers on a collective basis. Governments did not start holding regular lobby briefings until well into the twentieth century. But reporters helped one another and most worked in small, informal syndicates, with individuals from two or three different papers pooling almost all their information and competing fiercely against the rival lobby operations.

Although the lobby correspondents were to become the most powerful group of reporters working in Parliament, their status at the end of the nineteenth century was relatively low. 'It is to be feared . . . that much of the gossip of the lobby is fiction, or at any rate supposition and exaggeration. The London news-papers attach little importance to the paragraphs as news and make a sparing use of them as hints to the leader writers,' wrote Maxwell, a parliamentary corre-spondent on the *Standard*.[18] Michael MacDonagh, a gallery reporter on *The Times*, was equally sceptical. A stickler for accuracy, he devoted just 15 of the 454 pages in *The Reporters' Gallery* to 'lobbying', and he quoted with glee Sir William Harcourt's 1891 declaration: 'You will hear more nonsense in the House of Commons lobby in one hour than anywhere else in one month.'[19] Although he acknowledged the diligence of reporters like Pitt, MacDonagh essentially distrusted lobby journalism. To prove his point, he told a story about an early lobby correspondent who was sitting on the stairs wondering what to write when Gladstone came by, asked to be allowed past, and went on his way. The reporter went straight to the telegraph office to file: 'Meeting Mr Gladstone this evening in the lobby, I had a brief but interesting conversation with him,' etc. The report then went on to regurgitate some points made by Gladstone in recent speeches. Gladstone could not repudiate the piece because it accurately reflected his views. MacDonagh wrote rather pityingly about the unnamed fantasist. 'When there is little news to be had, when the lobbyist is (as he himself would say) "gravelled by lack of matter," can he be blamed if he has recourse to his imagination and invention in order to supply his newspaper with the column or so of gossip expected nightly of him?'[20] He would have been incredulous to learn that within a hundred years this kind of 'gossip' would have virtually replaced the parlia-mentary reporting he cherished so much.

The Gallery Enters the Democratic Age

Winston Churchill made his maiden speech in the House of Commons on 18 January 1901. Among the sketch-writers who wrote about it, one of the most important was Henry Massingham, the radical journalist who took over the

'Pictures in Parliament' slot from Lucy in the *Daily News*. Massingham had already been editor of the *Daily Chronicle*, but had resigned and gone back to a writing job because the paper's owner would not let him speak out against the Boer War. According to Charles Masterman, a colleague on the *Daily News* and later a liberal MP and minister, Massingham was at the height of his power in this period.

> His influence was certainly greater than that of most ministers and ex-cabinet ministers of the time. Indeed, quite a number of these used to solicit policy or praise; and he was making the reputations of the new men, such as Mr Lloyd George and Mr Winston Churchill. Everybody who mattered in the world around Westminster read the parliamentary sketch he wrote night by night; and those who knew nothing of the actual debate very largely took their opinions from it.[21]

On the eighteenth, Massingham wrote about Lloyd George and Churchill, because the one spoke after the other.

> Mr George has many qualifications – a pleasing face, animated and expressive, with the natural refinement of the Celt, a voice of that rare quality which unites passion and the finer silver tone one associates with a true tenor voice, feeling and fire, the power of a continuous narrative and of sustained argument, and above all, the true parliamentary style, simple, easy and clear. All these powers Mr George displayed in his speech last night – a speech to which the Tories listened with singular quietness, though Mr George did not abate one letter of the anti-war gospel . . .
>
> Mr Winston Churchill's reply was in very striking contrast to the speech to which it was indeed only nominally an answer. The personal contrast was as striking as that of treatment and method. Mr George has many natural advantages. Mr Churchill has many disadvantages. In his closing sentences he spoke gracefully of the splendid memory of his father. Mr Churchill does not inherit his father's voice – save for the slight lisp – or his father's manner. Address, accent, appearance, do not help him. But he has one quality – intellect. He has an eye – and he can judge and think for himself. Parts of the speech were faulty enough – there was claptrap with the wisdom and insight. But such remarks as the impossibility of the country returning to prosperity under military government, the picture of the old Boers – more squires than peasants – ordered about by boy subalterns, the appeal for easy and

honourable terms of surrender, showed that this young man has kept his
critical faculty through the glamour of association with our arms.[22]

The whole sketch runs to around 3,500 words. It is a good showpiece for
Massingham's qualities, which Masterman described as 'a complete fearlessness,
a brilliance of phrasing, a disinterestedness, and that sudden seizing of the
effects of the events of the moment, with all their implications, which make the
difference between a first-class and a second-class journalist in the extraordinary
rapid hour-by-hour changes in the discussions of Parliament'.[23] Others thought
just as highly of Massingham, and when he died the *Daily News* claimed that his
'Pictures in Parliament' column was 'in its force and originality the best example
of its kind that has ever appeared'.[24]

The press gallery that housed Massingham was a much more comfortable
place than it was around the time Lucy started. Towards the end of the nineteenth century the Commons authorities created more space for the reporters
and the facilities improved considerably. By the time Michael MacDonagah
wrote *The Reporters' Gallery* in 1913, members had access to one of three
writing rooms near the chamber ('the first black', 'the second black' and 'the
long room'), as well as committee room 18, which was reserved for writers who
did not smoke. There was also a smoking room, a library, a dining room, a tea
room and a bar, providing the journalists with 'the comforts and conveniences of
a well-equipped club'.[25]

There might have been more room, but the press gallery was still a relatively
closed shop and the spirit that had kept the *Scotsman* out for so long still
prevailed. When the *Daily Mail* and the *Daily Express* were launched, they both
applied to the Speaker for a seat in the press gallery. They were told it was full.
'There was an arrangement whereby . . . once a newspaper had secured the
privilege of a box, its claim to that box became, by a sort of freehold, its own
indefeasible right, apparently for all time. It became almost impossible to shift a
paper from its freehold box,' wrote Ralph Blumenfeld, who edited the *Daily
Express*.[26] The *Mail* got round the problem by buying up a provincial newspaper
that enjoyed press gallery membership, while the *Express* hired a box in the
gallery from an Irish title that did not use it.

Women reporters and foreign reporters had difficulty getting in, too. In the
early years of the twentieth century Britain was said to be the only country in the
democratic world where representatives from foreign newspapers were denied
access to the legislature.[27] Foreign correspondents working in London
campaigned for admission, but were told that there was not enough space for

them. They had to rely on the news agency Reuters for their parliamentary news. In the case of the women, different considerations seem to have applied. In 1890 the *Women's Penny Paper* asked: 'Is there any reason why women should be prevented from reporting the proceedings of Parliament?'[28] The paper wrote to the Serjeant at Arms asking to be allowed to send a woman to work in the press gallery. The Serjeant, David Erskine, wrote back with a polite no. 'Not only have I no authority to admit ladies into the reporters' gallery, but the gallery is already quite filled,' he said.[29] When Charles Bradlaugh raised the matter with the Speaker, Arthur Peel, he was told that letting women in 'would lead to consequences which at present it is difficult to conceive'.[30] At the time women were not even admitted to the strangers' gallery; if they wanted to listen to a debate they had to sit in a separate ladies' gallery. In ruling against the *Women's Penny Paper*, the Speaker seems to have been reflecting the views of the reporters, or at least some of them. 'Some were apprehensive of being ruined by female cheap labour, and others supposed that their free and unaffected social intercourse would be fettered and made artificial by the presence of women,' MacDonagh concluded.[31]

During the First World War the Press Association applied for permission to use 'girl messengers' in the press gallery 'on account of the extreme difficulty of finding boys'.[32] It was granted. But it was not until 1919 that a woman actually got the chance to report from the gallery. On 1 December Lady Astor became the first woman to take her seat as an MP and Marguerite Cody, a reporter on the *Daily News*, was in the gallery to watch. Cody was one of two women given a ticket for the gallery (the other worked for the Central News Agency), but that did not stop her paper using the headline: '*Daily News*' Reporter First Woman Journalist in the Press Gallery'. Cody was a Cambridge-educated linguist who had started in journalism on the *Belfast Evening Telegraph* and who, by 1919, had already notched up several 'first woman' achievements. For example, she was the first woman to swim the six and a half miles across Belfast Lough. While the paper's parliamentary correspondent wrote the main story about Lady Astor's first day (which led the front page), Cody contributed a long descriptive piece. She wrote positively about her reception in the gallery, although her experience was one that women reporters would find familiar more than eighty years later. 'The men were awfully kind to me . . . After Lady Astor had taken her seat they crowded round me, not to get my impressions, but to find out exactly how she was dressed.'[33]

Cody and the woman from the Central News Agency were sent to the press gallery only for a day and, if their arrival represented a breakthrough, it was no more than a symbolic one. Other women made an appearance in the years that followed, but without changing the essentially male-dominated nature of the place. Writing in 1932, R. G. Emery said that, while during his time in Parliament there had been women reporters in the gallery and two women representatives in the lobby, 'the gallery experiment was not wholly successful and of the two ladies in the lobby, one was only there for a short time, the other is very well known and very popular there, but I fancy that her work has little to do with politics and more with the social side of London life.'[34] Women did not achieve a significant presence in the place until well after the Second World War.

The reporters continued to complain about the acoustics in the Commons, but in the Lords, where hearing was even harder, peers found a solution to the problem. In November 1925, partly at the instigation of a Reuters correspondent, they installed microphones. Reporters were able to hear what was picked up using headphones in the gallery. Beforehand some peers were worried that the press would be able to eavesdrop on their private conversations, but in the event this did not cause much of a problem. On the plus side, the peers found that they were reported more thoroughly. 'Reporters discovered with astonishment that a small wizened figure whose lips had frequently been seen moving as he stood at the box was talking excellent copy. It was Lord Haldane,' William Barkley recalled. 'No complete sentence of his had ever been heard before. He must have been surprised in the last two years of his life at winning more space in the newspapers than he had secured in the previous fourteen years in the Upper House.'[35] For the next fifteen years the press gallery tried unsuccessfully to get the Commons to follow suit.

One solution for reporters faced with hearing difficulties was to get hold of a text of what was being said. This had been going on for some time, although the reporters were reluctant to admit that they were getting a service not available to MPs. When Charles Ross gave evidence to the select committee in 1878, he was asked how *The Times* made sure it reported answers given by ministers in the Commons accurately. Ross suddenly went all coy. 'I would ask to be allowed to decline answering that question. It involves confidential communications. I never betrayed one in my life, and I would not begin to do it now,' he replied.[36] The reporters continued to get this kind of help in the twentieth century, and they tried hard to keep it confidential. Even the tiniest diary item suggesting that an advance text had been available in the press gallery was enough to prompt a letter of complaint from the press gallery chairman to the offending newspaper. The committee appears to have been constantly worried that this system would break down. While lobby journalism was secretive, parliamentary reporting was supposedly open. But in fact both used sources of information that the reporters refused to discuss.

Twenty-eight years after making his maiden speech, Churchill was delivering a Budget as Chancellor of the Exchequer and a different sketch-writer
was writing about it for the *Daily Express*. William Barkley was an argumen-
tative, thirsty *Scotsman* with a Glasgow degree, a sharp sense of humour and
a curious obsession with simplifying English spelling, about which he wrote a
book. When he joined the paper in 1925 after just nine months in the press
gallery as a parliamentary reporter on the *Glasgow Herald* he was only twenty-
seven; for the next forty years, as the *Express* went through its glory days, he
was one of its star writers. In April 1929 his report of Churchill's Budget
started like this.

> For two and a half hours the Chancellor of the Exchequer unfolded, slowly
> but tantalisingly, in a voice that never seemed to tire, the Budget upon which
> the Government are going to the country.
>
> Mr Churchill took page by page from the despatch box before him the
> speech introducing his Budget, and at length won through the confusing
> maze of statistics which make up the country's balance sheet, to the central
> surplus of twelve million pounds.
>
> 'What shall we do with it?' he asked. His tense audience almost forgot to
> breathe. There was still silence in every corner of the crowded chamber . . .
>
> Mr Churchill took a sip from the suspicious amber liquor in a glass at his
> elbow, which he had audaciously sent Mr Boothby to collect just as he was
> speaking of the growth of the temperance movement, and he proceeded to
> explain the fighting front that he was to propose for the Government.[37]

The *Express* did not run traditional parliamentary reports and Barkley's job was
to combine recording what was said in the chamber with the lighter qualities of
a stand-alone commentary. Other papers adopted the same approach, but
Barkley was probably the master of this relatively new genre, the mass-market
report-cum-sketch.

Some journalists had their doubts about this new approach to covering
Parliament. Ralph Blumenfeld, who was the *Daily Express*'s editor-in-chief by
the time Barkley joined the paper, described the reduction of debate reporting
as 'one of the most significant changes that have taken place in British journalism
during my time' in a book published in 1933.[38] He attributed this development
largely to the *Daily Mail*'s founder, Lord Northcliffe. Blumenfeld accepted that
very few people were interested in reading long debate reports, but he thought
that if they were getting all their information from the sketch, then it was

important for the writer to be impartial. Without naming names, Blumenfeld complained that contemporary sketch-writers were biased.

> The descriptive sketch is scrappier than of old and is more flagrantly partisan. It is unfortunately too often the case that no attempt is made to provide the reader with a fair summary of the day's debate, or to distribute the limelight equally. Just those points are singled out from the speeches which accord or disaccord with the policy of the paper, and emphasis is laid on these to the exclusion of everything else. Often the emphasis is entirely unwarranted, with the result that the reader gets a false impression of the significance of the debate and of the relative importance of the various speeches delivered.[39]

In the 1920s and 1930s newspapers were reducing the proportion of space devoted to parliamentary affairs.[40] Blumenfeld thought this trend was going too far. But he accepted that there was no point filling newspapers with debate reports that nobody read. Northcliffe , he admitted, 'realised . . . that if the newspaper was to reach the vast new public of semi-educated readers that had grown up since the Education Act of 1870, it must function on a broader basis than any of the existing journals . . . He knew that what this public wanted was not political speeches, but news and incident and the varied drama of human life.'[41] Following franchise reform, by the time Churchill delivered his Budget all adult members of this 'vast new public' had the vote. Barkley was writing for this democratic audience and that explains why his work was so unlike Massingham's, in style, language and pace. Mass-circulation newspapers brought a new voice into parliamentary journalism, indeed into journalism as a whole, and it was one that more or less everyone would eventually end up using.

Hansard: Debate Reporting Gets Nationalised

If newspapers were no longer going to publish full debate reports, then Parliament was going to produce its own. In January 1909 the Commons itself took responsibility for producing the record known as *Hansard*. Debate reporting, an activity pioneered by entrepreneurial printers operating outside the boundaries of parliamentary legality, was nationalised. In the long term at least, the move can be seen as one that had a significant effect on the way newspapers covered politics at Westminster.

That is not to say *Hansard* started in 1909. It goes back to 1800 when William Cobbett began publishing *Cobbett's Weekly Political Register*. Two years later he started publishing debate reports as supplements to the *Register*, and from 1803 (coincidentally, the year the Speaker 'founded the press gallery' by setting seats aside for the reporters) the reports appeared separately under the title *Cobbett's Parliamentary Debates*. They were printed by Thomas Curson Hansard, whose father, Luke Hansard, had won the contract to print Commons papers in the late eighteenth century. Cobbett produced his *Debates* because he felt strongly that some kind of objective record should be available to the public. (For the same reason he compiled a multi-volume parliamentary history of England from the time of the Norman Conquest.) He was not trying to compete with the newspapers, and generally he obtained his material by lifting it straight from the pages of papers like *The Times*. The work was actually done by John Wright, his editor. Although the overheads were low, the *Debates* failed to make a profit and when Cobbett was gaoled and fined for printing a seditious libel, he sold the enterprise to Hansard. Wright went with it.[42] From 1812 the reports continued to be published under the title *Parliamentary Debates*.[43] They were bought by MPs, newspapers and certain institutions. In 1855 the Government became a customer when the Stationery Office took out a subscription for 100 copies, for distribution to departments in Britain and abroad. What people were buying was a work of reference. There were still no reporters and it did not compete with the newspapers because it tended to come out only once a month. Even as a historical record its value was questionable, because MPs were invited to 'correct' their speeches before publication and were allowed considerable leeway when they did so. Many Members sent in 'a composition which is no more the speech uttered by them in the House of Commons than it is a Welsh ballad', the *Daily News* complained in 1853. 'Observe, that whatever they return, is adopted . . . We are duping the unborn generations. With open eyes we are sowing the seeds of dissension between historians of another age.'[44]

Towards the end of the nineteenth century, with the parliamentary workload getting heavier, MPs began to worry about the speeches that were not getting reported under the existing arrangements. There were particular problems with committee stage, private bill and supply debates, which were of little or no interest to the newspapers, and debates after midnight, which were often too late to be covered properly. In 1877 Sir Stafford Northcote, the Chancellor of the Exchequer, started negotiations with Hansard over these four issues and the following year, in return for a grant of £3,000, Hansard employed a reporter in the gallery to ensure these areas were not neglected. This was the start of debate coverage as a public enterprise rather than a private one. In 1889 the Commons started putting the work out to tender. The money was not generous and over the next ten years five successive contractors provided the reports, two of them going bankrupt. Suppliers were not expected to compile a full report of the kind provided by *Hansard* today, and they were allowed to continue lifting from newspapers. But their service was reasonably thorough. Generally, they were required to fill in the gaps left by newspaper coverage, to report all speakers at least in part and to publish within a week.

In 1907 a Commons select committee considered whether the work should be contracted in-house. Arthur Balfour, the former Prime Minister, gave evidence, and argued that the growth of sketch-writing at the expense of debate reporting would have a serious effect on the quality of public debate in the country.

> I feel myself that the House of Commons is losing by the fact that the reporting is less good of its proceedings in the papers, and I do not believe that these sketch accounts of what goes on within our walls, even if they were impartial (which they rarely or never are), are in any sense a substitute for reasoned argument. I am aware it is rather the fashion to attack the House of Commons, but I still think there is no place where difficult questions are better thrashed out than on the floor of the House, and that you will never get the same closeness of argument in any newspaper articles. It is therefore a real loss to the public that they should be deprived of a very full statement of the arguments on either side, for they have in my opinion no other way of getting them.[45]

Balfour accepted that newspapers appealing to a mass readership would have only a limited interest in parliamentary proceedings. 'Nothing that government can do, of course, will induce the newspaper owner or newspaper editor to overload his paper with materials which he thinks the public do not desire to have,'[46] he said. The committee decided that the House should employ its own staff to keep a proper *Hansard*-style record of what was said. At the time it was almost the only legislature in the world that did not do so, the committee pointed out. Eleven shorthand writers were taken on, and in January 1909 the new arrangements came into force. A similar agreement was struck in the Lords.

Hansard was not set up to compete with the newspapers and it has never done so. Even though it has been on sale to the public, its 'circulation' has always been tiny.[47] But that does not mean that the decision to commission an official report did not have an effect on newspaper coverage. Charles Ross, who ran *The Times*'s parliamentary operation, was asked in 1878 if the production of an official report would be detrimental to the interests of the press. Not at all, he replied, but it would be detrimental to the interests of Members. 'It seems to me that the inevitable consequence would be that *The Times* would no longer feel it a point of honour to give reports at such length when at the public expense they are printed in full . . . As Members live in public estimation, this official report would be perfectly useless. The public would only know them by what appeared in the newspapers, where they would get less than they have heretofore.'[48] Although it is hard to prove a direct link between the start of the comprehensive *Hansard* service and the decline of debate reporting, Ross was almost certainly right. News demands a degree of exclusivity, and originally the reporters in the press gallery were presenting their readers with information that was not publicly available. After 1909 that was no longer the case. Their only advantage over *Hansard* was one of time, but even that was less marked than it used to be, because under the new arrangements *Hansard* appeared within twenty-four hours of the debate. For those editors who were wondering why they still covered proceedings in the Commons in such exhaustive detail, the MPs had provided them with just the excuse they were looking for to stop doing so.

'Definite Times and a Room at No 10': The Lobby System Starts

Political journalists created the lobby long after they invented 'lobbying'. When they started loitering in the Members' lobby of the Commons in the late nineteenth century to gather news, they were there as individuals, or at the very most as members of one of the unofficial syndicates that pooled intelligence and shared stories. The 'lobby system', involving collective briefings held on the confidential basis that already applied to one-to-one conversations outside the door of the chamber, was a later invention. In the absence of full records from before 1941, it is hard to say for certain when this started. James Margach, who started working in Parliament in the early 1930s, identifies 1926 as a key date. In his book *The Anatomy of Power* he claims that the lobby journalists were first invited into Downing Street as a group during the General Strike. 'After cabinet meetings during the grave crisis ministers found themselves being lobbied vigorously by lobbymen, as well as having to pass through milling crowds of angry strikers. To avoid the risk of contradicting each other in "off-the-cuff" comments . . . the Cabinet decided that during the emergency a cabinet secretary should give "guidance" to the political correspondents.'[49]

Among the few lobby papers that do survive from the period is the committee's annual report for 1926/7, which confirms that the year was 'important in the history of the lobby' because 'precedents' were set which would be of future use.

'During the General Strike the committee ensured that the Government's official informant saw lobby correspondents separately from the rest of the press,' the report says. 'When ministers conferred late at night at the House of Commons with parties in the coal dispute they received lobby correspondents at their rooms in the House. For lobby correspondents who had to watch late conferences at 10 Downing Street during the General Strike and the coal dispute the committee secured permission to wait in No. 12.' In other words, lobby correspondents were starting to get special treatment. They were already used to receiving briefings from the Government, but 1926 was a year in which they made a concerted effort to kept outsiders out. In a separate paragraph the report says: 'On certain occasions journalists who are not members of the lobby attended meetings arranged to be held between ministers and lobby correspondents. The committee regard it as important that only members of the lobby should attend those confer-ences, as ministers often speak confidentially and the committee can only assure ministers that our own members will respect confidences.' The report goes on to say that members of the lobby decided at a special general meeting that only those journalists whose names were on the lobby list should attend the ministerial briefings, and that the committee 'was authorised to take steps to see that this rule was observed'.[50] All this does not necessarily make 1926 the year the lobby started, but it does mean that by the time the General Strike was over, the lobby was acting as a unified group with a strong sense of its own self-interest and a close relationship with Downing Street.

Three years later Ramsay MacDonald became Prime Minister and the lobby committee approached the new Labour Government 'with a view to the provision of regular machinery for facilitating press enquiries'.[51] Some accounts say that George Steward, the man credited with being the first Downing Street press secretary, started in the post in that year. But the lobby's annual report for 1929/30 tells a different story. 'Conferences took place between the government chief whip and the lobby committee as a result of which arrangements were made for Mr WW Henderson, MP, to act as liaison officer between the Government and the lobby, and to make himself available for individual press enquiries.' William Henderson was MP for Enfield, head of the Labour Party's press and publicity department and the son of Arthur Henderson, Foreign Secretary from 1929 to 1931 and erstwhile party leader. Despite his connections, Henderson's appointment was not a success. The annual report goes on: 'The committee regret that the arrangements have not succeeded in the purpose for which they were intended, and have now appar-ently lapsed. The view of the committee is that the Government itself has not adequately supported its own scheme, and has made little or no information available through this channel.'[52]

As well as being uncommunicative, the Government could also be unduly heavy-handed. In the spring of 1930 Jack Kirk, a lobby correspondent on the *News Chronicle*, was interrogated by Special Branch officers for five hours in his own home and threatened with arrest for supposedly breaking the Official Secrets Act. He had written a story saying that the Viceroy of India, with London's approval, was about to arrest Mahatma Gandhi for his civil disobedience campaign. It was not even Kirk's story. According to Margach's account,[53] Frederick Truelove, a journalist on the *Daily Sketch*, got the information from John Clynes, the Home Secretary, and shared it with Kirk and William Forse from the *Daily Telegraph*. It is a good example of the way stories were routinely pooled. All three papers carried the story, but Kirk was the only man to get the Special Branch treatment because the *Daily Sketch* and the *Daily Telegraph* refused to give their correspondents' details to detectives. Kirk had to ring Truelove, his source, who then told Scotland Yard that the leak came from the Home Secretary. Clynes, when he was told, apparently sided with the journalists. A delegation from the lobby later went to Downing Street to see MacDonald and Sir William Jowitt, who as Attorney General ordered the Special Branch leak inquiry. The journalists argued that the Official Secrets Act was designed to deal with enemies of the state and not journalists doing their job. MacDonald and Jowitt expressed regret at what had happened, and agreed that if a similar situation occurred in the future, the lobby journalist concerned should have the right to see the Attorney General before being interviewed by the police.

At the same meeting the general state of relations between the Government and the lobby was discussed, and it seems that the journalists had something to say about the failings of Henderson junior. 'The Prime Minister expressed his astonishment that the arrangements he had made for the purpose of conveying information were not being effectively carried out,' according to the minutes of the meeting.[54] MacDonald asked the lobby to come up with some ideas and the journalists got involved in protracted negotiations with Herbert Usher, the Prime Minister's private secretary. Eventually there was another meeting with MacDonald. 'After a frank discussion in which the deputation suggested the appointment of a liaison officer to act as a medium between the Government and lobby journalists, the Prime Minister promised to consider the matter, but pointed out that he could not interfere in any proposal which involved an addition to the Civil Service pay roll.'[55] It is sometimes suggested that the modern lobby was a government invention, but this shows that it was the journalists who took the initiative. They wanted a liaison officer, just as in 1926 they were demanding customised briefings. MacDonald would not give them precisely what they wanted, but shortly afterwards Usher met another delegation to say that he had been given the job of supplying government information. 'In future he would be available at No.10 between 12 noon and 12.30 p.m. each day, and in the lobby at various times. During the recess he would also be available between 5 p.m. and 6 p.m.'[56] The committee concluded that, while this arrangement was not considered satisfactory, 'it was regarded as the best that could be secured in the circumstances'.[57]

In 1931 the Labour Government collapsed. With sterling going through the floor and half the Cabinet in revolt, there is no reason to believe that better media relations would have done MacDonald much good. But those lobby journalists who had called for the appointment of a liaison officer felt vindicated. 'The events which preceded the fall of the Labour Government provided ample evidence of the necessity of better provision being made for contact between the Government and the press,' according to the author of the 1931/2 annual report. 'The absence of machinery at the time of the crisis in August was a handicap alike to politicians and journalists. In practice it resolved itself into mass bombardment of the door of No. 10 Downing Street, and lobby journalists were compelled to take part in much undesirable questioning of cabinet ministers in Downing Street.'[58] A National Government was formed with MacDonald as Prime Minister and, according to the lobby's account, that was when Steward started. He was appointed private secretary to the Prime Minister and given the job of handling press relations.

Steward is seen as the original Bernard Ingham or Alastair Campbell because he institutionalised the lobby briefings. 'Definite times were arranged for conferences, and a room was provided at No. 10,' the lobby recorded.[59] No. 10 Downing Street was even extended to accommodate him; it was said to be the first time anyone had added to the building since the days of Sir George Downing in the seventeenth century. Steward used the system to distribute material like the New Year's honours list, and he also arranged for the lobby to meet the Prime Minister from time to time. The committee noted its gratitude to him for his 'personal helpfulness'.[60] At the same time the lobby journalists also seem to have been slightly wary about the new development. Having got what they wanted, some of them at least were asking whether it was such a good idea.

> The new system is an improvement on the old, though it carries with it certain dangers. There is a danger that it may become a personal service of the Prime Minister and ignore the wider and more important sphere of govern-

ment information. So far it has not had the effect of putting members of the Government further away from the lobby, though the possibility that this may be one of the consequences of an active development of the service cannot be overlooked when considering the desirability of its continuance.[61]

In June 1932 Steward informed the lobby that, although he was appointed primarily to act for the Prime Minister and the Treasury, he was 'also required to act for the Government as a whole, in all matters of a general character'.[62] He was prompted to make this statement because the lobby had arranged a briefing with a minister without consulting him first. Steward said that in future, if the lobby wanted to see a minister, it should make its request through him (although he accepted that if he failed to get the minister to turn up, the journalists were entitled to issue their own invitation). This arrangement made it abundantly clear that Steward was not going to ignore the wider sphere of government. But, if anything, this unsettled the journalists even more. The committee met to consider Downing Street's new ruling and agreed 'to inform Mr Steward that the lobby reserved their right to make direct approaches to any minister and could not accept any press officer as the only channel of communication between themselves and the Government'.[63] The lobby journalists were worried because in the 1920s and early 1930s it was relatively easy for them to get to talk to ministers, the civil servants running their private offices and their permanent secretaries. They correctly sensed that, as Whitehall developed its own information machine, the key decision-makers would become more elusive.

The procedures established by Steward and his counterparts in the press gallery were to survive for about sixty years. When people used to talk about the lobby system, this is what they were referring to: Downing Street briefing the political correspondents on a regular, collective and unattributable basis. There are at least five different levels of attribution or non-attribution available to a reporter, and the language used to describe them is generally not precise. (Or at least, it isn't in Britain, where 'off the record', for example, means different things to different people. The Americans, with their graduate journalism culture, are more particular.) First, a reporter can talk to a source on the basis that the information will not be used at all. Used properly, this is what the phrase 'off the record' means. Then there are two forms of clandestine, or unattributable, briefing. You can talk on the basis that information will be used but not sourced to anyone (which the Americans call 'not for attribution', or 'deep background'), or you can talk on the understanding that it will be attributed to some non-specific 'source' (or 'background', as the Americans say). Finally, there are on-the-record conversations, which can involve identifying the speaker by name, or alternatively as a spokesman of some kind. The phrase 'lobby terms' has in the past been used to describe both kinds of unattributable briefing, but in the early years 'deep background' prevailed. The lobby was very secretive, and it did not want to risk giving anything away about its methods. 'It is desirable that members should not talk in public of the source of their information, or discuss with others – especially those who did not attend a meeting and are, therefore, not bound by any pledge of secrecy – any information given at a confidential talk,' the reporters were reminded in 1936. 'Nor should any phrase or word be used in the stories written which might indicate the source of information. Such expressions as "I learn on the highest authority", "a member of the Cabinet", "in ministerial quarters" should be avoided where concealment of source is especially desirable.'[64]

Lobby journalists accepted these rules. None of them was clamouring for the kind of openness that press gallery reformers started demanding from the 1960s. They were worried that Steward might restrict their access to ministers, but they were not inviting ministers to speak to them on the record. The official reason for operating in this manner was that ministers were accountable to Parliament, and that if the Government had any news to announce, it was supposed to do so in the chamber. This was not just an excuse; many of those who have operated the lobby system over the years have genuinely believed in the primacy of Parliament. But the system also offered significant advantages to both sides. The journalists belonged to a prestigious clique that offered them the chance to write authoritatively about politics in a way that must have mystified and impressed most of their colleagues. And the Government got the chance to get its 'line' into the papers and trail its ideas without the awkward business of being held to account for what it was saying.

The lobby was able to operate a considerable degree of self-discipline because it was small. There were around forty-five British journalists on the lobby list in the 1930s. Technically the total size of the lobby was much bigger, because around the same number of foreign journalists were on the list and allowed into Parliament to gather news, but they were not allowed to attend the lobby briefings. With relatively little news coming through the official channels, much of the story-chasing during that decade was still done by correspondents acting as individuals, or as members of one of the story-sharing syndicates. But at the briefings, and on other occasions, they were capable of working collectively. When Bill Deedes went to the Commons as the *Morning Post*'s political correspondent, he encountered a Tory MP, Sir George Courthope, who had known his father at Eton. Courthope was sitting on a select committee dealing with the King's Civil List and revealed all to the grateful Deedes. His story led the paper the following day. But it turned out that Courthope had been blacklisted some time before for being rude to a journalist, and Deedes was told sternly by one of his elders that he should not even have been talking to him. More than a hundred years after the parliamentary reporters boycotted Members like William Windham, their successors were still capable of acting like the most restrictive producer cartel.

Appeasement and the Approach of War

George Steward stayed in Downing Street throughout the 1930s. He served MacDonald, Stanley Baldwin and Neville Chamberlain and, according to one commentator, 'did as much as anyone to shape the way politics is reported in Britain'.[65] At a time when the post of public relations officer (PRO) was still a relatively new one in Whitehall, Steward built up the most important PRO job in government. In the long term this had a considerable effect on the lobby; contact with ministers became less routine because the most important news source on a day-to-day basis was the Downing Street press secretary. Baldwin did not speak to the lobby collectively (he felt he had been let down in his dealings with journalists in the 1920s). Chamberlain felt no such inhibitions and, according to Margach, was the 'first PM to try to shape the lobby as an arm of government'.[66] Steward was his assistant in this endeavour, and the issue that preoccupied the two men, from Chamberlain's taking office in 1937 until war broke out on 3 September 1939, was appeasement.

Along with Parliament, the Conservative Party, the Royal Family and the press in general, the lobby did not emerge with much credit from the events leading up to the outbreak of the Second World War. The charge against the lobby correspondents is that they colluded with Chamberlain in presenting the pro-appeasement case and that they did not sufficiently challenge what Downing Street and the Prime Minister were telling them. Margach, who was in the lobby at the time, accuses Chamberlain of 'news management on a grand scale', and he accepts that the journalists allowed themselves to be grossly misled.

> [Chamberlain] persisted in giving optimistic forecasts of international prospects which were lies. In all situations and in all crises, however menacing, he always claimed that the outlook was most encouraging, with not a cloud in the sky; he claimed his contacts with Hitler and Mussolini were

very good and that the dictators were responding with understanding and promise, and if only Left-wing newspapers would stop writing critical and insulting things about them, he was confident that Herr Hitler and Signor Mussolini . . . would cooperate with him in his peace initiative . . . Alas, all too often we were caught napping. We would report Chamberlain's assessment in good faith, and write news reports and articles reflecting a strong mood of Government optimism on the eve of this or that recess. All too often we would be compelled to come rushing back within 24 or 48 hours as some new outrage by one or other of the dictators created a war threat which made nonsense of the Premier's dearest hopes.[67]

In accordance with lobby practice, the Downing Street briefings, including those given by Chamberlain himself, were unattributable. This meant that readers could not tell with any certainty where the pro-appeasement propaganda was coming from, and at times it allowed Chamberlain to convey a message that even the Foreign Office could not accept. On 9 March 1939 he met a few lobby journalists for one of his routine 'sunshine tours'.[68] *The Times* wrote it up under the headline 'Brighter Outlook' in a report that started: 'The more optimistic feeling in political circles is attributable not only to the consciousness of a swift growth in our armed strength, but also to an improvement in the international outlook. Difficulties and dangers enough remain, but in general the international situation seems now to give less cause for anxiety than for some time past.'[69] Other papers covered it in similar terms. At the Foreign Office, Sir Robert Vansittart, the Government's chief diplomatic adviser, read the reports, learned that Chamberlain had inspired them and concluded that the Prime Minister had given 'an entirely misleading estimate' of the international situation.[70] Vansittart was proved right when on 15 March Hitler invaded Czechoslovakia. According to Margach, some lobby correspondents eventually complained to Chamberlain that they were starting to look silly, reporting his wishful thinking at face value. But by then the damage had been done.

The gullibility of the lobby attracted some comment at the time. Two antiappeasement newsletters, the *Week* and the *King-Hall Newsletter*, revealed details of lobby briefings (in the manner of the *Independent*'s exposés in the late 1980s). 'The political correspondents were so startled by all this that they forgot to doll it up in their own words to give the impression of diversity, and on Friday one had the curious impression as one studied the papers that they were all employing the same writer,' Commander King-Hall's journal reported after Chamberlain spoke to the lobby on 9 March.[71] The historian Richard Cockett has also explored the lobby's conduct during this period at length in his book *Twilight of Truth* (1989). He argues that the press surrendered its independence in the run-up to September 1939 and that the lobby system was partly to blame. 'Due to the incestuous relationship between Whitehall and the press that had developed during the 1930s, the press in fact could do nothing but help Chamberlain pursue appeasement, as the "free" and "independent" press of Britain is at best merely a partisan political weapon controlled by politicians for their own purposes, and at worst a mere arena at the disposal of Whitehall to play out a game of interdepartmental warfare.'[72] When Cockett wrote his book in the 1980s the lobby system was under intense scrutiny and, reading between the lines, *Twilight of Truth* is in part about Bernard Ingham. The problem with Cockett's analysis is that he takes it for granted that governments will always be able to manipulate the lobby to their own advantage. This was a common belief in the 1980s, but not a theory that still had much credibility by 1997. Chamberlain may have managed to get the coverage he wanted, but the lobby system did not make that inevitable. That is not to say that the lobby deserves any credit for its reporting during this period. Cockett points out that by 1940 radio (the BBC) was seen as a more reliable source of information than the press, and he suggests that this was a result of those appeasement stories. The newspapers never regained their position as the nation's most influential provider of news.[73]

One of the papers that supported appeasement most enthusiastically was *The Times*. In 1937 Geoffrey Dawson, its editor, wrote a notorious letter to one of his correspondents saying that he could not understand why his coverage had upset the Germans because he had been doing his utmost 'night after night, to keep out of the paper anything that might have hurt their susceptibility'.[74] A year later these censorship tactics contributed to the resignation of Anthony Winn, a member of the paper's political staff. When Alfred Duff Cooper resigned as First Lord of the Admiralty after Munich, Winn wrote a positive story about the speech he made in the Commons explaining his decision. (Churchill described it as one of the best parliamentary performances he had heard.) Winn's story was spiked, and replaced with another, written by Dawson, which was 'satirical in tone and much more critical of Duff Cooper'.[75] Winn (who had already lined up a new job on the *Daily Telegraph*) resigned almost immediately, writing to his editor to say that he disapproved of the paper's pro-appeasement stand. 'My distaste for what I frankly regard as a silly and dangerous policy has been hardening for many weeks,' he said.[76] Winn was one of the few political journalists to emerge from the appeasement era with any credit. An old Etonian who was in his late twenties when he was on *The Times*, he was killed in action in 1942.

As war approached, members of the press gallery also had some more routine matters to worry about. Ever since 1925, the reporters had been anxious for the Commons to acquire a microphone system similar to the one that was used in the Lords, but they had resigned themselves to the fact that MPs would never accept the idea. In 1938 the Lords installed a new, less obtrusive version, and the press gallery committee decided that this gave it the excuse to try to get the Commons to think again. The Speaker, Douglas Clifton Brown, approved an experiment, but the committee was subsequently told that microphones were unacceptable. MPs objected to the thought that the reporters might be able to overhear private conversations in the chamber. Although this was not a problem in the Lords, they thought that in the Commons the opportunities for eaves-dropping would be greater. The committee persevered, and in July 1939 it sent a letter to all MPs drawing attention to the 'increasing difficulty' of hearing what was being said from the gallery. It argued that ministers and MPs were getting used to using microphones when appearing in public and that this meant they were developing 'a technique of speaking to which the acoustics of the House are totally unsuited'. It pointed out that the new, single microphone in the Lords (which was suspended from the ceiling) did not pick up asides. 'The press gallery feel,' it went on, 'that under the exceptionally trying conditions of today, they are entitled to the same measure of assistance in the House of Commons as they have received in the Lords – more particularly as statements of vital and worldwide importance are of more frequent occurrence in the Commons than ever before.'[77]

At around the same time William Barkley came up with a more novel way of trying to achieve progress on this issue. Noting that Herwald Ramsbotham, the newly appointed First Commissioner of Works, was an accomplished classical scholar, Barkley wrote him a letter in Latin inviting him to go up to the press gallery to sample the acoustics for himself. Ramsbotham was much taken with the idea of being able to correspond with a fellow classicist, and he replied (in Latin) to say that he would indeed come up to the gallery. The visit took place in August, just four weeks before the outbreak of war. According to Barkley, it was a propaganda masterstroke.

> We gave him one of the best seats and a sharp pencil. It took two or three weeks for anyone to tune in on the hearing in the old chamber and we were not surprised to see a look of incomprehension and bewilderment spread over the scholarly features. After a while he gave up, saying he did not know how we did it, for not one complete sentence he had heard.[78]

Ramsbotham agreed to carry out another experiment. This duly took place, but the reporters were not invited to participate and the conclusion, which was announced in February 1940, was the same. Microphones would not be allowed because the MPs were worried that they might lose the opportunity to gossip in private. Britain had already been at war for almost six months, and within a few more weeks Hitler would be threatening to invade. The British were fighting for a political system that was based upon elected MPs having the freedom to speak as they wanted in the Commons. But Parliament, with its customary disdain for the media, was not interested in making sure that the words they came out with were actually audible.

FOUR

War, Deference and Responsibility

The policy of the lobby has always been against quotations from an informant, even if he has no objection to this course. It is felt that the individual member of the lobby should take personal responsibility for his own stories, and that quotation reduces lobbying to mere reporting.

Guidance for lobby correspondents, May 1945

There might come a time when major measures were introduced by a minister, not first in this House, but first on the wireless. That may sound absurd, but we have had examples of what happens when the wireless is used in totalitarian countries.

Clement Attlee, House of Commons, 30 November 1955

Without conjecture there is no lobby journalism. The events or the proceedings that take place at any cabinet meeting are never officially revealed, nor are the meetings that take place between smaller groups of ministers, cabinet ministers or indeed those that take place between individual ministers . . . And of course it is a lobby correspondent's duty to deduce what has happened, because quite clearly what has happened at a cabinet meeting is of immense public interest.

Douglas Clark, political editor of the Daily Express,
evidence to the Vassall Inquiry, 18 January 1963

The War Years

Parliament flourished during the Second World War. Even though MPs regularly sat in secret and the general election was suspended, the norms of democratic life, by and large, carried on. The House of Commons became not just a law-making body, but a permanent reminder of what the country was fighting for. Parliamentary journalists have often seen themselves as contributing to the democratic process, but the sense of self-worth they seemed to feel between 1939 and 1945 was probably stronger than at any time in the gallery's history. 'We felt proud to be part of Parliament: proud to be sharing in the loss which the Commons had suffered: more confident than ever of victory; and determined to play our part in the struggle right through to the end,' wrote Arthur Baker in his memoirs, recalling his emotions after the destruction of the Commons chamber.[1] Given the fact that hundreds of thousands of other Britons had much more dangerous roles to play in the fight against Adolf Hitler, Baker's comments sound a touch melodramatic. But as an expression of what the reporters probably felt at the time, they come over as entirely genuine.

Before the war, members of the press gallery were fully involved in the plans drawn up for the possible evacuation of Parliament from London. It was proposed that Parliament would sit in Stratford-upon-Avon. The Commons would meet in the auditorium of the Shakespeare Memorial Theatre, the press would sit on the stage and the Lords would gather in the Shakespeare museum. It was envisaged that around a hundred men, or about half the press gallery, would make the move. Officials from the gallery committee were even taken to Stratford to discuss logistics such as accommodation. The chosen reporters were not told where they would be going, but they were issued with detailed instructions about what to do in the case of 'Black Plan A', which would operate if trains were running from Paddington, or 'Black Plan B', which would involve travel by bus from designated picking-up points. Parliament met on Sunday 3 September 1939, the day war was declared, and at the time the reporters expected to be leaving for 'somewhere in England' the following week.[2] Evacuation remained a possibility until Winston Churchill became Prime Minister the following May.

In the opening days of the war, the lobby correspondents had to deal with what they perceived as an even more unwelcome form of relocation. A Ministry of Information was set up with the intention that it would disseminate all government news and deal with censorship at the same time. It arranged to hold open, on-the-record briefings at its London headquarters, where there were facilities for journalists to file their copy and check their material with the censor at the same time. At the end of the 1930s most government departments employed press officers who answered enquiries from reporters, but the lobby correspondents had better access to Whitehall information than other journalists and when Downing Street wanted to release something important, the lobby enjoyed a total monopoly. Under the new arrangements, the lobby would lose its exclusivity. On 21 September Trevor Smith, the chairman of the lobby committee, wrote to Neville Chamberlain urging him to think again. He said the Ministry of Information briefings were 'unsuitable for confidential relations between the Government and the British and Dominions press' because foreign journalists were present. (Smith thought the Government would want to release some information to the British public but not 'the world at large', as if spying was not a possibility.) Even discounting the threat from foreigners, Smith claimed that the new arrangements still did not suit the needs of the Government and the public.

> Under the new system many ministerial conferences are held which are attended by journalists with no experience in the political field. They may be first-class crime reporters, for example, but it is not expected they can interpret or present matters of political importance in the manner to which lobby journalists, by their experience and training, are accustomed.

Conveniently forgetting all the tendentious appeasement guff, Smith said the lobby would like Chamberlain and other ministers to resume the personal lobby briefings 'which have proved so mutually valuable in the past'. He suggested that they should not take place at the new ministry, 'where publicity about them would be inescapable', but instead at the Commons.[3]

Other journalists who used the ministry wanted it to survive as a central source of government news. But most Whitehall departments were on the side of the lobby because they wanted to carry on disseminating their own information, and this view prevailed. At the beginning of October the Government announced that the Ministry of Information would lose certain functions and that departments would handle their own public relations. For critics of the lobby system, this was an important moment. In *Twilight of Truth* Richard Cockett suggests that, had it not been for the 'selfish considerations of a few journalists', the Ministry of Information would have allowed Britain to develop a more open system of government.[4]

Censorship had very little effect on the activities of reporters in the press gallery. Shortly after the start of the war Sir John Simon, the Chancellor of the Exchequer, declared that the Government had 'no desire to avoid parliamentary criticism or other fair criticism',[5] and from then on journalists operated on the basis that they were free to report whatever was said in the chamber. According to William Barkley, when the military censor sent an order to the press gallery saying that a question tabled by an MP should not be reported, the Speaker, Edward FitzRoy, immediately replied to the effect 'that there was only one censor of the House of Commons, namely Mr Speaker'.[6] That was apparently the last intervention of its kind. Reporters were asked on some occasions to leave out certain comments, but the requests came from the Speaker and the journalists seem to have been happy to oblige. In September 1940, at the request of the Ministry of Information, the Speaker ordered reporters not to file debate reports until after the House had adjourned. The Commons sat during the day during the war and the censors wanted to stop evening papers publishing stories that would reveal that the House was still in session. This rule was gradually watered down until it was abandoned in June 1941. The only other restrictions that applied were those in force when the House sat in secret. The 'I spy strangers' mechanism allowed the Commons to ban the press when MPs wanted to discuss the war candidly, and defence regulations were passed making it an offence to report proceedings from these sessions. In 1940, in a case with eighteenth-century overtones, a clerk who had written about a secret session in a publication called the *Uncensored British News Bulletin* was gaoled for eighteen months. It was the only prosecution of its kind. On another occasion the *Observer* was accused of disclosing information given out during a secret session; the matter was not taken to court, but the committee of privileges, which investigated it, did conclude that there had been a breach of parliamentary privilege and the reporter apologised.

While the most dramatic events of the war years happened at the battlefront, there were occasions when the House of Commons could compete. William Barkley covered the Norway debate in May 1940 for the *Daily Express* and shortly afterwards described what happened in a letter to Arthur Christiansen, his editor, mentor and hero. (Christiansen was in hospital at the time.) It was as important a parliamentary occasion as Barkley or anyone had ever covered, and he knew it. Most of the academic writing about political journalism overlooks the fact that it is an activity carried out by people who are enjoying themselves, and that, while some of it might be dull, there are also moments of sheer professional exhilaration. Barkley's letter is worth quoting at length because it captures that excitement.

> I should think my performance on Wednesday, 8 May for Thursday's paper
> was an all-time high record for a one-man effort, and I do not mean to set

myself up in competition with it in future merely for record-breaking purposes. Gunn [Herbert Gunn, acting editor] purred next day and said I was worth a thousand a week . . . I had John Redfern to assist me. He is an admirable reporter. He did the account of Duff Cooper. Otherwise every word was mine including the scene on the front page. Not a word of agency copy in the report. When it came to Churchill's closing speech my heart sank. Gunn had asked me to do it because the agencies lately have been so slow and inaccurate. But when Churchill was first of all held up by the previous speaker taking quarter of an hour over his time and then, being a great deal interrupted, he set off to speak at a pace such as I have never heard. This was at the end of an exhausting day. There was not a second to check with anyone because he finished at 11. When I came out of the gallery feeling hopeless of getting it through in time I found a gang of reporters still arguing the toss about what he had said at the beginning of the speech.

So I said 'blow' and banged into the telephone box. Hearing the shout from inside the House at the announcement of the majority I looked into the chamber – the Palace of Westminster being so arranged that the *Express* private telephone is only two yards from the gallery door. I had just got the Churchill report started. I broke off to slap through the outstanding bits of the 'Go, go, go!' to Chamberlain and was finishing that when Eden [Guy Eden – the *Express*'s lobby correspondent] rushed out to say that Chamberlain had almost 'slumped out' when he got out of sight of the House. So I tagged that on and turned back to report Churchill. It was now 11.20. I was finished at 12.20 – four columns due to one of Smith the telephonist's pieces of super-contraction. I have never known such a job done in my life. For one hour and 10 minutes Smith typed as fast as I could speak, and I was speaking as fast as I could read shorthand. Every word of the more than two pages of the paper was typed by Smith that day. I told Gunn what a hero he was. Net result I caught the first slip edition with the whole speech.[7]

In his memoirs Christiansen describes Barkley as 'the only reporter I have ever known who can dictate columns of coherent copy direct from the briefest of notes'.[8] The account of the Norway debate that appeared in the *Daily Express* under Barkley's byline on 8 May is around 6,500 words long. The Churchill material, which was dictated in those frenetic seventy minutes, runs to around 2,500 words on its own. The debate finished Chamberlain, and on 10 May (the day before Barkley wrote his letter to Christiansen) Churchill became Prime Minister.

Exactly a year later, on Saturday 10 May 1941, the chamber of the Commons was destroyed during a heavy German air raid. Westminster had been bombed before, but the damage caused in May meant that the chamber was not used again for almost ten years. By the time of the attack the Commons had already started holding some meetings in Church House, which offered much better protection against air raids, and for a few months this chamber, which was referred to as 'the annexe', served as its home. Here the reporters were provided with rooms and telephones, and for the first time some seats in the gallery were reserved for foreign journalists. There was no equivalent of the members' lobby, and the lobby correspondents plied their trade around the corridors of the building. MPs continued to hold meetings in their offices in the Commons in the spring of 1941 and, as the threat of air raids diminished, it was decided to return Parliament and sit in the Lords. The reporters did not particularly welcome the move because their accommodation in the Upper House was cramped. Most of them had to work from committee room 10, which was some distance from the chamber, halfway between the Lords and the Commons. But the arrangements stuck and, apart from a period in 1944 when they moved back to Church House because London was being attacked by doodlebugs, MPs made the Lords their home for the rest of the war.

Although in many ways life in the press gallery continued as normal during the war, Britain changed between 1939 and 1945 in ways that were to have important repercussions for political journalism. One development was the emergence of the broadcast media, in the form of the BBC, as the nation's prime source of news. Another was the expansion of the state, and in particular the massive increase in the numbers employed in the Whitehall communications industry. The first government organisation to take an interest in public relations is said to have been the Post Office, which was investing in publicity in the 1850s. A Department of Information was set up during the First World War, and during the interwar years, as George Steward created a press office in Downing Street, most other government departments set up their own public relations departments. However, following the creation of the Ministry of Information, the Whitehall information machine became more powerful than ever. At its peak the ministry employed 2,950 staff in Britain and 3,600 abroad. Another 1,700 people were doing similar jobs in other departments. After the war the ministry was disbanded; but large numbers of press officers remained in Whitehall, where Clement Attlee's Government needed an army of PROs to explain its programme of social and economic reform to the public.

George Orwell was not the only man to worry about the state investing resources in trying to control what people thought. The development of government public relations in the late 1940s was the subject of so much controversy that it makes the concerns about Bernard Ingham in the 1980s, or Labour 'spin' in the late 1990s, look rather tame. The press, Parliament and democracy all seemed to be at risk. Journalists (at Westminster and elsewhere) were worried that the PROs would stop them speaking to the politicians or officials who mattered. It was also suggested that reporters might become too dependent on the press officers employed to give them stories. 'If newspapers get out of the habit of finding their own news and into the habit of taking all or most of it unquestioningly from a government department, they are obviously in some danger of falling into totalitarian paths,' said the Royal Commission on the Press in 1949.[9] Some MPs thought that if the Government were allowed to spend money persuading the public to support a new initiative, then Parliament would be sidelined because it would become much harder for MPs to object. There were also concerns that PROs would destabilise Britain's two-party system by giving the government party a permanent advantage. These fears turned out to be unfounded. But that is not to say that the arrival en masse of the PROs did not fundamentally alter politics, and political journalism. Originally the job was all about covering MPs and what they said in Parliament. After the Second World War, interrogating officials about the work of their departments mattered almost as much too.

The war left another, more practical legacy. By the time the old Commons chamber was destroyed in 1941, there were sixty-nine seats in the press gallery: almost double the number in 1852, but still not enough for all the journalists who wanted one. There were also complaints about lack of office space. When Parliament began planning the reconstruction, the press gallery committee requested a larger gallery with ninety-five seats, more space, better telephone facilities and a smarter entrance. The authorities gave the committee largely what it wanted and when the new chamber opened on 26 October 1950, the journalists were in better accommodation than they had ever known. One feature was particularly welcome. For the first time since reporters crept surreptitiously into the gallery in the eighteenth century, the acoustics in the Commons chamber were not a problem. Having refused for so long to use microphones, MPs accepted them during the war when they sat in the Lords chamber (where the proceedings had been amplified since 1925). The first debate in the Lords took place on 24 June 1941 and it was agreed only at the last minute that the microphones would be turned on. Afterwards there was no desire to return to inaudibility. The MPs accepted that their concerns about being overheard were largely unfounded, and when the new chamber was being planned, microphones were incorporated into the design. In terms of facilitating the reporting of debates, it was one of the more significant reforms of the twentieth century. Unfortunately, the only 'moderniser' who could really take any credit for it was Adolf Hitler.

Guy Eden and his Secret Lobby Rules

As the war in Europe came to an end, the lobby decided to issue a mini code of conduct. It filled just one side of A4 and there were only seven 'suggestions' on the list. As the opening paragraph said, the committee decided to produce the document for the large number of members 'new to the traditions and customs of the lobby'.[10] The authors, John Carvel, chairman in 1945, and Guy Eden, secretary in the war years and afterwards, were probably not saying anything particularly original. The lobby, after all, had had its own code of behaviour for many years.[11] But Carvel and Eden seem to be the first people to have written it down. Their text is effectively the earliest surviving version of the lobby rulebook. Over the years this was rewritten several times and much ridiculed by critics of the lobby system. The original is worth studying in some detail.

The first three points are about lobby etiquette:

1 When a member of the lobby is in conversation with a minister or a private MP in the lobby, another member of the lobby should not join in unless invited to do so. This is one of the oldest traditions of the lobby.

2 Stay to the end of meetings. If it is quite impossible to do so, you are under an obligation of honour not to make use of any information gained at the meeting until the meeting is over, and all other members of the lobby are free to write their stories.

3 Normally, the lobby's guest should be left to complete the opening statement before questions are asked. The chair will indicate when questions may be put.

None of these is particularly controversial and, as a guide to behaviour least likely to annoy colleagues, they broadly apply today.

The next rule is more revealing because it shows how anxious the lobby was to preserve its monopoly as a provider of Westminster news.

4 When meetings are arranged on behalf of the lobby, it is strongly urged that all members of the lobby should endeavour to attend, even if the subject is not of first-class importance. The policy of the lobby is to

encourage ministers and members to work through its machinery when they have anything to communicate, and this can only be done if the officers are sure of an audience for the lobby's guests.

But the most significant of all is the one that follows.

5 Don't quote informants. Meetings of the lobby are on the same basis as individual lobbying, and, unless the informant gives special leave for his name to be mentioned, it should not appear. The policy of the lobby has always been against quotations from an informant, even if he has no objection to this course. It is felt that the individual member of the lobby should take personal responsibility for his own stories, and that quotation reduces lobbying to mere reporting.

In later years lobby journalists defended their preference for non-attribution on the grounds that ministers and officials giving collective briefings were always likely to say more if they were talking on that basis. But the lobby in the 1940s went further than that; it was opposed to quoting from a source 'even if he has no objection to this course'. Why? Because to do so would diminish the status of the lobby correspondent. Reading paragraph 5 today, one is struck by the hubris of Eden and his colleagues. A lobby correspondent did not need to attribute anything to a figure of authority because he *was* the authority. To do otherwise would be 'mere reporting'. Reporting is at the heart of all effective journalism, yet the lobby of the 1940s appeared to view the activity with a measure of contempt.

The final two 'suggestions' are about secrecy and the collective good.

6 Don't talk about lobby meetings, before or after they have been held. If outsiders appear to know that a lobby meeting is to be, or has been held, do not confirm their conjectures. Steps have been taken to prevent leakage of such information through PROs and others in the government departments.
7 In short, it is suggested that all members of the lobby should, in matters of common interest, keep in mind the importance of communal life, and do nothing to prejudice it, while of course preserving the free competition which has always been a strong feature of lobby life.

In a few short paragraphs Carvel and Eden had set out a model for lobby journalism that was to survive for at least another forty years. Like many lobby documents of the period, it was headed: 'Strictly private and confidential'.

Eden was the key figure. Born in 1901, he was brought up in London where his father founded and ran the *Wimbledon Gazette*. He worked briefly for the local paper in his teens and then moved on to the Press Association. In 1924 he joined the lobby as a Press Association correspondent and in 1933 he was made political correspondent of the *Daily Express*, a post he held until 1952. A conformist with a strong sense of propriety, Eden, as lobby secretary, probably did more than anyone else to cement its reputation as an organisation that could keep a secret. Lobby journalists were respecting confidences long before 1939, but the war made this aspect of their work seem more important than ever. As we have seen, they objected to the original plans to hold open press conferences at the Ministry of Information because, they said, they did not want to take the risk that sensitive information would be picked up by foreigners. They were even able to keep the official censors out of their meetings. There is some evidence that these acts of self-importance were justified. Eden was given information in advance about important military and diplomatic events on the understanding that he would pass it on to other lobby journalists at the appropriate time.[12] When he died *The Times* described him as 'a shrewd observer, both amiable and dependable and the repository of innumerable confidences'.[13]

After the war, the lobby journalists still had to tiptoe around the convention that government announcements were supposed to be made in Parliament, but in theory they should have been able to relax a little about sharing their information with foreigners. In practice, protectionism still applied. There were many journalists from other parts of the Empire covering Parliament, and some of them were on the lobby list. But the lobby committee was anxious to ensure that the foreigners allowed into the Members' lobby were not given access to the collective briefings too. In May 1946 Norman Robson, the acting lobby secretary, wrote to the Serjeant at Arms, Brigadier Sir Charles Howard, asking for a ruling on the matter. Robson said the lobby room was too small to accommodate both the British journalists and the foreigners. 'The meetings held in it are of a highly confidential character and provide ministers and spokesman of all parties with a valuable opportunity of confidential talks with lobby correspondents,' he went on. 'The admission of dominion and foreign correspondents to these meetings would destroy the value of these meetings and do serious damage to an institution which has proved of great value for more than half a century.' Robson argued that foreign journalists generally did not stay in the country long enough to acquire knowledge of lobby traditions or to build up the 'intimate personal contact' that was the basis of lobby confidentiality.[14] Three years later, in a letter to Sir Stafford Cripps, the then Chancellor, Eden put it even more bluntly.

Writing as lobby secretary, Eden complained about the fact that Cripps had unveiled his White Paper on the balance of payments at a press conference rather than a closed lobby briefing. At the open press event, 'there was no opportunity for the sort of questions lobby journalists seek to ask,' Eden said. 'I would emphasise, in this connection, that the lobby journalists are reluctant on grounds of public policy and the national interest to ask highly political questions before foreigners. There are many points which may properly be dealt with in the privacy and confidence of a lobby conference, which cannot be dealt with in the semi-public atmosphere of a general press conference.'[15]

For all their patriotic protestations, Eden and his colleagues turned out to be just as hostile to the idea of letting British non-lobby journalists invade their territory as they were to the notion of allowing the foreigners in. In 2002, when Alastair Campbell changed the pattern of Downing Street briefings, he made a deliberate attempt to break the monopoly of the lobby by making sure that other specialist correspondents were regularly invited. In 1947 Francis Williams, Attlee's press secretary, had the same idea. He asked members of the lobby what they would think about Downing Street briefings being open to non-members. The committee rejected the idea smartly, on the grounds that 'it would be impossible [to have] the same confidence between informant and informed'.[16] Doubtless the reply came as no surprise to Williams. He worked on the basis that his dealings with the lobby were confidential, and in September 1946 he complained formally to the committee that what he had said at a briefing had been disclosed to an outsider. Interestingly, he was irritated not by something that had appeared in a newspaper but by the fact that 'members of the lobby had quoted him to a government department'.[17] Lobby briefings were evidently so secretive that even Whitehall officials were not supposed to know about them.

The committee took the offence quite seriously. It suspended lobby briefings for three working days while it tried to find out who the culprit was, and it agreed to introduce a new lobby rule saying that facts and figures given by a source should not be checked with a government department.

Members of the lobby seem to have relished the undercover aspects of their work. There is always a danger that journalists will enjoy having secrets more than reporting them, and the lobby of the 1940s was particularly vulnerable to this charge. For many years members went to remarkable lengths to try to stop anyone finding out what was going on in the briefing room, or even that there *was* a briefing room. When Chris Moncrieff started as the Press Association's lobby correspondent in the late 1960s, he was told by his predecessor – apparently in all seriousness – that he should not discuss the workings of the lobby even with his wife. Moncrieff took no notice. But generally, at least until the 1970s, the rule about not talking about lobby meetings was upheld, even to the extent that non-lobby members of the press gallery were not supposed to know what was going on. The lobby communicated through messages on a notice board and, just to create an authentic air of subterfuge, a code was used to indicate who would be giving a briefing: 'Blue Mantle' for the Conservatives, and 'Red Mantle' for Labour. Other peculiarities included the occasional reading of a note at the beginning of some lobby meetings reminding members that the proceedings were secret and the practice of formally 'introducing' newcomers.

Eden encouraged a lot of this self-indulgent cliquishness. In the late 1940s only around thirty journalists attended the lobby every day, and that made it easier to impose collective standards of behaviour than it was later when the numbers soared. Eden took the view that the lobby rules were no more than the expression of 'the ordinary usages and courtesies of gentlemanly conduct',[18] but what struck Eden as 'gentlemanly' now looks unduly deferential. He seemed to hate causing offence. On one occasion he even considered resigning from the lobby committee because some of his fellow journalists had rushed out of the lobby room after one briefing, pushing past the next guests (prison commissioners) who were waiting to go in to hold theirs.[19] (He thought his colleagues should have stayed. See rule 4.) In retrospect, much of the lobby practice of this era seems hard to justify. The argument used to explain why foreigners should not be allowed to attend a Treasury briefing comes over now as just a spurious excuse for the preservation of a cosy little cartel. Some of the rules, the fawning, and the attempts to enforce a Soviet-style news blackout on any reference to the way the lobby ran its business seem absurd. They were. But they were also, partly, a consequence of what happened between 1939 and 1945. 'The lobby journalists have handled official secrets of the highest importance and there has never been a well-founded suggestion that they have been misused or carelessly handled,' Eden wrote in 1947 with evident pride.[20] The modern lobby was not created during the Second World War, but the journalists who lived through it developed an understandable conviction that not revealing Whitehall secrets was a way of serving the national interest. One of the reasons why Eden and his colleagues seem so odd today is that contemporary journalists believe precisely the opposite.

'Jobbery, Bribery and Corruption': 1947

There was at least one journalist in the 1940s who was instinctively opposed to the prevailing culture of non-attribution.

> I do not believe that anything should take place, concerning the political
> welfare of the nation, that should be kept secret from the public . . . The duty
> of the press is to find out what is afoot and inform the public. Cabinet
> ministers and MPs have no right to go into huddles, hold secret meetings to
> define public policy. They are merely servants of the public and their masters
> – indeed, their paymasters – the public, have a right to know what their
> servants are doing in their name and under their authority.[21]

When Garry Allighan wrote that in April 1947, he had been in journalism for
more than twenty years and had worked as a reporter, a war correspondent, an
industrial editor, a news editor, a picture news editor and a political correspondent. Unfortunately, at the time, he also happened to be Labour MP for
Gravesend. His commitment to the public's right to know, combined with a
marked reluctance to be quite so open when it came to telling fellow parliamentarians about his own activities, was to cost him his seat.

Allighan's trouble started when William Nally, a Labour MP and a journalist
himself, asked Clement Attlee for an inquiry into 'the circumstances under
which a newspaper of the *Express* group continues to pay bribes to members of
this House to supply the report of private and confidential meetings of this
House'.[22] The allegation that unnamed MPs were susceptible to bribery of this
kind went down very badly. Nally was ordered by the Speaker to withdraw the
remark, and he did. But a few days later, under the headline 'Labour MP reveals
his concept of how party news gets out', the *World's Press News* set out to explain
what Nally was on about. Allighan was the author and his revelations were
extraordinary.

> Every newspaper in the street has anything up to half a dozen MPs on its
> 'contacts' list. They always have had – what's the contacts file for otherwise?
>   Some of the 'contacts' are on a retainer, some get paid for what they
> produce, some are content to accept 'payment in kind' – personal publicity. I,
> as news editor of the *Daily Mirror*, used to okay payments to several regular
> MP contacts, both for stories, 'info' and tip-offs . . .
>   That is one way any enterprising newspaper gets what the party calls 'leaks'.
> Another way more accurately justifies that description. MPs 'leak' around the
> bar. Being no less human than subs, some MPs 'knock 'em back' at the bar and,
> being less absorptive than reporters, become lubricated into loquacity . . .
>   No worthwhile reporter could fail to get the stuff. If he knew no other way,
> and had no other contacts, all he would have to do would be to spend his time

and paper's money, at the bar, and if he did not pick up enough bits and pieces from MPs in search of refreshment to make a first rate 'inside' story, he ought to be fired.

Just to endear himself more to his Commons colleagues, Allighan ended with a plea for meetings of the parliamentary Labour Party to be open to the press. 'To discuss public policy behind locked doors is not only to deny knowledge to the public, but deny to the public its right to know,' he concluded.[23]

Quintin Hogg, a Tory, complained that the article was a breach of the privileges of the Commons and the matter was referred to the privileges committee for investigation. At the time there was considerable interest in leaks from PLP meetings. The *Evening Standard* was regularly printing the best material and fellow lobby journalists were struggling to work out who was supplying it with information. Naturally, the committee invited Allighan to give evidence. He said that he was describing 'past methods of news gathering'[24] on the assumption that that was how it still worked. He repeated the assertion that stories were leaking because MPs were either being paid, or talking under the influence of alcohol, or providing information in the expectation of favours in the future. And was that how the stories were getting into the *Evening Standard*? 'Those are the only ways I can imagine of their leaking,' he said.[25] When he was asked if he knew of any MP who had taken money in return for supplying information, or any Member who was still receiving payments, he replied 'no' both times.

Unfortunately for Allighan, the committee subsequently found out, as it put it in its report, 'that he had no need to draw on his imagination in the matter'.[26] Since he was unable to provide evidence to back up his allegations, the committee decided to interview various editors and journalists to see if they could shed any further light on the affair. Most witnesses rejected the suggestion that they paid MPs for stories. But Herbert Gunn, editor of the *Evening Standard*, admitted that he paid an agency called the Trans-Atlantic Press Agency £30 a week (at least £700 in today's terms) for reports of PLP meetings and other parliamentary news. At first he was reluctant to name the author of those reports. But when it was put to him that disclosure was in the public interest, Gunn said they were written by Allighan, and that he had been supplying them to the *Evening Standard* for a considerable period of time. When Allighan was later asked to explain why he had lied, he said that he preferred the committee to discover the truth for itself.

The committee took Allighan's offence very seriously. 'It has long been recognised that the publication of imputations reflecting on the dignity of the House or of any Member in his capacity as such is punishable as a contempt of Parliament,' it concluded.[27] To suggest that MPs were willing to betray the confidence of private party meetings for money or because their discretion had been 'undermined by drink' was just such an imputation.[28] Bizarrely, the committee also ruled that the fact that such a charge was true was not necessarily a defence. It said that it would be if the allegations were published with a view to ending such a discreditable practice, but that Allighan could not use that as an excuse because that was not his motive. As well as writing the offending article, Allighan was judged to be at fault for having supplied information about a meeting he attended in his capacity as an MP in return for money. The committee described this transaction as bribery. The MP had also 'persistently misled' the committee. He was judged guilty of an aggravated contempt of the House and a gross breach of privilege.[29]

The Commons debated the affair on 30 October. Allighan apologised profusely and said that he had written the offending article during a period of 'intense mental strain'. In his 'journalistic zeal' he thought it was his duty to report all news in the public interest and, in working for the *Evening Standard*, he had put his duty as a journalist ahead of his duty as a Labour MP. The only allegation he rejected was the idea that he had taken a bribe; as a working journalist, it never occurred to him to view a payment as a bribe.[30] Allighan left the chamber after his statement. The committee, in its report, left it up to the Commons to decide an appropriate punishment and Herbert Morrison, leader of the House, moved that Allighan should be suspended without pay for six months. Quintin Hogg proposed an amendment to expel Allighan permanently and Churchill, then leader of the Opposition, spoke in its favour. 'How can you stigmatise a Member as dishonourable by the most formal and solemn vote and, and then, after an interval, long or short, immediately resume calling him an honourable Member? . . . I do not think that to bring about a situation of that kind has a grain of logic in it,' Churchill argued.[31] The Commons agreed, and Hogg's amendment was carried. Allighan was subsequently escorted from the building by a police officer, never to return. One of only three MPs to be expelled from the Commons in the twentieth century, Allighan subsequently went to South Africa to run a journalism school.

Allighan was not the only MP giving information to newspapers in return for money. During the committee hearings Guy Schofield, editor of the *Evening News*, and Stanley Dobson, his political correspondent, revealed that they too had a Member on their books. They refused to identify him, but Evelyn Walkden, MP for Doncaster, subsequently owned up in a statement in the

Commons. He was receiving £5 a week (at least £120 today) for his services. He told the Commons that he had been friendly with Dobson for many years, that he had helped the reporter 'in an advisory capacity' in the past and that he had only recently entered into a financial relationship with the paper. Under the arrangement he was 'invited to give frequent guidance . . . on a wide range of political and industrial subjects'. The payment did not affect the information he was willing to disclose, he claimed. As for leaking the proceedings of PLP meetings, 'it was only after garbled and very biased reports appeared in the *Evening Standard* that I took the opportunity when approached for guidance by Mr Dobson to try and render to him a little advice which would enable the *Evening News* to present a more balanced account of the proceedings without giving away anything of an essentially secret nature.'[32]

This revelation was also referred to the committee of privileges. Walkden was in a better position than Allighan, because he had not sounded off about the misdemeanours of his colleagues in print and he had not lied to the committee. But it took an 'unfavourable' view of his evidence nevertheless. To supply confidential information for a fee was to accept a bribe and so, 'although Mr Walkden thought fit to betray the secrets of his party meeting for a relatively small sum, he has been guilty of a breach of privilege.'[33] When the Commons debated the affair on 30 October, Walkden apologised. The committee had not recommended a punishment and, although there was some pressure for him to be expelled too, the House decided that instead he should receive a formal reprimand from the Speaker. This was delivered immediately.

In his *World's Press News* article, Allighan presented the practice of paying MPs as a necessary, almost commendable, form of journalistic enterprise. But that was not the conventional view in the Commons and, as the affair unfolded, the newspapers involved faced almost as much censure as their contacts. Schofield and Dobson were summoned to the Bar for refusing to tell the committee whom they were paying for information. In its main report the committee recommended that Arthur Heighway, editor of the *World's Press News*, should be reprimanded. On 30 October he was summoned to the Bar and told by the Speaker that he was guilty of publishing 'words which contain unfounded imputations against the conduct of Members of this House'.[34] In view of the fact that the Commons was spending the whole evening deciding what to do about two MPs who had behaved exactly as Allighan described, this charge was demonstrably untrue.[35] But that was not an argument that Heighway chose to make. In his statement he accepted full responsibility for the publication of the article and offered his sincere apologies.

Later that night, after the House had dealt with Allighan, Heighway and Walkden, Morrison brought forward a motion intended to make explicit the ban on paying MPs for confidential information and to introduce a tougher penalty for future offenders. It said that if a journalist did this again, 'that person and any other representative of the same newspaper or [press] agency shall, if the House thinks fit, be excluded from the precincts of this House, until this House shall otherwise determine'.[36] According to James Margach, 'it was an obvious threat to gag and expel correspondents and papers on a permanent basis.'[37] It was past 11 p.m., and it seems that Morrison expected the Commons to support him. But at this point in the debate, MPs came to the defence of the press. Haydn Davies, a Labour MP and a former lobby correspondent, complained that the House might be giving the impression 'that jobbery, bribery and corruption are the everyday stock-in-trade of journalists'. He insisted that this was not the case, and pointed out that, under the Morrison law, gallery staff on a newspaper could be excluded from the Commons for an offence by someone in the lobby.[38] Wilson Harris, editor of the *Spectator* and an independent MP (representing Cambridge University), argued that the House already had the power to expel journalists. With the debate turning against him, Morrison withdrew the motion. A few weeks later he introduced a revised version that was passed by MPs. It said that anyone offering to pay an MP for confidential information would incur 'the grave displeasure' of the House, but it did not mention the press and it did not set out specific penalties. At the time this was seen as something of a climbdown.

Although the committee of privileges was really interested only in the bribery issue, it also accepted the word of its journalist witnesses when they said they did not try to obtain confidential information by getting MPs drunk.

> The general effect of the evidence given [by the press] was an indignant repudiation of the suggestion that the press sought or obtained confidential information from Members of Parliament either by paying them . . . or when Members were under the influence of drink. It was stated on behalf of the lobby correspondents that any such conduct on the part of any one of their number would be regarded as wholly contrary to the standard of journalistic ethics maintained in the lobby.[39]

Sadly, the committee did not go into any more detail, or try to explain the difference between legitimate entertaining and getting an MP 'lubricated into loquacity'. If it had, it would probably have found the task impossible. Today, lunches between lobby correspondents and politicians are generally much more sober than they used to be. Robin Oakley, in his memoirs, charts the decline; first to go were the pre-lunch drinks; then guests gave up the post-prandial brandy; then it was just a glass of wine, rather than a bottle. 'Nowadays the most taxing decision as the wine waiter approaches tends to be "still or fizzy",' he observes.[40] But for many years heavy drinking was a routine part of Westminster professional life, and an important component in the relationship between politicians and the press. And journalists' motives were more than just social. Just as he was accurate about MPs being paid, Allighan was right about alcohol too.

A Leak and a Resignation: November 1947

Thirteen days after the Commons voted to expel Garry Allighan, Hugh Dalton, the Chancellor, was heading for the chamber when he saw the lobby correspondent John Carvel. Dalton was about to deliver the Budget and Carvel, who worked for the *Star*, a London evening paper, was after something to file for his paper's late edition. In a very short conversation, Dalton told Carvel the Budget highlights. Carvel was on the phone to his office within five minutes and, as a result, a story ran in the paper's second late-night edition. It was only fifty-five words long,[41] and it appeared only in the 'stop press' (or 'fudge'). Yet this was to become one of the most famous leaks in the lobby's history.

'Leak' is probably one of the most over-used words in political journalism. It conjures up the image of a disloyal insider surreptitiously posting a document in a brown envelope. Occasionally it happens like that. Those stories often attract the most acclaim although, in fact, they often involve the least enterprise; the envelope either arrives or it does not. More often, the word 'leak' is applied to information that comes from someone in authority willing to give it out. Security has not really been breached; just the embargo. Getting these stories normally involves developing good personal relationships, having the nous to ask the right question at the right time and being able to cajole, beg or bully someone into talking. Carvel's Budget leak was a good example.

Carvel would not have got his scoop had he not been 'on close drinking, lunching and gossiping terms with Dalton since early in the war'.[42] The Chancellor considered him to be one of his two or three best contacts in the lobby. When Carvel went down to the lobby on Wednesday 12 November, he was accompanied by his son, Robert, who worked for the *Daily Express*, and Willie Alison, from the *Evening Standard*. According to the account in Ben Pimlott's biography of Dalton, Alison was particularly interested in an item of 'colour'. He wanted to know whether the Chancellor would be drinking rum and milk as he delivered the speech, as he had done the year before. When the three men saw Dalton, Carvel peeled away with the words, saying: 'I'll find out for you, Bill.' Robert Carvel and Alison hung back. Item 1 in the Guy Eden rulebook was being followed to the letter. But it would be a mistake to think that the two of them were staying away just out of deference to 'one of the oldest traditions of the lobby'. The older Carvel, by virtue of his relationship with Dalton, was much more likely to get something out of the Chancellor on his own, and Alison seems happy to have trusted him with the task of solving the rum-and-milk mystery.

'Well, what is the worst you have for us today?' Carvel asked the Chancellor.[43] He did not seem to expect a serious answer. Dalton told him he would soon hear all about it. Then, as Carvel tried another question, the Chancellor offered him a summary. 'I cut these questions short, and told him, in a single sentence, what the principal points would be – no more on tobacco; a penny on beer, something on dogs and pools but not on horses; increase in purchase tax, but only on articles now taxable; profits tax doubled,' Dalton recalled.[44] Carvel wished him luck with the speech and the two men then parted. In their brief conversation they must also have discussed what Dalton would be drinking, because Carvel returned to his companions with the news: 'It's rum and milk.'[45]

Alison hurried off to file his titbit. Carvel also headed for the telephone and at 3.17 p.m. he sent his first message to the office. It read: 'I believe that when Mr Dalton introduces his Budget today the following will be among the proposals: penny a pint increase in the beer duty; no change in tobacco; profits tax to be doubled; purchase tax to be substantially increased but not to be applied to any new commodities.'[46] Carvel also spoke to his editor, Arthur Cranfield, who asked him if his Budget predictions were reliable. He said that they were and that his source was a good one. But he did not tell his editor to whom he had spoken. As he explained later: 'In this I was following my usual course and also the custom of the lobby journalists, the whole foundation of whose relationship with ministers and private members alike rests on the absolute understanding that sources of information should not be disclosed.'[47] Carvel then went to take his seat in the gallery. A few minutes later he realised that he had forgotten to mention the dogs, pools and horses and he went out to call the office a second time. The story was subbed by Cranfield himself and it appeared in the following form:

'PENNY ON BEER'
TAX ON POOLS AND DOGS LIKELY
'*Star*' Political Correspondent writes: It was expected Chancellor's proposals

would include:

1d a pint increase in the beer duty.

No change in tobacco.

Profits tax to be doubled.

Also likely to be a tax on dogs and football pools, but not on horse racing.

Purchase tax to be substantially increased but not to be applied to any new commodities.[48]

The second late-night edition started printing at 3.40 p.m. and within twenty minutes 260 copies from the first bundle were available for sale from a few vendors around Fleet Street. Dalton did not get to the section of his speech dealing with tax changes until just after 4 p.m. Carvel and the *Star* had beaten him by just a few minutes.

Given the relative lack of prominence of the story in the paper and the fact that publication more or less coincided with the Chancellor's official announcement, it would not have been surprising if no one had taken any notice. But the *Star* was one of three London evening papers in fierce competition with one another and the other two, the *Evening Standard* and the *Evening News*, had recently been pilloried for getting their own leaks by 'bribing' MPs. The *Star*'s two rivals recognised that Carvel's story was much better sourced than the usual pre-Budget forecasts and they knew that, if Dalton had leaked the contents of his statement before he announced it to MPs, then he had committed a serious parliamentary indiscretion. Probably because they wanted to embarrass Cranfield, they encouraged the Tories to raise the matter in the Commons. Dalton learned about the move the following day and offered Clement Attlee his resignation; the Prime Minister declined to accept it. In response to a private notice question from Victor Raikes, a Tory, Dalton told the Commons that he had spoken to the *Star*'s lobby correspondent before delivering the Budget and he apologised. Raikes seemed to be as critical of Carvel as he was of the Chancellor and he condemned the *Star* for its 'very grave breach of journalistic honour' in publishing the information.[49] MPs and the press assumed that that was the end of the matter. But, after leaving the chamber, Dalton again offered Attlee his resignation and this time it was accepted.

If the worth of a political scoop is to be judged according to a ministerial resignation index, then Carvel must get the credit for writing one of the most influential stories ever to come out of the lobby. However, that is not how people thought about the affair at the time. Carvel seems to have been as surprised as everyone else that Dalton resigned over a leak that could have been read by just a tiny number of people only minutes before the announcement was officially made. (In his biography, Pimlott explains Dalton's departure by saying that he was 'exhausted, disillusioned and depressed' at the time,[50] and that Attlee wanted to get rid of him.) Tempting as it might be to view the episode as evidence that the lobby was becoming subversive in the late 1940s, what the episode really shows is that Carvel was working within conventions that made lobby journalists extremely cautious when dealing with politicians.

For a start, consider the words Carvel actually filed. He was told authoritatively what some of the points in the Budget would be, yet the information was presented in a way that suggested he was only 95 per cent certain. The message to the office started: 'I believe that when Mr Dalton introduces his Budget today . . . ', and the story that appeared in the 'fudge' began: 'It was expected . . . ' These were standard lobby qualifiers at the time and the fact that they appeared, when, in this case at least, they were not necessary, suggests that Carvel felt some reservation about pushing his story too far.

Churchill demanded an inquiry into the leak on the evening of Dalton's resignation, and the select committee that was subsequently set up looked in detail at the question of whether Carvel had been entitled to use the information when he did. In his evidence, Dalton said that he could not remember whether he had said the information should be kept confidential until after the announcement. Carvel was certain that there was no such embargo. In those circumstances a modern lobby journalist would have no compunction about rushing into print. Yet, in the inquiry, Carvel revealed considerable doubt about whether he had done the right thing. In his evidence he said the information was given to him in such a way that he could use it, but he 'agreed that if he had stopped to think, at the time he received the information, he would have known then that his use of it was not legitimate'.[51] Cranfield told the committee that if he had known his lobby correspondent had got his information directly from the Chancellor, he would not have used the story in the *Star* 'as it would have seemed to him to be a direct Budget leakage'.[52] Eden also gave evidence on behalf of the lobby committee and in doing so helped to explain why Cranfield might have felt so nervous about what is supposedly a normal journalistic activity. An embargo could be implied as well as explicit, Eden said.

Carvel did not take any pride in the story afterwards. In his evidence to the committee he said he did not realise that Dalton had given him anything more than a few clues as to the contents of the Budget. 'I never expected that I was providing a story containing five of the main proposals, and I was astonished when I discovered how comprehensive my forecast had been.' The implication was that, if he had known at the time how much he had been told, that would have been a reason for not filing. Certainly, in the light of what happened, he was sorry the story every appeared. 'I would like your honourable committee to know that if I could have had any realisation of the tragic outcome for Mr Dalton, I should never have telephoned my office, and my regret that I did so, now that I am aware of the events that followed, is deeper than ever I shall be able to convey,' he said.[53] Any political journalist with a good relationship with the Chancellor of the day would be mad to throw that away for a 55-word story in a late edition 'stop press', and so at one level Carvel's expression of regret was hardly surprising. But his contrition went deeper than that. He genuinely thought he had made a mistake.

Almost fifty years later there was another notable Budget leak. The *Daily Mirror* got hold of press releases from the Treasury setting out full details of Kenneth Clarke's tax plans the day before he unveiled them in the Commons in November 1996. Piers Morgan, the *Mirror*'s editor, decided not to publish because he thought to do so would cause chaos in the financial markets. The two leaks were wholly different; Carvel's involved a one-sentence tip in the lobby, while the *Mirror*'s came in the form of a 94-page bundle of documents procured by Peter Hounam, a freelance investigative journalist. But the contrast between what happened says a lot about the breakdown of journalistic deference. Morgan was criticised by many fellow journalists for his act of supposed responsibility and he later identified it as one of his greatest professional mistakes.[54] Carvel did publish his leak, but later wished he hadn't. In the late 1940s, in the lobby at least, journalists still felt a strong sense of obligation towards politicians.

Parliament and the Press Gallery: 1945 Onwards

While the lobby was being accused of sins such as Carvel's supposed 'very grave breach of journalistic honour', the gallery was not enjoying an entirely comfortable existence in the postwar years either. The House retained its historic aversion to reporting, and the Labour landslide of 1945 did not necessarily make the relationship any easier. For the first time the Commons was dominated by Labour MPs, and many of them were inherently suspicious of the capitalist press.

Gallery reporters had generally prided themselves on being fair. Writing in 1913 about the men covering debates more than a hundred years earlier, Michael MacDonagh declared: 'That there was any deliberate misrepresentation due to political bias it is impossible to believe . . . Parliamentary reporters are liable to error, but as a class they have always been politically unprejudiced and incorruptible.'[55] In the narrow sense of note-taking being a neutral activity, he was probably right. But the broader process of deciding which speeches to report is much harder to do objectively, and by 1947 MacDonagh's 'unprejudiced' verdict was looking absurd. A Royal Commission on the Press was set up that year and it considered, among other things, the quality of political reporting. To enable it to reach conclusions, it analysed the reporting of several debates, including the second reading of a controversial nationalisation Bill. The commission's conclusions were mixed:

> The two quality papers [it meant *The Times* and the *Daily Telegraph*] gave straight reports which were fair and, so far as space permitted, adequate accounts of the debate. The popular papers each carried a combined report and commentary by the parliamentary correspondent; only from that of the *News Chronicle* was it possible to obtain a clear idea of the debate and of the points made on each side. The remaining accounts were in varying degrees distorted by over-emphasis on dramatic incidents and interruptions, or by reporting one side almost to the exclusion of the other, or by so reporting both sides that one was held up to ridicule and the other to approbation.[56]

The commission noted that some of these features might be explained by the shortage of space caused by postwar paper rationing.[57] But many of these 'deficiencies' were also to be found in reporting before 1939, it went on,[58] implying that bias was generic.

A few years later William Barkley complained that Parliament was biased towards him. A smoker, he noticed that the press gallery bar was selling only Co-op cigarettes and not more popular brands, like Wills or Players, and in 1951 he wrote a letter to the *Daily Express* with a suggestion. 'Since the catering here is now under a Co-op chairman (W Coldrick, MP Socialist, Bristol North-East) and the prices have gone up and for three weeks there have been no cigarettes on offer in this place except Co-op brands, I think that MPs and ourselves at the end of the session ought to get a divi,' he wrote.[59] Barkley claimed that he was not accusing William Coldrick of misusing his position as chairman of the kitchen committee, and that he was just trying to make a joke. Unsurprisingly, Coldrick took a different view and the kitchen committee called for the matter to be referred to the committee of privileges. Barkley was not worried at this stage, because he thought that if there were an investigation, it would show that he was right. The Commons discussed the kitchen committee's recommendation, but, in the course of a debate that started at one-thirty in the morning, Chuter Ede, Home Secretary and leader of the Commons, tabled a manuscript amendment saying that Barkley's letter was a 'gross libel'. He even hinted that he wanted Barkley expelled from the Commons. There were about two hundred Labour MPs in the chamber and only ten Tories and, despite protests that Barkley was being judged without being given the chance to put his side of the story, Ede's motion was carried. The following day Barkley wrote a letter to the Speaker, Douglas Clifton-Brown, apologising for causing offence, and the matter was dropped. But Barkley nevertheless deeply resented the fact that his professional integrity had been questioned by what was effectively a one-party kangaroo court sitting without prior notice in the middle of the night.

Five and a half years later another Beaverbrook journalist was actually summoned to the Bar of the Commons. As editor of the *Sunday Express*, John Junor was responsible for an editorial about post-Suez petrol rationing which complained that politicians would be exempt because they would receive 'prodigious supplementary allowances'.[60] Sir Charles Taylor, a Tory MP, lodged a complaint and the committee of privileges investigated. It concluded that Junor was 'guilty of a serious contempt' because he had accused Members of 'contemptible conduct in failing, owing to self interest, to protest at an unfair discrimination in their favour'.[61] It recommended that Junor be severely reprimanded and on 24 January 1957 he was summoned to be censured by the Speaker. Junor's submission to the privileges committee had not been impressive. He argued, implausibly, that the article was aimed at 'politicians in general' rather than MPs. However, the statement he made at the Bar, which combined an unreserved apology with a declaration that petrol allowances were nevertheless a proper subject for comment in a free press, was admired. 'In saluting the dignity of Parliament he had asserted the freedom of the press without retreating an inch,' Margach said.[62] Junor's performance contributed to the growing realisation that summoning someone to the Bar was becoming pointless, or even counterproductive, as a punishment. The House has not tried to reprimand a journalist in the same way since.

Junor's appearance at the Bar, and his declaration that there were certain subjects on which the press had a right to comment, coincided with the collapse of Parliament's last wide-ranging attempt to censor the media: the fourteen-day rule. This would be seen as one of the most important moments in British media history were it not for the fact that it is hard to believe the rule ever existed in the first place. The fourteen-day rule was an arrangement whereby the BBC agreed not to broadcast discussions on subjects that were going to be debated in

Parliament within the next fortnight. The 'ban' also covered matters that were the subject of legislation going through the House. The BBC governors drew up the rule themselves in 1944 because they were worried their organisation would be drawn into party politics if ministers were allowed to make controversial announcements on the radio. After the war the BBC, the Government and the Opposition all agreed that the rule, which was still voluntary, should continue. Today the idea of trying to stop broadcasters discussing current affairs seems ludicrous. But the defenders of the rule realised, quite rightly, that if radio and television were allowed to fulfil their potential, then Parliament would have diffi-culty surviving as the nation's principal debating chamber. In February 1955 Churchill, who was only two months away from retiring as Prime Minister, was asked to relax the fourteen-day rule. He refused. 'It would be shocking to have debates in this House forestalled time after time by expressions of opinion by persons who had not the status or responsibility of Members of Parliament,' he told MPs. Then, in response to a further question on the topic, he explained:

> I have always attached great importance to Parliament and to the House of Commons. I am quite sure that the bringing on of exciting debates in these vast, new robot organisations of television and BBC broadcasting, to take place before a debate in this House, might have very deleterious effects upon our general interests, and that hon Members should be considering the interests of the House of Commons, to whom we all owe a lot.[63]

In a debate later the same year, Attlee said that he supported the rule because he believed in 'maintaining Parliament as the right and major forum for debate'. He invited MPs to imagine what would happen if the BBC had freedom to broadcast as it wished. 'There might come a time when major measures were introduced by a minister, not first in this House, but first on the wireless. That may sound absurd, but we have had examples of what happens when the wireless is used in totalitarian countries. It is an instrument the use of which has to be watched extremely carefully.'[64] With the first edition of the *Today* programme only two years away, Attlee would have been horrified if he had realised just how accurate his forecast would eventually turn out to be.

By this time the BBC had changed its mind about the fourteen-day rule; indeed, two years earlier it had suggested to the Government that the arrange-ment be abandoned. The Government and the Opposition dug their heels in, and for the next three years Parliament tried to cling on to its monopoly on topical debate. With the BBC reluctant to honour an agreement it no longer supported, the Government had to issue a directive in July 1955 making the rule compulsory. Independent television, which was just starting, was covered too. In a debate in November the Commons voted by a majority of 145 to keep the ban going. But it was looking increasingly anachronistic. 'I do not think this House has any historical claim at all to be the sole or even the main forum of public discussion,' said Sir Robert Boothby, a Conservative and one of the few MPs already to have mastered the art of television punditry. 'In a democracy it is madness to try to fetter, beyond an extent which is absolutely necessary, public discussion in every shape and form outside the House.'[65] The following year the rule broke down during the Suez crisis. Competition from independent television made the BBC bolder, and with Anthony Eden's plight dominating the news for weeks, the broadcasters simply decided to take no notice of Parliament's wishes. Bowing to the inevitable, the Government suspended the rule temporarily in December, and then for good from July 1957. Its abolition did not immediately affect the work of the political journalists in Parliament, because news reports, and all newspaper activities, were exempt anyway. But in the long run the scrapping of the fourteen-day rule was hugely important to the press gallery because it reflected, and perpetuated, a fundamental shift in the balance of power between Parliament and the media.

Parliament may have lost some control over what was said on the airwaves, but within the precincts of Westminster MPs still had the final say over what was reported, for the theoretical ban on reporting was still in force. This was established in 1949 when Raymond Blackburn, a Labour MP, complained that a speech he had given had been misrepresented in the *Daily Worker*. The committee of privileges investigated the allegation and concluded that the report was 'technically a breach of the privileges of the House' because the ancient rules banning the publication of debates had not been repealed.[66] It recommended no further action.

The old rules may have been unenforceable, but MPs were able to take other measures to limit the scope for reporting. During the 1950s it was normal for select committees to take evidence in private, and reporters had to wait until the minutes of evidence were published before they could find out what had been said.[67] Also, the 'I spy strangers' procedure still allowed MPs to clear the galleries. Writing in *The Reporters' Gallery* in 1913, nearly forty years after the rule had been changed so that the press could be excluded only after a vote of the whole House, MacDonagh said: 'It is probable that never again will the order of the House of Commons for the exclusion of strangers be put into operation. Failure has attended every attempt to close the doors since 1878. The right of the people to be informed through the press within the walls of St Stephen's may now be regarded as unconditional and superior to all other considerations.'[68] But he was wrong. In 1925 Labour MPs were able to use the device successfully on one occasion, and on 18 November 1958 Labour performed the same trick again. The Commons was debating a Bill to remove restrictions on the use of cars during general elections when George Wigg, as a protest against one of the Government's tactics, raised the standing order about strangers. When the Speaker called the vote, none of the twenty Tory MPs in the chamber objected because they did not realise what was going on. The Government would have won a majority if there had been a proper vote, but with the Tory benches silent, the motion was carried by acclamation. Reporters, members of the public and even *Hansard* staff were forced to leave. Having inadvertently decided to sit in private, MPs then discovered that their procedures would not allow them to bring the reporters back, and for the next two hours, as they carried on with the committee stage of the Representation of the People (Amendment) Bill, MPs debated without any of the people being represented in the gallery at all.

'Responsible Office': The Lobby in the 1950s

When Anthony Eden became Prime Minister in April 1955, one of his first tasks was to organise a reception for the lobby journalists at Downing Street. Churchill, his predecessor, had refused to brief them, or even meet them socially, but Eden was keen to re-establish contact. The drinks party evidently went well because two months later, after Eden had fought and won a general election, he decided to go one step further and turn up to a 4 p.m. lobby to give a personal briefing. He went on a Wednesday, the day when the lobby expected a cabinet minister to give them an overview of government events. Fife Clark, Churchill's old press secretary, was still in post, and he prepared a memo saying what Eden should expect.

> The lobby meetings are very informal, and held in conditions of physical discomfort in a small room reached by an iron staircase at the very top of the House of Commons building. The traditional style for these weekly meetings is chatty, personal and not too heavy. On the other hand, every word said, particularly by a Prime Minister, is most carefully examined for all possible implications, and may be 'written up' well above the level of ministerial intention. The strict rule is, however, that nothing must be attributed to the speaker or quoted in inverted commas and the fact that the meeting has taken

place is never published – although one must reckon that before long the overseas correspondents and the diplomatic representatives of foreign powers in London will know that the Prime Minister has seen the lobby.

Clark said that the meeting would last for no more than half an hour and that Eden would sit to the right of the lobby chairman, Leslie Way of the *Western Morning News*. The memo suggested four subjects the Prime Minister could talk about (a forthcoming summit, an announcement about Dorneywood [at that time the country residence of the Foreign Secretary], ongoing industrial talks, and a Monopolies Commission report out that day) and also covered some of the topics likely to be raised by the journalists. Top of the list was a possible cabinet reshuffle.

> When things are quiet at Westminster, as at present, it is an old custom to write about cabinet reconstruction. Clearly, any word the Prime Minister may speak on this subject to the lobby will be accepted as having great significance. I would therefore suggest that he should treat it fairly lightly . . . If the lobby get anything they could regard as the slightest encouragement for forecasting, press Cabinet-making will go on and on, uncertainty among government members and supporters will be built up, the Prime Minister will lose the initiative and, worst of all, the press will feel disappointment if they do not get their reconstruction!

At the end of the memo Clark included a line advising Eden to keep his entourage to a minimum. 'The lobby like as much informality and as few "henchmen" as possible,' he said. The general rule was private secretary and a press officer only.[69]

Eden's arrival in office must have been particularly welcome because the lobby had received relatively little prime ministerial attention in the years immediately after the war. Clement Attlee was not interested in the press and, although he met the lobby, his refusal to reply to questions with answers that were more than a few words long meant that the encounters were not illuminating. According to James Margach, typical responses were along the lines of: 'Nothing in that'; 'You're off beam again'; 'I've never heard that, have you?'; 'That idea seems bonkers to me – the Cabinet's never looked at it,' and 'You can't expect me to answer that one.'[70] Attlee agreed to install a news agency tape service at Downing Street only when Francis Williams told him that he would be able to use it keep up to date with the cricket scores, and apparently the Prime Minister was amazed when he went past one day to find that it was churning out information about what was said at Cabinet. Churchill was even less accommodating; he would deal only with editors and proprietors. Lord Swinton, as minister in charge of government communications in Churchill's postwar administration, once tried to persuade the great man to meet the political correspondents. 'They're the chaps who are writing the stories every night which make the front pages of all the papers next morning. Have you ever met them? Do you know any of them, to ask along for an informal chat and a drink, off the record, background; that's how to get the real facts about the Government put across,' he suggested. Churchill replied: 'I'm too old, Philip, to learn these tricks [he was seventy-nine]. I suppose it's the new American style of trying to persuade journalists they're important.'[71]

Although Attlee and Churchill had their own personal reservations about using the political correspondents, other ministers and officials were more obliging, and the lobby system continued to develop during the postwar years. In a memo for Churchill, Fife Clark described the routine as it was in 1954. He would meet the lobby twice a day, in the morning in his own office and in the afternoon in the Commons, for a routine briefing. Lord Swinton would take the lobby on Wednesday afternoons; other ministers would attend on an ad hoc basis, normally when they had a specific announcement to make; and the leader of the House would speak about forthcoming Commons business at the 4 p.m. meeting on Thursdays. With the leader of the Opposition also seeing the correspondents every week, there could be as many as four lobby briefings an afternoon. Clark said that relations with the lobby were 'cardinal' and that the system was working better than it had been a few years earlier. 'Not only has the flow of news swelled but the prestige of the lobby itself, which slumped following the Dr Dalton "leak" and the report of the committee of privileges criticising two other evening paper correspondents, has been enhanced. Three years ago ministers were not sure they could "trust the lobby". Now they know they can.'[72]

At the time it was taken for granted that the lobby had to work on an unattributable basis. Charles Hill, who as Chancellor of the Duchy of Lancaster was Harold Macmillan's first Minister for Information, said in his memoirs that non-attribution had 'considerable advantages' for the lobby. 'Obviously a spokesman can be much more forthcoming in guidance if he knows that the actual words he uses will not be quoted. He can talk in the plainest of plain English.'[73] For Paul Einzig, a lobby correspondent until 1956, the key advantage of the system was that it provided 'a permanent channel through which ministers are able to reach the public at a stage at which they are not yet prepared to commit themselves to a formal public announcement.'[74] There seems to have been no one arguing at this stage for greater openness.

But that does mean that ministers felt entirely safe when they ascended the stairs to the lobby room for a 4 p.m. briefing. According to Hill, there was a noticeable division in the 1950s between the members of the lobby's old guard, who saw themselves as 'students of politics' and specialised in analysis, and the majority, who were after hard news. 'This is what their editors and their public want and their snappier pieces have a far bigger public than the sterner stuff produced by their predecessors. They make palatable for the many what formerly could be assimilated by the few.' The older correspondents wanted a spokesman who would 'think aloud', but Hill said this was impossible in the presence of the new breed of lobby journalist, 'to whom a nod is as good as a wink in his quest for clues to tomorrow's news'.[75] Harold Evans, Macmillan's press secretary, was even more critical of the lobby's willingness to over-speculate. 'Lobby journalists quickly catch whatever fever is running round the place,' he wrote in his memoirs.

> If one of their number has a story which seems to be new or novel they are at once under pressure (not least from their offices in Fleet Street) to expand it, embroider it and find a new angle to it. Even when they know the foundation is flimsy they are under compulsion to write, so that within very short order a story which may have been based on little more than a rumour or a piece of speculation can be blown into dramatic headlines.[76]

The lobby rules did not have anything to say about journalistic exaggeration. Although the committee was obsessed with propriety, it never tried to enforce any accuracy standards on its members. This was understandable; it would have been impossible. But the committee nevertheless tried to police other aspects of lobby behaviour. At the time the lobby rules were set out in a small booklet known as the 'Black Book'. In 1956, shortly after Eden addressed the journalists for the first time, there was a debate about revising one of its most draconian provisions. Lobby journalists were under an obligation to keep secret the fact that briefings took place. But it was also accepted that it was sometimes appropriate for lobby journalists to tell their editors about them. This was tolerated, but not encouraged. During the Second World War, journalists attending the lobby briefings held at the Ministry of Information had to sign a confidentiality agreement and, although this made an exception for communications with editors, it was a very limited one. The relevant rule said: 'Confidential memoranda to editors, based on information given at lobby conferences, should be limited to the barest essentials, and those who receive them should be impressed with the imperative necessity for secrecy. Even in these confidential memoranda, it is highly undesirable to mention the identity of informants.'[77] In July 1955 the committee decided that it was unreasonable to maintain a blanket secrecy rule when journalists were allowed to tell their editors about lobby briefings, and it was decided to amend the 'Black Book' rules accordingly.

There are no copies of the early 'Black Book' surviving in the lobby records, but a revised version was issued in July 1956. Its contents were first disclosed to the public when Jeremy Tunstall printed them in full in *The Westminster Lobby Correspondents* in 1970. Headed 'Notes on the Practice of Lobby Journalism', the rulebook builds on the set of rules drawn up by Eden in 1945 (some of the phrases are identical), but it is more extensive. It is also more deferential.

This shows particularly in the section about protecting the identity of sources. After stressing the importance of not naming informants ('experience has shown that ministers and MPs talk more freely under the rule of anonymity'), the rulebook goes on:

> Sometimes it may be right to protect your informant to the extent of not using a story at all. This has often been done in the past, and it forms one of the foundations of the good and confidential relationship between the lobby and members of all parties . . .
>
> Again, all embargoes, whether openly stated or merely understood, must be observed. This is important. Where the embargo is an explicit one, no difficulty can arise. Where it is merely implied it is equally important that there should be no breach of confidence.
>
> Remember always that you hold a responsible office, and that ministers, Members and officials have a right to rely on your tact and discretion.[78]

It is not clear exactly when the 'Black Book' was first drawn up, but the comments about protecting informants, implied embargoes, and ministers having a right to rely on the 'tact and discretion' of lobby correspondents are likely to have been inserted as a direct response to the repercussions of the Dalton Budget leak. When the rules were reissued in July 1969, in a little booklet called 'Lobby Practice', these paragraphs were all omitted.

The 1956 document also contained a section under the heading 'General Hints' setting out some rules of lobby etiquette. These are worth quoting at length, not least for their comedy value.

Do not 'see' anything in the Members' lobby, or in any of the private rooms or corridors of the Palace of Westminster. You are a guest of Parliament, and it has always been the rule that incidents, pleasant or otherwise, should be treated as private if they happen in those parts of the building to which lobby correspondents have access because their names are on the lobby list. This rule is strictly enforced by the authorities.

Do not run after a minister or a private Member. It is nearly always possible to place oneself in a position to avoid this.

When a member of the lobby is in conversation with a minister or private Member, another member of the lobby should not join in the conversation unless invited to do so. Nor should the lobby activities of any colleague ever be the subject of published comment.

Do not crowd together in the lobby so as to be conspicuous. Do not crowd round the Vote Office when an important document is expected. In general, act always with the recollection that you are a guest of Parliament.

Do not use a notebook, or, as a rule, make notes when in private conversation, in the Members' lobby.

NEVER, in ANY circumstances, make use of anything accidentally overheard in any part of the Palace of Westminster.[79]

For all the apparent absurdity of a ban on running, these rules make a serious point about the status of the lobby correspondents in Parliament. They were drawn up in response to the perception that reporters had no right to be in the lobby, and that a certain degree of obsequiousness was necessary to appease the MPs who might be tempted to throw them all out. 'If we don't crowd together, they won't notice we're here,' seems to be the message. Just as the gallery reporters had no automatic right to hear a debate, and could be thrown out by the House 'spying strangers', so the lobby correspondents were there on sufferance too. These 'General Hints' reappeared almost verbatim in the 1969 rulebook, but they had been dropped by the time 'Lobby Practice' was reissued in July 1982.

As lobby confidentiality broke down in the 1980s and 1990s, 'published comment' on the activities of lobby journalists became increasingly common. In the 1950s such comment was rare. But there were times when newspapers did take an interest in how the lobby operated. On 1 June 1959 *The Times* published a story on its front page saying that Macmillan was planning to dismiss his Foreign Secretary, Selwyn Lloyd. It was instantly denied by Downing Street, and Macmillan expressed his confidence in Lloyd in the Commons. Other newspapers started speculating on who had tried to knife the Foreign Secretary, and David Wood, the *Times* political correspondent who wrote the story, was ridiculed by some of his lobby colleagues for making such a hopeless prediction. It later turned out that the story came from Macmillan himself, who had spoken to Wood about Lloyd's future at a Downing Street reception.[80]

Wood, a Grantham-born labourer's son who had left school at fourteen, was one of the most diligent, well-connected and high-minded political correspondents of the postwar period. One of his first steps after being appointed was to forgo the right to approach MPs behind the Speaker's chair. This was a privilege granted to *The Times* when Stanley Baldwin was Prime Minister, and it meant that Wood's predecessors could speak to ministers who were avoiding the Members' lobby. After his Lloyd story backfired, he was angered by the lobby reaction and towards the end of the month he wrote to the lobby committee saying that he was resigning from the lobby 'organisation', although he still planned to attend meetings.[81] Much agonising ensued about whether this was possible. Eventually Wood relented and withdrew his resignation (although he refused to pay his lobby membership subscription, and it was assumed that someone did so on his behalf); but he remained sceptical about the lobby until he left Westminster in 1977.

The Lobby and Conjecture: The Vassall Inquiry 1962–1963

William Barkley, who was not a member of the lobby, once told a joke that made him pretty unpopular with the reporters who were. 'What is a lobby man?' he asked, and answered: 'He is a man who begins every paragraph with the words "I understand" – when he doesn't.' As he recalled in his memoirs, 'it was a cut just too near the bone.' Percy Cater, a *Daily Mail* reporter, later offered his own variation on this theme. After one unproductive stint in the lobby, he told Barkley: 'I have reaped all day and harvested nothing. So I will write a piece beginning "I gather".'[82] Barkley's jibe was neater, but both encapsulate one of the main problems with lobby journalism.

Stories from the lobby often contained phrases along the lines of 'I understand' or 'I gather' because information was disclosed unattributably. In later years it became more common for lobby correspondents to use a slightly more specific form of non-attribution ('background', in American jargon), such as 'sources close to the Prime Minister'. But in Barkley's era rule 5 of the 1945 code still applied, and the journalists tried to write up what they were told during lobby briefings, and on an individual basis, without attributing anything to anyone at all. Quotes had to be avoided, because quotes implied a source. (ministers even objected to a phrase from a briefing appearing in quotation marks without any reference to a speaker.[83]) Many stories appeared, as it were, out of thin air. Using the 'I understand' formula, or an equivalent, was a slight variation, implying there was some basis for the story, even if the reporter could not say what it was. By the end of the twentieth century there was a strong presumption against journalism based on unattributable sources; the history of the lobby is largely an account of how attribution became more transparent. But there is nothing intrinsically wrong with non-attribution. Journalists regurgitate pieces of information all the time without giving sources and, as long as the information is accurate, there is no reason why they should not do so. Attribution becomes important only when reporters are dealing with sources that are one-sided or unreliable, when they are writing about matters that involve a strong degree of interpretation, or when they are engaged in conjecture.

Unfortunately, ever since the days when Sir William Harcourt denounced the 'nonsense' buzzing about in the lobby, this is exactly how political journalism has operated. Informed forecasting was – and is – a legitimate part of the service. But the combination of speculation and non-attribution had serious potential disadvantages. The reader had no way of knowing whether 'I understand' meant the journalist was writing a story that was measured and well-sourced, or whether, as Barkley implied, he was just taking a wild guess.

These problems did not seem to worry many journalists in the 1950s. But in 1962 the Vassall case exposed some of the flaws of lobby journalism very publicly. John Vassall was a gay Admiralty clerk who was gaoled for spying for Russia. Following his conviction, a series of lurid stories appeared in the press suggesting that the affair was more serious than it appeared. Much of the innuendo was about Vassall's relationship with Thomas Galbraith, a Scottish Office minister, and Macmillan accepted Galbraith's resignation, even though the only thing the minister had done was to have been friendly to Vassall when Vassall was working in his office. Macmillan then set up an inquiry under the chairmanship of Lord Radcliffe to look into all the allegations. Many of the journalists responsible for producing nuggets of Vassall sensationalism gave evidence, and the quality of Fleet Street reporting quickly became one of Radcliffe's main concerns.

Part of the inquiry involved the lobby. On Thursday 8 November the *Daily Express* published a story saying that Lord Carrington, the First Lord of the Admiralty, had known for the past eighteen months that there had been a spy at work in his department. The following day Douglas Clark, the paper's political editor, wrote a story saying that Carrington had been summoned to see Macmillan to explain why he had not told the Prime Minister earlier about the spy. That weekend the *Sunday Telegraph* published a story by Ian Waller, its political correspondent, which started: 'John Vassall, the convicted Admiralty spy, was known to British diplomats in Moscow as a homosexual. His contacts with the Russians were also well known. But, according to Foreign Office circles, reports on him by the embassy were ignored by the Admiralty.' Both stories were wrong. Carrington had not known there was a spy in the department until April 1962, and he had not been summoned to see Macmillan to explain why the Prime Minister had been kept in the dark. There was no evidence that it was widely known in Moscow that Vassall was gay, and the embassy did not send reports on him back to the Admiralty.

Waller's story sounded authoritative. Yet, when he was asked to justify what he had written, he wriggled because he could not produce firm evidence. He mentioned two articles he had read about Vassall's Moscow lifestyle, and he said he had discussed the matter with MPs. 'The impression I got that week, backed by what I had read and by my own judgement, was that it was inconceivable that Vassall was not known to the very limited number there for what he was,' said Waller. He could not name a single person who had told him, as a fact, that Vassall's homosexuality was recognised, or that his contacts with the Russians were known. 'There was no single source for this. It was a reflection of the views expressed by a number of Members of Parliament, allegations that they thought were justified and which I thought, on the balance of probabilities, seemed to me to be equally justifiably made.'[84] As for the reference to 'Foreign Office circles', Waller admitted that he had not talked about the matter with anyone in the Foreign Office. But he had discussed it with his paper's diplomatic correspondent, who said that he was reflecting the Foreign Office view. In his evidence Waller conceded that he was basically just reporting tea-room speculation. The inquiry concluded that the speculation was wrong.

Clark's story was based on even flimsier foundations. He said that a senior minister had told journalists at a lobby briefing that Carrington had met Macmillan on 8 November and that the minister had said they were not discussing Galbraith's role in the Vassall affair. Clark said that because the only other aspect of the case in the news at the time was the allegation in that day's *Express*, he assumed that was what Macmillan had wanted to talk about. When he learned the meeting had not been in the diary the night before, Clark was even more certain that he knew why it was taking place. In his evidence, he explained that lobby journalists made assumptions of this kind all the time.

> Without conjecture there is no lobby journalism. The events or the proceedings that take place at any cabinet meeting are never officially revealed, nor are the meetings that take place between smaller groups of ministers, cabinet ministers or indeed those that take place between individual ministers . . .
>
> And of course it is a lobby correspondent's duty to deduce what has happened, because quite clearly what has happened at a cabinet meeting is of immense public interest.[85]

On this occasion, he got it wrong. 'Mr Clark's allegation was based on deductions only and the facts show that his deductions and allegation were incorrect,' the Inquiry concluded.[86]

Clark was asked why he did not include a qualifying phrase like 'it is believed' or 'it is assumed' in his copy. If he had done so, and acknowledged an element of doubt, his story would have been slightly less misleading. But Clark dismissed this approach. 'If I had not believed it, I would not have written it, so it seems to me those words are redundant; they are also, I think, faintly cant.'[87] Maybe this was just arrogance. But Clark had a point. Journalists writing speculative stories did – and still do – insert small qualifying phrases ('set to', 'expected to', etc.) into their copy to protect them if things go wrong.[88] Technically, these devices enhance accuracy. But readers probably overlook them and their main function is to serve as an insurance policy (in the eyes of other journalists) if a story goes wrong. In some respects Clark's candour was quite admirable.

Relations between the Government and the press were badly damaged by the Vassall inquiry. Radcliffe had two reporters gaoled for not disclosing their sources to the tribunal, and many journalists thought that was an outrage. Journalists also resented the way that a government spy scandal was turned into an inquiry into the ethics of the press. But that is what happened and Radcliffe's report, which was published in April 1963, depicted Fleet Street at its shabbiest. Lobby journalists, with their reliance on conjecture, were exposed as being capable of getting it woefully wrong. When John Carvel filed his Budget leak in 1947, he used 'I believe' because he felt the need to qualify what he knew to be true. Fifteen years later lobby correspondents were doing the opposite, and recycling as the truth what was little more than second-hand rumour. Guy Eden in 1945 sneered at the notion that lobby correspondents should be 'mere reporters'. But mere reporters specialise in telling the facts, and getting them right; and in the immediate wake of the Vassall Inquiry that should have seemed not such a bad thing for the lobby to aspire to.

FIVE

Secrecy and Openness: The 1960s and 1970s

The press, constitutionally and historically, is here on sufferance. That is the position.

Sir Barnett Cocks, Clerk of the Commons, 22 April 1964

In what is meant to be an open political system it has always struck me as extraordinary – and I frankly think unhealthy too – that so much secrecy and mystery should surround the work of the parliamentary lobby. For men whose task it is to find out things about other people, the lobby journalists traditionally display a really remarkable wariness and resentment when anyone tries to investigate the nature of their own activities.

Anthony Howard, Listener, January 1965

I think many people rightly suspect the validity of stories which lean heavily upon thin air. From now on, it will be my general rule that if a statement needs to be made on behalf of the Prime Minister, that statement will be made on the record.

Joe Haines, letter to lobby journalists, 19 June 1975

Broadcasting and Parliament: To 1970

The British Broadcasting Company was formed in 1922.[1] A year later, in its first issue, the *Radio Times* said that the broadcasting of Parliament was inevitable.

'It's bound to happen this century or next,' it predicted.[2] In the event, the BBC did not have to wait quite that long. By the time the Speaker's 'Order, Order' was heard on the airwaves in April 1978, the *Radio Times* had been hanging on in anticipation for a mere fifty-five years. Radio and television, of course, reported Parliament long before they were allowed to broadcast its proceedings. But in the early days they could not compete with newspapers as the principal medium through which people obtained information about politics. The press gallery in the House of Commons really was just that – a gallery for the press.

It was not that the BBC did not try to get in. John Reith wanted to broadcast Parliament from the moment he was put in charge of the fledgling organisation. He suggested getting the King's Speech or the Budget statement on air, but the Government rejected the idea. Successive Prime Ministers also said no whenever the idea of broadcasting Parliament was raised in the chamber, as it was periodically in the 1920s and 1930s. The BBC even had trouble getting an ordinary reporter into the building. News was not a priority for the organisation before the Second World War, and it normally relied on Reuters for information about what was happening in Parliament.[3] If the BBC wanted to send one of its own reporters to listen to a debate for a special reason, it had to apply in writing to the Speaker. In 1932 it requested permission to put someone in the gallery on a permanent basis, on an equal footing with the newspaper correspondents. The proposal was turned down. According to a note in the BBC files, 'the Speaker explained he had obtained the views of the Prime Minister and others, and it was decided unanimously that it was undesirable to have an account of proceedings in the House broadcast daily by a BBC representative in the press gallery.'[4]

BBC journalism acquired new authority during the Second World War as radio became the main source of headline news for the public. The corporation was finally allocated two places in the gallery in April 1940, although the seats had a poor view and the reporters using them were not allowed to take notes. The BBC was not given better facilities until a year later.[5] In 1945 Teddy Thompson, a former *Manchester Guardian* journalist who had worked as a government press officer before the war, became the corporation's first lobby correspondent. In the same year Sir William Haley, the BBC's director general, decided that the Home Service should carry a fifteen-minute programme about Parliament every night summarising what was said. *Today in Parliament* started in October and Haley, who complained that some of the first few broadcasts contained adjectives like 'pointedly', declared that the programme should be 'as unblemished as the parliamentary report of *The Times*'.[6] It went out at 10.45 p.m. to make it easier to provide a balanced account of the day's debate. Two years later *Yesterday in*

Parliament was launched for morning listeners. But there was still no enthusiasm for broadcasting actual proceedings. The Labour Government set up an inquiry into broadcasting under Sir William Beveridge, and his committee advised in 1949 that the effects of putting the proceedings on air would be harmful.

Over the next decade broadcasting, and in particular television, became much more important to politicians. In 1950 the BBC did not cover the general election campaign because it thought that it would not be safe to do so under the Representation of the People Act. The Act made it illegal for third parties to spend money presenting the views of a candidate to the electors. Newspapers and periodicals were exempt, but broadcasters were not and, on a strict reading of the legislation, a BBC executive could go to jail for transmitting an entirely objective election report before polling day. For the first time a television programme presented the general election results, but only a small number of homes had sets. (The press gallery did not get a television of its own until 1951.) However, by 1955, when independent television was launched, 40 per cent of homes had a set. The following year current affairs broadcasters threw off the shackles of the fourteen-day rule. ITN, the independent television news service, was less deferential than the BBC and in 1958 it broke another taboo in political broadcasting when it covered candidates campaigning in the Rochdale by-election. There was some concern that the camera crew might be arrested, but no action was taken and ITN's coverage established the principle that broadcasters could report an election without breaking electoral law. In the general election the following year the BBC and ITN both reported on the campaign with some confidence. As television became more assertive, there were renewed calls for the proceedings of Parliament to be broadcast, with the emphasis now on cameras as much as microphones.

When Labour came to power in 1964, a select committee launched an inquiry into the case for televising the Commons. It recommended that the cameras should be allowed in for a trial period, with the results shown only to MPs so as to allow them to make a permanent decision. By the time the Commons debated the matter on 24 November 1966, the Lords had already decided in principle to go ahead with its own experiment. It was assumed that the Commons would vote in favour and Richard Crossman, who opened the debate as leader of the Commons, used much of his speech to reassure MPs worried about the practical consequences. If the experiment became permanent, lighting levels in the chamber would be raised 'only very slightly' and it would be possible to install highly sensitive, remotely controlled cameras which would be 'built into the panelling of the chamber and be completely unobtrusive'.[7] But Crossman underestimated the level of opposition there was from MPs who thought that the character of the Commons would be spoiled by the cameras. 'I think this is one of the great institutions on this planet, of the human race, and I would not risk its being fundamentally altered for the world,' said Quintin Hogg, the Tory future Lord Chancellor.[8] Crossman did not even have the support of his government colleagues. He was left alone on the front bench during the debate and when the vote came he was the only member of the Cabinet in favour. Against expectations, MPs decided that an experiment would be over-stepping the mark and Crossman's motion was rejected by a single vote.

The result, which was partly attributed to MPs in favour of television staying away because they thought victory was a foregone conclusion, may have put back the cause of televising the Commons by twenty years. There were subsequent broadcasting experiments in the decade, but after 1966 the campaign for change lost some momentum. The Lords went ahead with its own three-day experiment in 1968. Its proceedings were recorded on radio and television but not transmitted publicly. Peers had mixed feelings about the results and the idea was dropped. A few months later the Commons tried a similar, private experiment with radio coverage. The microphones were admitted for four weeks and the response was broadly favourable. But the committee in charge decided the Commons could not afford the money it would have to spend to make the project viable and the plan was shelved.

Even with the microphones and cameras kept outside the chamber, broadcasting had a profound effect on Westminster political journalism in the 1950s and 1960s. As politicians became increasingly keen to appear on television, the newspaper journalists realised they were losing the monopoly they used to enjoy as the purveyors of political news. One theory is that competition from television encouraged newspapers to run more speculative, forward-looking stories. That may be true, although lobby journalists had been engaged in speculation long before television was even invented. What is certain is that the print reporters did not like being usurped. Members of the lobby were particularly aggrieved because in the 1960s it became common for a minister to give an unattributable briefing to the lobby, only to go out and say it all again on the record in a television interview. The lobby was being used as a warm-up act. To make matters worse, the television cameras sometimes got priority. On one occasion in 1969 there was 'something of an altercation' between members of the lobby, who had been waiting three hours for a statement on Ulster, and Harold Wilson, who walked into a room to see them at No. 12 Downing Street having just made his announcement on television.[9] One solution to this dilemma was the old-fashioned press gallery strategy of a boycott, and by 1970 the lobby was experimenting with a policy of not inviting a minister to speak if it was known that he or she would be appearing on television later that day.

Press Gallery Reform: To 1971

While the broadcasters were still clamouring to get their cameras into Parliament, the print journalists were becoming increasingly conscious of the fact that life on the inside was not as amenable as it could be. The reporters who had moved into the new premises after the war with a sense of gratitude were retiring, and they were being replaced by a new generation that was more demanding. The incomers felt they had a lot to complain about and in March 1963 the gallery launched an inquiry into 'the status, rights and working conditions of parliamentary journalists'. It was to be the most thorough exercise of its kind ever undertaken by the political journalists at Westminster.

Not everyone approved. The initiative was launched by the press gallery committee, which represents all journalists working in the building. All lobby correspondents are members of the gallery, but not vice versa. The lobby is smaller and more exclusive. According to David Wood of *The Times*, the lobby committee 'curdled in displeasure at the harsher focusing of the limelight on its "mystique"'.[10] The working party, which was chaired by Andrew Webster, the Provincial Newspapers chief political correspondent, was careful not to encroach on its territory.

Webster ran the inquiry very formally. Gallery members were invited to make written submissions and senior politicians, including the Prime Minister, were interviewed in private. By the time the working party started drawing up its conclusions, it had nearly 80,000 words of evidence to consider. The picture that emerged was one of a reporting corps not happy with its lot.

When the Commons was rebuilt after the war, the space was deemed sufficient for the 140-odd daily attendees. But less than fifteen years later, with 297 people holding tickets admitting them to the gallery and around 190 attending every day, the lack of space, the shortage of phones and the quality of the accommodation emerged as the biggest complaints.[11] Ronald Butt, the *Financial Times*'s donnish political correspondent, described the problems graphically.

> No journalist that I know working inside a newspaper office is quite so unaided as we are and I have met none who has seen the writing conditions in the House of Commons who has not been appalled by them . . . On a big day

the work is concentrated between the hours of, say, four to eight o'clock. At that period I think about 15 people are liable to be in the room I occupy. The noise is fearful; there are no facilities for records; there are no outgoing telephones . . . If, during the writing of a story, it becomes necessary to telephone a ministry to check some point, one has to run along the corridor to a call box and (supposing one is fortunate enough to find one empty) to use 3d pieces which both limit and inhibit the conversation. If one's office telephones, one has to leave the room and telephone back if the conversation is in any way private, as it may be.[12]

Even the politicians were unhappy with the phone system. 'I don't know who answers your telephone in the gallery,' Harold Wilson told the deputation from the working party that went to see him early in 1964. 'Apparently he goes away to find someone, then he comes back and generally says that the person cannot be found. In our experience it is terribly difficult during the recess.'[13] In the working party's report, the section headings told the whole story: Too many people, Too few rooms, Too many desks per room, Too much heat, Too much air, Too much dirt and noise and Too few telephones. In an exercise of (mock?) bureaucratic pedantry, the report even compared the space available per person with the legal limit laid down in the Offices, Shops and Railway Premises Act 1963. The Act set a minimum of 40 square feet per person. In the eight rooms on the upper corridor of the press gallery, space varied between 30 square feet per person and 23 square feet per person. At least the occupants were better off than Exchange Telegraph. 'Their lobby correspondent still prefers to work in the three square feet of telephone kiosk which has been his office for the last 14 years,' the report said.[14]

There were also complaints about the eating and drinking arrangements. Ever since the press gallery committee was set up in 1881 and given the task of 'making arrangements for the supply of refreshments', the quality of food available to the reporters had been a periodic cause for complaint. The report recommended various improvements. It also tackled an even more sensitive grievance. During the war, lobby journalists could drink with MPs on the Commons terrace. This privilege was withdrawn when the new building opened in 1950, but thirteen years later the reporters were still angling for readmission. Offering advice in his retirement, Guy Eden said he thought the concession was 'much over-rated' when he was lobby secretary. 'It was not a great success, for there was always a "sheep and goats" atmosphere, with even the friendliest of Members and officials slightly resenting our presence . . . It was, in any case, out of bounds for "lobbying".'[15] The working party took a different view. It said that journalists should be allowed back on to the terrace 'as a useful and pertinent step towards improving relations between the gallery and Parliament',[16] and that a new bar should be opened as a meeting place for MPs and journalists. In one of his benevolent contributions to British journalism, Robert Maxwell gave the working party what it wanted. As a Labour MP and chairman of the Commons services committee in the late 1960s, he was credited with letting the lobby correspondents back on to the terrace and opening Annie's Bar as an off-the-record drinking hole.[17]

The inquiry also considered the press's status in Parliament. The Commons was still in theory bound by the resolution of 1738 stating it was a 'high indignity and a notorious breach of privilege' to report what was said in the chamber, and members of the working party saw this as a dangerous anachronism. Their worst fears were probably realised when they went to see Sir Barnett Cocks, who, as Clerk of the House, had the job of articulating the institutional prejudices of the Commons. 'The press, constitutionally and historically, is here on sufferance. That is the position,' he told the journalists.

> The attitude of the House that newspapers are 'dangerous publications' is a traditional one . . . It is based on the constitutional power and right of the Houses of Parliament to control its own publications. There is a certain amount of rivalry in the fact that the House prints its own reports as well as relying on reports in newspapers . . . Whatever recognition you have, on a lobby basis and so on, seems to be grudgingly given on pain of cancellation should the press once step out of line.

As Clerk, Cocks held a post that dates back to at least 1363, and so it was hardly surprising that his outlook was rather conservative. But although he did stress repeatedly the House's instinctive suspicion of the press, he told the reporters that they should try to get the Commons to reconsider. 'At present you are tolerated but not respected . . . which I think you ought to be as members of a great profession. You ought not to be treated as slightly suspect characters sitting up in the gallery.'[18]

Some journalists in the press gallery were strongly opposed to the idea of tampering with the 1738 decision, or any of the other resolutions banning debate reporting. They thought that if MPs abandoned the old, defunct rule, they would replace it with something they were more likely to enforce. 'The more codification there is about the relationship between press gallery and House, the less palatable life will be for us. The fewer rules the better,' Robert Carvel said in his submission.[19] The ever-cautious Guy Eden said that there was 'not the slightest chance' of getting the 'breach of privilege' rule revoked and that the journalists should not worry at all about their status as 'strangers' in Parliament. 'Like so many British customs, it works until somebody starts rationalising it,' he wrote.

> We are, at present, a very special and privileged class in Parliament, and I am convinced that any examination of that position by the authorities (and still more by Members) would result in a cutting down of our privileges, rather than an increase. These privileges have been gained, over the decades, slowly and with travail, and it would be sad to see them cut by insistence on supposed 'rights'.[20]

One worry was that the Commons might introduce a new resolution along the lines of the one proposed by Lord Hartington in 1875, allowing debate reporting except in cases of 'wilful misrepresentation', and that this would be used to punish newspapers for publishing reports that annoyed MPs. But the working party decided to take the risk and, when it published its report in July 1964, its first recommendation was that the 'breach of privilege' rule should be rescinded.

Following the publication of the working party's report, *Partners in Parliament*, the press gallery obtained various concessions from the Commons authorities. For example, in 1967 the reporters were allowed to see division lists showing how MPs voted on the night, instead of having to wait until the lists were published the following morning. But it took seven years for the theoretical ban on reporting to be lifted. In December 1967 a select committee on parliamentary privilege said that whenever strangers were admitted to debates or committee meetings, the publication of reports of those proceedings should not be considered a contempt of Parliament. It did not propose any new conditions relating to 'wilful misrepresentation'. Wilson's Government did not pursue the matter, but on 16 July 1971 William Whitelaw, the Tory leader of the House, finally got round to implementing the committee's report. 'The old resolutions forbidding reporting have been a dead letter for many years. I agree with the committee that the time has come for theory to come into line with practice,' he told MPs.[21] Without the need for a vote, the Commons decided that, notwithstanding earlier resolutions, it would 'not entertain any complaint of contempt of the House or breach of privilege in respect of the publication of the debates or proceedings of the House or of its committees, except when any such debates or proceedings shall have been conducted with closed doors or in private, or when such publication shall have been expressly prohibited by the House'.[22] There were no new conditions of the kind that Carvel and Eden had feared. By happy coincidence, the reforms came almost exactly two hundred years after Onslow's Pyrrhic victory over the printers led to newspapers publishing debate reports as a matter of routine. It had taken that long for the rules to catch up with reality.

'An Essential Thread': The Lobby in the 1960s

The press gallery inquiry did not cover lobby practice. Secrecy was still paramount, and most members of the lobby in the 1960s seem to have been happy with the status quo. But the election that brought Wilson to power roughly coincided with the start of the first prolonged, public questioning of the lobby system. Peter Hennessy, Michael Cockerell, David Walker, Anthony Bevins, the *Independent*, Alastair Campbell and everyone else agitating for reform in the 1980s and 1990s were taking up a debate that started twenty years earlier.

One of the first to speak out was the academic David Butler, who delivered a talk on the subject on the BBC's Third Programme in 1963. 'It has long seemed to me that the reporting of British politics needs much more and much deeper examination than it normally receives – and that the examination should be devoted primarily to the so-called serious press,' Butler said. He identified at least six problems. First, 'scoops are surprisingly rare . . . The *Daily Mail*'s scoop in forecasting the great cabinet purge of July 1962 was chiefly remarkable for being so remarkable.' Second, 'informed atmospheric stories are in short supply . . . In the eighteen hours following Sir Anthony Eden's resignation from the premiership the press had a golden opportunity to pick his successor – but all the serious papers, with more or less confidence, tipped Mr Butler . . . Why, then, were the lobby correspondents and newspaper editors so ill-informed about the state of opinion in the party that was, after all, governing the country?' Third, there was little reporting from Whitehall and the leaking of official documents was 'astonishingly rare'. Fourth, political portraiture (or profile writing, as it would be called today) was 'oddly unenterprising'. The public learned more about the party leaders from television than from print, and the personalities of other senior politicians were 'almost completely unknown' to the reader at large. Fifth, there were not many analysis pieces explaining the mechanics of how politics worked. (Unsurprisingly, Butler thought the lobby itself was just the sort of subject that merited this kind of 'case study' treatment.) And sixth, there was not enough use of the background story, 'the retelling of how a situation developed'. Butler said that papers reported events but did not do enough to put them in their long-term context.[23]

Butler blamed the system rather than individuals. He identified a series of institutional obstacles, including the unwillingness of civil servants to talk to reporters in the way that officials did in Washington, Parliament's obsession with hearing announcements first, the rules of parliamentary privilege, Britain's libel laws and parliamentary hours inimical to newspaper deadlines. There should be better political reporting, not better political reporters, Butler said, because there was nothing much wrong with the lobby journalists themselves. But the journalist Anthony Howard, who was to emerge as one of the decade's other main critics of the lobby, went further, and made it more personal. 'In what is meant to be an open political system it has always struck me as extraordinary – and I frankly think unhealthy too – that so much secrecy and mystery should surround the work of the parliamentary lobby. For men whose task it is to find out things about other people, the lobby journalists traditionally display a really remarkable wariness and resentment when anyone tries to investigate the nature of their own activities: not even the vestal virgins guarded the secrets of their craft more zealously.' In his own talk on the BBC, Howard suggested that the public got a 'far cleaner, tougher standard of political reporting' during the 1964 election campaign because much of the coverage came from reporters outside the lobby who were not 'cribbed, cabined or confined by all the sanctimonious self-denying ordinances of Westminster'. Like Butler, he argued that political journalists should break out of the informal censorship of the lobby system and concentrate on the new centres of power like Whitehall. Speaking in the early days of the Labour Government, he looked forward to 'a new era of thrusting, radical, inquisitive, political reporting'.[24] His talk coincided with his move from the *New Statesman*, where he was political correspondent, to the *Sunday Times*, where, in the new post of Whitehall correspondent, he had been set the task of pioneering the kind of journalism he espoused.

The Butler–Howard analysis was not shared by most lobby correspondents. The *Sunday Telegraph*'s Ian Waller wrote a reply pointing out that other groups of reporters spoke to informants on an unattributable basis. 'The phrase, "lobby terms", which attracts so much abuse, is not more than an ordinary journalistic convention,' he said.[25] In his own act of retaliation, David Wood of *The Times* stressed that the lobby journalists were not operating in an open political environment. 'The lobby's activities have always been and still are on sufferance. Its members are not free to discuss them because reserve, or confidentiality, has been imposed on them in the terms of their relationship with the other contracting party – the members of the Commons and every administration in turn.'[26] But both journalists accepted there was room for improvement. Waller said that the expansion of government activity was swamping the critical resources of the press (and Parliament) and that newspapers needed bigger reporting teams. Wood said that it was 'absurd' for the lobby to go on accepting unattributable briefings from ministers when their informants were increasingly giving the same information out on television. Lobby journalists should also be 'much more on guard against the uncritical acceptance, in private, of statements that are no more than public relations exercises'.[27]

One person who was even less critical of the lobby correspondents was Harold Wilson. In the early 1960s he cultivated them assiduously and heaped praise on them. 'The relationship between politicians (Conservative and Opposition) and lobby journalists is a relationship of complete trust, and no politician has even been let down,' he said in 1962 (conveniently forgetting about his old ministerial colleague Dalton). 'This unique phrase of only three words, unknown in any other country, more binding than any legal contract, these three words "on lobby terms" are an essential thread of precious metal in our British parliamentary democracy.'[28] While previous party leaders had treated journalists with some reserve, Wilson appeared to revel in their company. He remembered their Christian names, attended their parties, entertained them at Downing Street and sent them Christmas cards. In the words of one aide, he 'elevated them as a profession'.[29] And if this involved laying it on with a trowel, he was willing to do so. 'It would be possible, I think, in a single day to take articles written against deadlines, sometimes late at night, by some of the gallery writers and get from them examples of English literature which I do not think you would get anywhere else in the country,' he once told a press gallery dinner.[30] After the 1964 election, lobby correspondents assumed that Wilson's arrival in Downing Street would give them better access to the executive, and at first they were proved right. In the early days there were up to three lobby briefings a day, many of them conducted by Wilson personally. Waller put this down to the fact that Wilson was 'the first occupant of 10 Downing Street ever to show any signs of understanding the press', and he declared that the country would never go back to having distant, aloof Prime Ministers.[31]

Within a few years the relationship had soured. One of the early victims was tation in the newly invented post of Whitehall correspondent. He was not based in Parliament and he was not a member of the lobby. Howard had very good Labour Party contacts and assumed that he would be able to use them to produce the kind of journalism he described in his anti-lobby manifesto. However, Wilson objected strongly to the idea of journalists writing about civil servants and he ordered ministers and officials not to cooperate with the *Sunday Times* newcomer. 'We can't recognise any such Whitehall animal,' Wilson told the Cabinet on 22 February 1965. 'This is a very dangerous man doing a very dangerous job.'[32] Howard found that people were reluctant to talk to him, and within a few months of launching his experiment, he left to become the *Observer*'s Washington correspondent.[33]

It took slightly longer for relations between the Government and the lobby to break down, but by the end of the 1960s Wilson's 'essential thread of precious metal' was looking a bit frayed. Partly that was because Wilson became paranoid about the press in general. But he also developed obsessive, green-ink grudges against specific lobby correspondents. One of them was David Wood. In 1966 Wilson told Roy Thomson, who was trying to buy *The Times*, that he should sack Wood if he won control. 'Get rid of him first, that's what I would do if I were the new owner of *The Times*,' Wilson said, before launching into a long rant about Wood's alleged deficiencies.[34] This became a common theme when the Prime Minister met *Times* executives, and they responded appropriately in 1968 by promoting Wood to the post of political editor.[35] Another correspondent on Wilson's hate list was Nora Beloff. Beloff, the daughter of Russian émigrés, worked in the Foreign Office political intelligence department during the war, became a foreign correspondent afterwards and reported for the *Observer* from Moscow and Washington before joining the lobby in 1964. She was the first woman to do a prominent job in the press gallery. A campaigner on an assorted range of causes (for: Soviet Jews, the Serbs; against: Trotskyists in the Labour Party, the closed shop for journalists), Beloff had a cosmopolitan self-confidence that was admirable and working methods that were not. 'She was famous for grasping the wrong end of any stick that might be in sight,' says Alan Watkins, who attributes this in part to her habit of getting material for stories by eaves-dropping on fellow journalists.[36] When David Astor, the *Observer* editor, went to see Wilson on one occasion, the Prime Minister produced reams of Beloff's cuttings and started sounding off at length about her supposed mistakes. 'That woman hates me, she hates me,' he told Astor. 'She's always slanting things against me; she repeats in your paper all the gossip she picks up from my enemies.'[37] Wilson even claimed that he was having Beloff tailed to find out what she was up to. As with David Wood, Wilson's hysteria only served to enhance Beloff's reputation.

At one stage in the late 1960s Wilson tried to deal with what he perceived as the hostility of the lobby by setting up what came to be described as the 'White Commonwealth'. A select group of lobby correspondents from mostly upmarket (but not necessarily pro-Labour) papers were invited to Downing Street, where Wilson would act all avuncular as they discussed politics for several hours over drinks. The group included Walter Terry, who as well as being political editor of the *Daily Mail* was conducting a relationship with Marcia Williams, Wilson's adviser and confidante. She had two children by him in the late 1960s before the affair became public knowledge. Terry was one of the outstanding story-getters in the lobby at the time and, although he was close to Downing Street, he was no pushover. In 1967 he anticipated the devaluation of the pound, partly because Williams was refusing to talk to him that week and he guessed that meant she was afraid of giving away a sensational secret. At the 'White Commonwealth' evenings, Wilson wanted Terry and the others to take a considered, almost academic view of his achievements. But unfortunately he failed to cure them of their undignified obsession with news reporting. 'It was run like a seminar,' recalled Williams. '[Wilson], therefore, became incensed when those same people proceeded later to write what seemed to him further trivial pieces based on a short-term, often sensational political event, rather than on the longer-term implications and background to which Harold had tried to direct them.'[38] Although Wilson became strongly associated with his 'White Commonwealth', there were in fact only a handful of meetings. The *Daily Express* (which was not invited) caught the select few coming out of Downing Street one night and ran a story exposing the whole operation, after which the experiment was abandoned.

Just as Wilson had his doubts about the lobby correspondents, they developed their doubts about him. They particularly objected to being given wrong information, and, as the decade went on, the reliability of Wilson's press operation became an increasingly sensitive issue. At times this caused problems for Trevor Lloyd-Hughes, the *Liverpool Daily Post* political correspondent appointed as Wilson's first press secretary. After one briefing about the Department for Economic Affairs that turned out not to be true, the lobby committee was told that the matter had been taken up with Downing Street and that 'Mr Lloyd-Hughes was himself aggrieved with the Prime Minister for having misled him, although he had not said as much in so many words'.[39] Joe Haines, who took over as Wilson's press secretary in 1969, recalled a similar experience. He was told to brief Robert Carvel that Wilson was going to sack Hugh Jenkins, the Arts

Minister; the *Evening Standard* ran with it, Wilson changed his mind and Carvel was left with a dud story. Wilson appeared not to be unduly bothered by all this. 'There is a certain amount of imaginative writing by lobby journalists, but there is also a certain amount of imagination by politicians too,' he once said.[40] He seemed to assume that a bit of dishonesty was par for the course.

In May 1969 the *Observer* published a full-page article – with no byline – about Wilson's relations with the press. 'The honeymoon came to an end some time in 1966,' it said.

> It was a slow process, owing something to the fact that the lobby gradually came to feel that they had been conned, something to the widening gap between Wilson's words and his actual performance, something to the uneasy realisation that there were too many non-news stories coming out of Downing Street . . . and, perhaps most important, a growing realisation that the economy, the object of the Prime Minister's greatest euphoria, was out of control. Few political journalists can take pride from reading, in cold blood today, what they wrote during the early part of Wilson's premiership.[41]

The article described in broad terms how the lobby operated, and it mentioned some of the correspondents by name. In the era of the ubiquitous media page, it would not be remarkable. But in the 1960s it was unusual for newspapers even to acknowledge that the lobby existed. Writing about briefings or the activities of colleagues was firmly against the rules and the lobby committee was furious. Astor insisted that none of the *Observer* lobby staff was responsible, but the committee threatened to expel the paper from lobby meetings unless Astor gave an assurance that he would 'do his utmost to prevent any further breach of lobby practice'.[42] Several journalists in the press gallery thought the committee was mad to make an issue of the matter. At first Astor refused to give in, and the row was resolved only in October, after a meeting in the *Observer* boardroom, when both sides agreed a face-saving formula. Reforming the lobby clearly had a long way to go.

Heath's Struggle with the 'Opaque Windows' of Whitehall

Edward Heath came to power in June 1970 eager to change the way the lobby worked. 'It is only when the opaque windows of Whitehall and around our working lives are opened that we shall find ourselves braced to make the immense efforts which are required in Britain today,' he declared as leader of the Opposition.[43] As

well as disapproving of the secrecy of the lobby, Heath thought its members did
not have the necessary technical expertise to explain government and all its
workings to the public. In a speech to the Institute of Journalists in 1968, he
argued that the lobby's relative ignorance of a subject like economics left it open
to manipulation. He gave an example.

> When the Vote on Account was published earlier this year it showed – just
> over two months after the Government's so-called expenditure cuts – a
> £1,000 million increase in government spending. The government spokesman
> – if one reads correctly between the lines – explained to the lobby that the
> Vote on Account was of no importance and this year was largely meaningless.
> One lobby correspondent – but one only – refused to accept this bland
> assertion, and it was largely due to him that this deliberate attempt to mislead
> the public failed.⁴⁴

In the Conservatives' election manifesto for 1970, Heath promised to make
government more open and accountable. When David Wood had defended the
lobby against some of the Butler–Howard criticisms five years earlier, he had
implied that he and his colleagues were not to blame for the fact that they
operated in such a clandestine manner. Confidentiality was 'imposed' on them
by the parliamentary system, Wood argued. Heath's administration was to show
that, when offered a choice, this was an imposition the lobby was not willing to
give up.

The new press secretary at No. 10 was a diplomat called Donald Maitland
who had been ambassador to Libya and head of news at the Foreign Office. He
was the first person without any journalistic experience to do the job since
George Steward, and he found at least one of the lobby conventions rather hard
to understand. The system still operated on the basis of non-attribution. But the
rules of lobby journalism were so strict, at least in theory, that it was impossible
for Downing Street to say something on the record even when it wanted to. The
only solution was to issue a written press notice. As Maitland explained in a
letter to the lobby chairman, Keith Renshaw, this meant that ordinary journalists were in some respects getting a better service from Downing Street than the
lobby was. 'If a non lobby correspondent who makes an enquiry by telephone
asks for the answer to be put on the record, we may well agree. However, this
same answer may normally only be given to a lobby correspondent non-attribut-
ably.'⁴⁵ Maitland's solution was for the Downing Street press secretary to be
allowed to brief – just sometimes – on the record.

In his letter he said that much of the information given out since he started the Downing Street job could have been on the record. Briefing on that basis would benefit both sides.

> The correspondent is protected should he have reason to doubt the validity of the guidance he is given; and the spokesman for his part can be assured that his words will be correctly reported. If the spokesman's non-attributable language is inaccurately interpreted and then virtually attributed by some such phrase as 'sources close to the Prime Minister were yesterday at pains to emphasise . . . ', he finds himself saddled with words he never used. The correspondent is equally disadvantaged if he is debarred from pointing to his source when his story is challenged.[46]

Maitland said that he did not expect to go on the record frequently and that it would happen least of all when the Commons was sitting. He insisted that there should not be a problem mixing unattributable remarks with on-the-record ones at the same briefing. And he promised that the flow of information on lobby terms would continue.

This all sounds relatively uncontroversial. But the lobby was distinctly suspicious. Rather than recommend accepting the Maitland proposals for a trial period, the committee ruled that the decision should be taken at a meeting open to all members of the lobby. Renshaw summarised the issues for his colleagues in a memo. He acknowledged that some members of the lobby were in favour of change, and that in the past on-the-record quotations had been offered at some briefings. He said that Maitland's proposal would make it clear where the 'responsibility' for a story lay and that it would enable the lobby to get away from some of the 'shadowy myths' surrounding it. But he also suggested that going on the record might make 'news management' easier for the Downing Street spokesman. 'What is favourable to his case he might pronounce with full authority on the record. What is unhelpful he might prefer to leave for the correspondent to write on his own authority. Put slightly differently, there may obviously, on occasion, be pressure upon a correspondent to give prominence in his report to quotable information.' Renshaw also invited his colleagues to consider whether such a fundamental change in their practice would 'dilute the atmosphere of confidentiality and confidence which has been our greatest asset in news gathering for decades, and from many sources'.[47]

Forty-eight members of the lobby met to discuss Maitland's idea in the lobby room at the Commons on 2 December 1970. George Gardiner, the chief political correspondent for Thomson Regional Newspapers, proposed the motion, saying that on-the-record briefings should be tried on an experimental basis. He pointed out that it was increasingly common for reporters to write up a story on lobby terms, only to have to insert quotes taken from the television when the minister who gave the briefing was interviewed on the record a few hours later. In view of the way the media was changing, 'the lobby really could not afford not to try this experiment', he said.[48] Proposing an amendment on behalf of lobby conservatives, Leslie Way, of the *Western Morning News*, claimed that the proposal was all about manipulating the media. 'Was it suggested that an odd "quote" from a No. 10 spokesman would put the lobby in a better position? This was purely and simply a desire for "news management", and unless the lobby wanted to commit suicide it had better throw the proposal out altogether.' Way's comments make it clear that some members of the lobby were still alarmed by the prospect of having to carry out what Guy Eden described as 'mere reporting'. Going on the record would 'erode the very foundations of the basis on which the lobby worked', Way argued. 'If they could not do without "quotes", which was what supporters of the motion were trying to pretend, it seemed to him that they were just demoting themselves to the role of general reporters, and they ought to face the consequences.'[49] After a long discussion, Way's amendment was carried by twenty-five votes to twenty-one. Maitland's proposals were rejected.

With the lobby refusing to go on the record, Heath and Maitland resorted to two new strategies in an attempt to get their message across in their own words. Maitland started issuing government statements in the form of press releases, which were handed out at the lobby. The news agencies and the broadcasters reported them fully, with the result that the lobby correspondents also felt obliged to quote from them directly. Heath also tried holding on-the-record press conferences at Lancaster House, modelled on the grand, presidential audiences that General de Gaulle used to hold at the Elysée. Maitland thought that these events would enable Heath to display his intellectual coherence and mastery of detail. But Heath was criticised for bypassing Parliament and the lobby correspondents complained that the meetings were boring. Heath held just four of them, and they did not become an alternative to lobby briefings.

Having failed to get the lobby to alter its attribution rules, Maitland decided a year later to alter one of the aspects of the briefing arrangements that he could control. For years the lobby correspondents had been going to Downing Street for their regular morning briefing, with the lobby room in the Commons being used in the afternoon. When Maitland arrived, he was amazed that these mini press conferences actually took place in his office. 'There were not enough seats, and some of the reporters were trying to take their notes standing up leaning against the mantelpiece,' he recalls. 'I thought it was ridiculous that the Prime Minister's press secretary and the national press should have to put up with those sorts of conditions. It was carrying the British obsession with amateurism to extremes.'[50] In late 1971 Maitland wrote to the lobby committee saying that the lobby was getting too big to meet in Downing Street and that he wanted to hold his briefings instead at 47 Parliament Street, in the old Welsh Office building. He explained that the room in No. 10 where the reporters used to gather before briefings was being turned into a proper office because the press team was expanding, and he said that the result would be a better service for journalists.

On 9 November a meeting was held to discuss Maitland's letter. Some of the correspondents were not bothered where the lobby met (the *Guardian*'s Francis Boyd reminded everyone that Churchill had kept the lobby out of Downing Street) but most of them were pretty unhappy about the thought of not being allowed to walk through the most important front door in the country. In truth, the only thing that was really at stake was lobby vanity, but there were some heroic attempts to make it an issue of principle. 'There is a certain symbolic significance in going through that door at No. 10,' John Egan argued. Lobby correspondents were the only journalists allowed into the building every day, and that affected the way they were viewed within the profession, by MPs and ministers and also outside Parliament. 'I think that for us to get shuffled off to some unknown part of Whitehall . . . would be misunderstood.'[51] The correspondents agreed unanimously that they were opposed to the move. Negotiations with Maitland continued over the next few weeks. At first he offered to allow the briefings to carry on at No. 10 on Mondays, to preserve the symbolic link with Downing Street. This raised the obvious question why, if it was practical to use No. 10 one day a week, it was not practical to do so every day of the week. Eventually Maitland came up with a compromise that at least allowed the lobby correspondents to carry on going to Downing Street. On Mondays, Tuesdays and Thursdays the briefings would take place in a new room provided by the government whips in their offices at No. 12; on Wednesdays, for the sake of preserving a tradition, they were held in No. 10.

Contempt and Privilege: Press Rights in the 1970s

With hindsight, the press gallery reformers of the 1960s who campaigned so vigorously against the ancient resolution banning the reporting of Parliament were fighting the wrong battle. They may have achieved an important symbolic victory in July 1971 when the Commons formally resolved that publishing debate reports was not a breach of privilege. But the decision was of no practical benefit whatsoever to reporters . If the reformers had wanted a more challenging task, they should have focused on the arcane rules governing the reporting of select committees. The inquiry report did not cover the subject at all yet, only three months after the supposed liberalisation of the privilege rules, the *Daily Mail*'s Gordon Greig was to give Parliament a fresh chance to demonstrate its enduring antipathy to newspaper coverage of its affairs.

Greig was another of the pre-eminent lobby correspondents of the postwar period. Like Walter Terry, he was an old-fashioned newspaperman with no discernible party or ideological loyalties who excelled at befriending politicians and working them for stories. He had been on the *Daily Mail* for about a year when he fell foul of the Commons authorities. His offence was to write a story in October 1971 about proposed increases in the civil list that appeared under the headline 'The million pound Queen'. Greig said that the Queen's pay was going to be fixed at £890,000 and that other expenses would add another £100,000 to the total. At the time the select committee on the civil list was looking into the matter. In the story, Greig said that the figures were based on government proposals but that they were 'not the last word' because a select committee was also discussing the claim.[52] As it happened, the select committee had already come to its conclusions, and three days before Greig's exclusive was published its members had been circulated with a draft report recommending that the royal household should receive £980,000. The *Daily Mail* story included rises for Prince Philip, the Queen Mother and Princess Margaret that were all identical to the equivalent figures in the draft report, and increases for Princess Anne and the Duke of Gloucester that were slightly different. Committee members assumed that Greig must have seen a copy and one of them, Willie Hamilton, made a formal complaint.

Hamilton was able to do this because the Commons still acknowledged a rule making select committee proceedings secret. 'Evidence taken by any select committee of this House and the documents presented to such a committee, and which have not been reported to the House, shall not be published by any member of such committee or any other person,' the House resolved in 1837.[53] This rule was not enforced when reporters covered the evidence given to a committee during a public hearing. But publishing the private deliberations of a committee was still seen as a serious contempt.

Greig acknowledged this when called before the privileges committee to explain himself. 'I have tried to avoid the possibility of committing a contempt in the story in every way I can think of,' he said.[54] He would not, of course, identify his source. But he stressed that he had been given the information on the basis that the figures were government ones, not committee ones. 'As far as I was concerned these were the Government's own private thoughts on what in fact the Royal Family might or might not have.'[55] When it was put to him that the proposals might have been submitted to the committee as evidence, Greig said the thought had not occurred to him. 'My impression was, rightly or wrongly, that these were in isolation, these were calculations made in isolation of the select committee.'[56] In fact, as both Greig and his interrogators knew, the civil list committee was chaired by Anthony Barber, the Chancellor, and its conclusions were always going to bear the Government's hallmark. There seems to be a strong element of feigned naïveté in what Greig was saying, and it is hard to avoid the conclusion that his 'government figures' line was a ploy to camouflage a story that he knew broke the rules.

Greig clearly realised that he was in trouble. He apologised to the committee when he gave evidence and later, in writing, he was even more abject. 'On reading the proof of the hearing, I feel that I failed to convey the full and sincere apology which I wished to convey to your committee and through your committee to the House,' he said. 'I did not, and do not, wish to qualify my apology. It is whole-hearted and unqualified.'[57] When it met to consider its report, the committee concluded that Greig knew, 'or on reasonable considera- tion ought to have known', that the information in his story came from a document presented to the civil list committee. 'Mr Greig's part in publishing the information he received was a contempt of the House and reprehensible, particularly as he is a journalist who enjoys the facilities and corresponding obli- gations of the parliamentary lobby and benefits from privileges which he has abused,' it said.[58] But on the question of punishment, the committee was split. George Strauss, a Labour MP, proposed an amendment suspending Greig from the lobby for a month and three other members voted with him. Another four voted against, and Greig was saved from temporary expulsion only on the casting vote of the committee chairman, Sir Derek Walker-Smith, a Tory.[59] In its report, the committee recommended no further action. Greig's non-confronta- tional tactics had paid off.

A fresh restriction was almost imposed on newspapers in 1973 when the *Daily Telegraph* lost a libel action relating to what was written in a parliamentary sketch. Since 1868 the courts had accepted that reports of parliamentary proceedings were covered by qualified privilege, and that such reports could not be libellous provided they were fair and accurate. At the time of the original decision sketch-writing barely existed. The 1973 case arose after Ivor Cook, a teacher who had exposed a school physical punishment scandal, was himself criticised in a House of Lords debate. The *Telegraph*'s sketch writer, Andrew Alexander, wrote up the allegations and Cook sued on the grounds that the report was unfair to him because it was only a partial account of the debate. (Alexander had virtually ignored a pro-Cook speaker.) Cook won. Given that all sketches are partial, the verdict set a dangerous precedent for newspapers. The case went to appeal and Lord Denning ruled that Alexander was protected by privilege because a partial report could be a fair one. 'If the reporter is to give the public any impression at all of the proceedings, he must be allowed to be selective and to cover those matters only which appear to be of particular public interest,' Denning said.[60]

The ruling came at a time when many people probably thought parliamentary sketch-writing was becoming less fair. In the 1950s Bernard Levin heaped scorn on MPs when he was writing a sketch for the *Spectator*; he is credited with being the first twentieth-century journalist to make a career out of writing about politicians disrespectfully. Newspapers were slow to follow his lead, but by the 1970s sketches were becoming increasingly aggressive. They were also getting more polemical, and Alexander himself used his platform to attack Heath's Government on political grounds. 'He was the first example of a sketch writer as a Right-wing ideologue,' says Frank Johnson, who joined the *Telegraph* as one of Alexander's replacements when Alexander went to the *Daily Mail*.[61] In retrospect, Denning's ruling can be seen as evidence of the way conventional 'fairness' in parliamentary reporting ('on the one hand, on the other') was coming to be seen as less important.

In 1975 another journalist got hold of a select committee leak, and this time the House adopted a much harsher stance. On 11 October the *Economist* published a story giving details of a draft report that had been circulated to members of the select committee on a wealth tax. It was written by Mark Schreiber, who combined being a journalist (but not a member of the lobby) with working part-time as an adviser in Margaret Thatcher's office. He and his editor, Andrew Knight, were called to give evidence to the privileges committee, and it became clear that their approach to the rule about reporting select committee deliberations was rather more cavalier than Greig's. Unlike Greig, who said he had not seen the draft report relevant to his story, Schreiber had got his hands on the confidential committee document. 'I fully realised it was not a report intended for publication because it said so at the top,' he said. But at the time he did not consider that a problem. 'I did not believe that once this thing had come to me as a journalist I had any obligation to keep it confidential.' As the committee concluded, 'Mr Schreiber considered that it was for him to decide what confidential information he would treat as secret, and what he would not, irrespective of the views of the House.' In doing so his conduct was 'wholly irresponsible'.[62] Knight said that he would not have published if he had known for certain that he was committing a contempt, but he admitted that at the time he thought it '60 to 70 per cent' likely that he was breaking the rules. The committee took the view that he was 'reckless in deciding to go ahead when he suspected that he was acting in contempt of Parliament'.[63] Strauss was by now chairman of the privileges committee and, having failed to get Greig suspended, he was not minded to let the two *Economist* journalists escape unpunished as well. Although Schreiber and Knight both expressed regret for what had happened, the committee recommended that they both be excluded from the Commons for six months. The only exception would be if either man wanted to come into the building to speak to his MP as a constituent.

The Commons considered the recommendation on 16 December. Strauss opened the debate, claiming that, if the House allowed the deliberations of select committees to be leaked, 'members of the committee as a whole would be subject to constant pressure from outside.' He further claimed that Schreiber would not have been allowed to act as he did had he been a member of the lobby, that the punishment was 'not a severe one' and that if the House were to reject a unanimous report from the privileges committee, the consequences would be 'grave and seriously damaging'.[64] Jeff Rooker, the Labour MP who originally complained about the leak, referred to the fact that Schreiber worked for Mrs Thatcher. Even though Schreiber had insisted in his evidence that the leak had nothing to do with her, Rooker said that if one of Harold Wilson's aides had done the same thing the press would have made political capital out of the affair and for that reason he supported Strauss. Jeremy Thorpe, the Liberal leader, also spoke in favour of the six-month suspension. But many Members complained that the proposed punishment was excessive. The Conservative Kenneth Baker pointed out that the last two committees to have recommended excluding journalists did so in 1899 and 1901. 'Those reports lie upon the table of the House. As far as I know they are still lying there, because our predecessors had the good sense not to take any action upon them at all,' he said.[65] John Pardoe, a Liberal, told MPs: 'If we pursue the line that the committee has recommended to us we are far more likely to bring ourselves into ridicule and contempt than may anything that has been done by anyone who is not a Member of this House.'[66] Douglas Crawford, a Scottish Nationalist, said the House was making itself a 'laughing stock' just by debating the recommendation.[67] The Conservative Jonathan Aitken accused the committee of 'a grave over-reaction and the use of a sledge hammer to crack a nut',[68] and his colleague Paul Channon argued that the committee was being inconsistent.

> Is it not somewhat farcical that we should tonight be asked to express our disapproval on this matter when extensive stories were leaked over the weekend about Chrysler, dealing with whether ministers were to resign, whether the Cabinet was split and so on? We all know perfectly well that governments of every political complexion, and individual ministers from time to time, leak stories to the press when it suits them. They do so on far more serious matters than the first draft report of the chairman of the select committee on the wealth tax. Is it not hypocritical of the House to condone one and to condemn another?[69]

Channon proposed an amendment to the suspension motion, regretting the leak but proposing no further action. After two hours and forty minutes of debate, the House backed him by sixty-four votes to fifty-five. Schreiber was allowed to stay. It was a victory, of sorts, for the press. Although MPs still had the power to chuck a journalist out of their building for breaking their rules in the course of routine newsgathering, the *Economist* episode showed that they were most reluctant to do so.

On and Off the Record: The Lobby 1974 to 1979

When Wilson was re-elected Prime Minister in 1974, he took with him to Downing Street Joe Haines and a renewed determination to do battle with the press. Haines had been a political correspondent on the *Sun* from 1964 to 1968 (in its pre-Murdoch phase). An acerbic Labour loyalist, he had replaced Trevor Lloyd-Hughes as Wilson's press secretary in 1969. ('Trevor was far too nice for that job at such a time in politics . . . Joe Haines's style was rougher and more direct,' Marcia Williams recalled later.[70]) But his moment of glory was to come during Wilson's second spell in power. Haines and his boss had watched Heath's attempts to impose change on the lobby fail dismally, and they were to try something much bolder.

Even in 1969 and 1970, when Haines enjoyed a honeymoon with the lobby, relations were not easy. As one set of committee minutes records, 'there was undoubtedly a feeling of unease among some members of the lobby about allegedly inadequate guidance from the Prime Minister's press office . . . Mr J. T. W. Haines, press secretary, deliberately referred many inquiries to other government departments.'[71] Lobby journalists had got used to being able to bounce a wide variety of questions off Downing Street, and Haines took delight in the fact that, once he stopped answering questions on behalf of all government ministers, they had to make their own inquiries. He justified the decision on the grounds that No. 10's practice of commenting on all aspects of government activity was an anachronistic hangover from the days when other departments did not have fully equipped press offices. Haines was already on his way towards acquiring the nickname the lobby gave him: the anti press officer.

In 1975 Haines (and Wilson) went one step further. Having given up using his regular meetings with the political correspondents to talk about matters not directly related to Downing Street, Haines declared that he was not going to use the briefings to talk about the Prime Minister either. In fact, 'as a step, albeit a modest one, in the direction of more open government', he was going to abolish his collective daily encounters with the lobby altogether. Haines had had objections to the principle of collective unattributable briefings ever since his own time in the press gallery, and he had discussed the idea of ending the briefings with Wilson. Two incidents triggered the decision. At one 4 p.m. briefing a reporter who had enjoyed a good lunch was so rude about 'Marcia' that Haines felt he had to walk out. ('Privately I was insulting about her too, but as the spokesman I could not accept that,' Haines recalls.[72]) Then, after another briefing, three lobby correspondents went to the Tory Chief Whip to say that Downing Street had discussed confidential discussions between the two parties about a forthcoming vote. Haines thought this was totally against the rules. In a letter on 19 June to John Egan, the lobby chairman, he explained why he wanted to abandon the traditional system.

> I appreciate the convenience of one person answering for the whole of Whitehall, but it is physically not possible and nor, from the point of view of the press, is it desirable. No journalist should rely on a single source for his information.
>
> More fundamental, however, is the question of whether a daily meeting between the Prime Minister's spokesman and political journalists on a non-attributable basis is good for government, good for the press, and above all good for the general public which sustains us both.
>
> In my firm opinion, and in the view of the Prime Minister, it is not. I think many people rightly suspect the validity of stories which lean heavily upon

thin air. From now on, it will be my general rule that if a statement needs to be made on behalf of the Prime Minister, that statement will be made on the record.

This will not lead to any loss of information to the general public. Indeed, they will then know its source. And it will eliminate the kind of extreme absurdity where, under the rules governing the present meetings, even the name of the annual poppy day seller who calls on the Prime Minister is given unattributably.[73]

Haines said that he would continue to make routine information available to the lobby, although he saw no reason why it should not be on the record. He would also carry on speaking to journalists individually, agreeing with them on a case-by-case basis whether or not he wanted to be quoted. Just in case Egan failed to get the message, Haines made eighty copies of his letter for circulation in the press gallery. In effect, the letter itself was one of the new, on-the-record press releases Haines was promising. For the next ten months the lobby had to get by without its regular fix of unattributable briefing. The arrangement created no desire among the correspondents for permanent reform, although Haines himself found it useful being able to deny stories on the record, rather than just on lobby terms.

When James Callaghan became Prime Minister in April 1976, he made Tom McCaffrey his chief press secretary. Unlike Haines, McCaffrey was a career civil servant. He had spent time in the Downing Street press office when Heath was Prime Minister, and he had worked for Callaghan as a press secretary both at the Home Office in the 1960s and at the Foreign Office since the 1974 election. He was a believer in the lobby system and on the night he took charge, he rang the lobby to say that it would be business as usual the following morning. 'I believe that as a result of lobby meetings over the years the public know more today than ever before of what the Government is doing in their name, and that if the unattributable element of these meetings is removed the public will be poorer,' he later explained.[74] He also thought that the arrangement was at least as useful to the Government as it was to the press. The lobby correspondents had strongly resented Haines's decision to cast them into exile, and McCaffrey's phone call was most welcome.

Ostensibly the lobby system that McCaffrey re-established was exactly the same as the one that operated in the 1940s and 1950s. Members were still bound by the rule saying: 'Don't talk about lobby meetings before or after they are held.' But there were signs that the old conventions were breaking down. In 1975

Haines was not the only person to complain that the lobby could no longer keep a secret. The *Spectator* was told in March that its lobby correspondent, Patrick Cosgrave, would not be allowed to attend lobby meetings after it published an account of an unattributable briefing. (The lobby committee decided that Cosgrave should be punished even though he did not write the offending article.) In the same month the *Sun* published a story based on off-the-record remarks given by Prince Charles at a press gallery lunch, and its reporters were subsequently banned from attending such events in the future. Although that was a press gallery event, rather than a lobby event, the episode reflected the fact that Westminster journalists were finding it increasingly hard to keep a secret. Part of the reason for this was that the press gallery was expanding. There were more than a hundred journalists in the lobby in the mid-1970s, which meant that it was getting more difficult for the old guard to use peer pressure as a restraining influence. But partly it was just that the press, like society at large, was becoming less deferential towards authority.

Appropriately enough, the big lobby crisis of the Callaghan years followed the Government's decision to get rid of an ambassador who supposedly represented the old, stuffy, forelock-tugging Britain where establishment secrets were always safe. The announcement that Sir Peter Ramsbotham, the 57-year-old Old Etonian son of a peer, was to leave the Washington embassy to be replaced by Peter Jay, a 40-year-old journalist, would have caused a stir in any circumstances. Since Jay was also Callaghan's son-in-law, the reaction was more one of outrage. On 12 May 1977, after a briefing dominated by questions about the appointment and Callaghan's supposed nepotism, McCaffrey fell into conversation with two journalists he knew well, Robert Carvel of the *Evening Standard* and John Dickinson of the *Evening News*. McCaffrey told them the real reason Ramsbotham had to go was that he was considered fuddy-duddy and a bit of a snob. A few hours later the information was the basis of a *Standard* front-page story under the headline 'Snob envoy had to go'. It said that Ramsbotham was being replaced because the Government had decided he would be 'a dead loss for Britain in the Jimmy Carter era'. There were no direct quotes, but Carvel said he was reporting the 'explanation available in government circles'. The *Evening News* reported the story in similar terms under an identical headline, although Dickinson sourced his information to 'the Callaghan camp'.

McCaffrey had not intended his remarks to be reported. He thought he was just talking 'amongst friends'.[75] In that respect his indiscretion fell into the same category as Hugh Dalton's. But the events that followed showed that the lobby had changed considerably since 1947. When John Carvel published the Budget leak that led to Dalton's resignation, there was a widespread assumption that, in the event of it being unclear whether a lobby reporter could use a confidential piece of information, he should keep it to himself. Thirty years after the Dalton affair, this convention no longer applied. The onus of responsibility had shifted, and when McCaffrey said something he did not mean to, it was accepted that the lobby correspondents were within their rights to report it. (Even McCaffrey conceded that he was the one who made the mistake.) What was even more significant was the way in which rival papers followed up the story. Lobby correspondents were still bound by the rule saying they should not discuss what happened at their meetings, and newspapers were generally happy to respect that. But after the two 'Snob envoy had to go' headlines appeared, other newspapers began to speculate where the remarks had come from and who was knifing the ambassador. Over the coming years, it became increasingly common for stories involving a sensational comment made on lobby terms to be followed up in this way. McCaffrey was soon identified as the source of the remarks and Callaghan was accused of running a deliberate government smear campaign against Ramsbotham. Eventually, on 16 May, he had to make a statement in the Commons denying this.[76]

Callaghan told MPs that he did not think the lobby system had worked very well on this particular occasion and that he was 'attracted . . . to having public briefings and not private briefings'. Although he did not commit himself to change, he urged the lobby to 'reflect' on what had happened.[77] The following day there was a special meeting for all lobby correspondents. David Holmes, political editor of the BBC and lobby chairman at the time, pointed out that many of the correspondents were concerned by what they saw 'as an abuse of the lobby system by No. 10 in the last few days'. Although McCaffrey's most inflammatory remarks had been made in a private conversation, he had used his official briefing to criticise Ramsbotham indirectly, and this was seen as a deliberate attempt to divert attention away from the nepotism charge. But Holmes also credited McCaffrey with trying to be 'as genuinely informative as possible' and with wanting to continue the existing system, against the wishes of the Prime Minister. He invited his colleagues to consider whether they needed to reform their 'shaky structure'.[78] Several people called for more openness, although there were also claims that on-the-record briefings would make news management easier. Nothing was resolved, but a week later there was another meeting at which a compromise resolution was proposed. It said that 'future meetings between the lobby and ministers, MPs and civil servants should allow for exchanges to be conducted, where appropriate, for quotation "on the record"', but that the journalists were convinced 'that a substantial part of the interchange between political journalists and politicians is better conducted through the convention of "non-attribution"'.[79] The motion was passed by forty-two votes to eleven, and the committee was instructed to start discussing the new arrangements with the relevant parties.

It did not make much difference. On 18 July McCaffrey gave his first on-the-record briefing as the Prime Minister's press secretary. He opened with a statement saying that there had been a two-hour meeting of various ministers at Downing Street and that Callaghan had later attended a charity engagement. David Harris, the new chairman of the lobby, asked for on-the-record questions and someone asked McCaffrey what the ministerial meeting was about. And how did McCaffrey greet the dawn of open government? With the reply: 'I regret – I am very sorry – but I cannot help you on that.' That was about it. 'It could not be described as dramatic, but it was the start of a new era in the history of the journalists' organisation,' said *The Times*, optimistically (and erroneously). The briefing quickly went unattributable, and the *Times* report includes four paragraphs in conventional lobbyese (no quotes, 'later the correspondents learnt', etc.) describing what happened at the ministerial meeting.[80] With McCaffrey reluctant to be quoted, the reforms were shown to be pointless, and on-the-record briefings were abandoned almost immediately. The new era was still twenty years away.

'The Dead Restored to Life': Radio Broadcasting

After the failure of attempts in the 1960s to allow the televising of Parliament, a fresh bid to get the cameras in was launched in October 1972. Robert Carr, the leader of the Commons, was personally in favour, but officially the Government was neutral and the motion was proposed by Brian Batsford, a Tory backbencher. It called for the proceedings of the Commons to be broadcast publicly on radio and television for an experimental period. Batsford and other pro-broadcasting MPs were worried by what they saw as growing evidence that Parliament was becoming irrelevant to ordinary voters. 'We are witnessing today a mounting lack of respect for authority in many walks of life, and Parliament is no exception. Ignorance of our procedure, of what we are trying to do here, and of our work in general, will create a lack of respect for politics and politicians,' he argued. Television was a means of 'restoring the people's interest'.[81] Michael Foot complained that the popular press had almost abandoned parliamentary reporting and that 'the so-called posh papers' were devoting less attention to it.

As a result, 'in some ways the safest place in which to utter something one does not want to be leaked by any journalist is in the secrecy of the chamber.' If MPs rejected an experiment, 'we shall be saying by implication that we are content with the relationship between Parliament and the people and with the fact that the argument about politics in this country is more and more being transferred from this central forum.'[82] But the case against television was argued as vigorously as it had been in the 1960s. Joe Ashton, a Labour MP, spent much of the afternoon holding up signs carrying slogans like 'Where is Ted?' in an attempt to highlight the way television would affect conduct in the chamber. When he was called to speak, he said that he had originally been in favour of admitting the cameras but that he had changed his mind. 'It would be derogatory to Parliament to introduce television,' he said. 'We shall have the evils of sponsorship, the protesters from the public gallery and the show-offs and I do not want to see politics degenerating in the same way as that in which I have seen religion and sport degenerate after going on television.'[83] Reinforcing the same point, Norman Tebbit asked whether there was anything, 'with the exception . . . of show jumping', that had not been trivialised by television.[84] The House agreed, and Batsford's motion was rejected by 191 votes to 165, a majority of twenty-six.

When Labour came to power two years later the new leader of the Commons, Edward Short, introduced the subject again. There was a debate on 24 February 1975, and this time MPs were invited to vote separately for public experiments on radio and on television. Members were still opposed to the idea of debating on screen. Peter Morrison, a Tory, invited MPs to imagine 'some poor chap' appearing before a Conservative selection committee. 'Perhaps he is a small fat man who wears glasses and does not look too prepossessing. He would make a good Member, but the members of the selection have to bear in mind the question of his appearing on television.'[85] The proposal for a television experiment was rejected by a majority of twelve. But many of the MPs who were anti-television were not averse to radio. 'I shall vote for the motion on sound broadcasting,' said Ashton. 'People will then be able to listen carefully to what has gone on and will not gaze at their televisions wondering why so-and-so is showing his braces and why somebody else appears to be nodding off.'[86] With 354 votes in favour and 182 against, the radio motion was approved by a majority of 172. The month-long experiment began on 9 June when, for the first time, the proceedings of the Commons were broadcast live to the public. The breakthrough came just ten days before Joe Haines made his own contribution towards parliamentary openness by suspending lobby briefings and deciding to distribute Downing Street information on the record.

In March 1976, following the publication of a report from the services committee about the experiment, MPs were invited to vote for the resumption of radio broadcasting on a permanent basis. Short, opening the debate once again, concentrated on the positive public response to the previous year's experiment. 'For those who favour the broadcasting of our proceedings it would, I suppose, be one of the principal aims of the broadcasts to widen public interest in what goes on here; to broaden the base of informed public opinion about parliamentary matters; and generally to sustain and stimulate interest in what Parliament stands for.'[87] The evidence suggested that this had happened, he went on. The live broadcasts of Prime Minister's Questions attracted an audience four times as large as the normal one for that time of day. The daily *Yesterday in Parliament* listener figures had risen by 300,000. According to a BBC poll, 76 per cent of listeners thought that the broadcasting of Parliament should continue. So did the Government, Short said, although he stressed that the final decision was one for the Commons itself.

During the debate, which started on 8 March and resumed eight days later for time reasons, all the old arguments against broadcasting resurfaced. John Stokes, a Tory, said MPs would become part of the 'huge and growing news and entertainment industry' if broadcasting were allowed. 'There is already in this once great but now, regrettably, declining country far too much talking, news and comment about current affairs,' he complained.[88] Bruce Grocott, a Labour MP, advanced a more sophisticated version of the same argument. He said that although broadcasting might make people interested in Parliament, it did not necessarily make them better informed. During the 1975 experiment his constituents seemed interested only in the theatre of the place. 'The reaction has not been to say, for example, "I was convinced by the argument I heard," or "That seemed to be a substantial case." The reactions were almost always related to the duels between the front benches being impressive or entertaining.' Grocott said that he did not want proceedings in the Commons to be 'over-dramatised' because that was not conducive to good government. 'All experience seems to me to suggest . . . that if the glare of publicity is brought into a particular decision-making situation, we inevitably move the decision-making situation somewhere else.'[89] But this time the opponents were in the minority. When the Commons divided on the proposal 'that the public sound broadcasting of its proceedings should be arranged on a permanent basis', there were 299 votes in favour and only 124 against, making a majority of 175.

It took another two years for the details to finalised, but on 3 April 1978 the permanent broadcasting of the Commons began. (A similar process took place in the Lords, and radio broadcasting from the Upper House began the following day.) The Commons event started with Welsh questions, an engagement that is normally of no interest whatsoever to MPs outside the principality. On this occasion it was, and there were something like eighty members in the chamber for the prayers that mark the start of proceedings. George Thomas, the Speaker, had been opposed to the installation of the microphones, but he soon changed his mind. He was convinced that broadcasting increased the public's interest in Parliament. His own postbag more than doubled and there was an increase in the number of people actually visiting the building. Within the chamber, the atmosphere was also transformed. 'Members who had been silent since I had been elected Speaker suddenly came to life. It was as though the dead had been restored to life and had found a new aggressiveness,' Thomas said later.[90]

Print journalists in the press gallery did not notice an immediate change in their circumstances after April 1978, although in the long run having the proceedings of the Commons on the radio certainly did not encourage newspapers to expand their parliamentary coverage. The BBC and Independent Radio News hired extra staff to cope with the new opportunities available to them. But although the broadcasting parliamentary teams expanded, the reporters doing the job, like Christopher Jones, the BBC's parliamentary correspondent, were eventually to lose out. 'Being a parliamentary correspondent was far more rewarding when people could only hear what had happened in the House of Commons through your descriptions,' says John Sergeant, who worked at the BBC with Jones. 'When that gap was filled, first by radio and then by television, the skills of the lobby correspondent . . . came much more to the fore.'[91] Although few people seem to have predicted this in advance, the advent of radio broadcasting turned out to mark another step in the gradual, century-long transfer of power from the parliamentary correspondents to their colleagues in the lobby.

SIX

Secrecy and Openness: The 1980s

The lobby is often passive; it waits for the information to be presented on the sugared spoon held out by government public relations officers off the record. It practises spaniel journalism, like those newspapers that roll on their backs to be tickled by the award of a knighthood to their editors or political editors.

Michael Cockerell, Peter Hennessy and David Walker,
Sources Close to the Prime Minister, *1984*

When I heard what the lobby journalists said about the report of the committee of privileges, I was reminded of two old dinosaurs locked in combat. The misuse of privileges and the lobby system are both designed to deny the public the information it should have.

Tony Benn, House of Commons, 20 May 1986

Some journalists are unwilling to receive briefing from No. 10 when we speak to the lobby collectively; but only too anxious to receive it from us one to one; and apparently only too delighted to receive it second hand, unattributably, from members of the lobby they affect to despise.

Bernard Ingham, 5 December 1986

Rattling the Lobby: To 1985

'Almighty God, to whom we are all attributable . . . ' So began the grace at the lobby's centenary lunch on 18 January 1984.[1] It was held at the Savoy, and it was attended by all the sources a political journalist could ever need. Margaret

Thatcher proposed the toast to the lobby, and her fellow guests at the top table included Neil Kinnock, David Steel, David Owen and Bernard Weatherill. In her speech the Prime Minister joked that she was 'not lost in uncritical admiration of the lobby, a feeling which I judge to be warmly reciprocated'. But, she told the assembled horde, at their best – for example, in a real crisis or when they were really up against time, as on Budget day – they were 'brilliantly professional', and the lobby was right to celebrate 'a successful hundred years in pursuit of press freedom'.[2]

For critics of the lobby system, the spectacle of the reporters sitting down on such cosy terms with their subject matter neatly illustrated why it was so ghastly. 'Can you think of any more nauseating scene in 1984 than the kept men and women of British journalism lunching with their keeper, and purring with pleasure at her witty remarks scripted by Bernard Ingham?' asks Peter Hennessy. 'It was toe-curling.'[3] At the time of the lunch, Hennessy, a broadsheet journalist in the process of transferring into academia, was writing a book with Michael Cockerell, a television journalist who had made a *Panorama* programme in 1982 'exposing' the lobby, and David Walker, a journalist on *The Times*. Published later in 1984, *Sources Close to the Prime Minister* was a polemic against Downing Street news management. The authors wanted to sound a discordant note amid the 'orgy of eulogy' surrounding the lobby's centenary celebrations.[4] (Hennessy says he still cannot decide whether Thatcher was being deliberately ironic in her remarks about the pursuit of press freedom.) In their book, Cockerell, Hennessy and Walker said that the lobby's reliance on unattributable briefings, 'coupled with the credulity of many of its members', had turned it into 'the Prime Minister's most useful tool for the management of the news'.[5] In the 1970s, some members of the lobby had claimed that on-the-record briefings would make it easier for the Government to manage the news; *Sources Close to the Prime Minister* argued precisely the opposite. Many of the anti-lobby arguments in the book had been doing the rounds since David Butler and Anthony Howard first called for reform in the 1960s, but this time the criticism was more vitriolic.

> Ask . . . what the lobby journalist wants, and the answer ought to be indiscretion, information that the powerful do not want to impart. In practice, however, the lobby journalist does not want a great deal. The lobby is often passive; it waits for the information to be presented on the sugared spoon held out by government public relations officers off the record. It practises spaniel journalism, like those newspapers that roll on their backs to be tickled by the award of a knighthood to their editors or political editors.[6]

Hennessy's views were informed by his own experience as a lobby correspondent on the *Financial Times* for a few months in 1976. 'I loathed it almost from the first moment,' he says. A journalistic loner, he disliked the way the lobby correspondents worked as a pack and gathered in a huddle to 'fix the line' after briefings. 'I thought that was a restraint of trade and bad for the general reservoir of information.' But, more importantly, he thought they were failing to uncover the really important stories. 'Even on a really serious paper, there was so much trivia one had to chase. I knew enough about Whitehall to know that the really interesting stuff was deep down in the cabinet committees, which were very hard to penetrate in those days. I thought our job was to write the first draft of history – I thought we had to strive for that, even though we could not do it – and yet we were not reporting things that were happening literally three hundred yards away from the lobby corridor where we worked. It drove me mad.'[7]

One of the chapters in *Sources Close to the Prime Minister* was called 'What the papers never said', and it covered three important policy decisions taken by the Attlee Government. Using government papers released under the thirty-year rule, and comparing them with contemporary newspaper reports, the authors showed that political journalists at the time largely failed to pick up or report crucial government developments relating to the atomic bomb, immigration and devaluation. *Sources Close to the Prime Minister* argued that the public was still not being properly informed, and that the behaviour of the lobby correspondents was partly responsible for this.

The book went down very badly in the lobby. Many political journalists did not accept the implication that their job was to provide a cuttings service for future historians. More importantly, almost all of them objected to the suggestion that they practised 'spaniel journalism' and that they allowed themselves to be spoon-fed by Downing Street. 'The assumption behind it was that we were all either extremely stupid or extremely forelock-plucking and I resented that,' says Ian Aitken, who was the *Guardian*'s political editor at the time.

> They got the wrong end of the stick, because the really important sources for lobby correspondents were not those boring old briefings, but the hundreds of other sources inside the Commons. The main thing was having access to the lobby and being able to talk to MPs and ministers, and if you thought you were being lied to at a briefing, you could go and speak to someone else.[8]

Looking back, Hennessy now thinks that that in some respects he 'overdid it'. But he believes that one of the strengths of *Sources Close to the Prime Minister* was that it 'annoyed all the right people', and he takes pride in the fact that he is the second most vilified journalist in Bernard Ingham's memoirs.[9]

Although members of the lobby objected to the way they were depicted in the book, many of them were keen to make the system more open, and in the autumn of 1984 one of the reformers, Glyn Mathias, became lobby chairman. Mathias, ITN's political editor, thought that the lobby needed to do something about its increasingly negative public reputation. In particular, he thought it was mad to insist that briefings had to be unattributable. 'On Thursday afternoons we would have the leader of the House and then the leader of the Opposition and then David Steel and David Owen and, if a story was good enough, they would come afterwards and do an interview,' recalls Mathias. 'Then you would have the sight of the lobby correspondents with their tape recorders crowding round the television set getting the same quotes that they had been given – but could not use – from the meeting they had just sat through. It was absolutely bizarre.'[10] He consulted Ingham, the Downing Street press secretary from 1979, and the opposition parties about putting the briefings on the record. Ingham made it clear that he would not speak to the lobby on those terms (he cited the constitutional argument, and the need for the Government to communicate through elected politicians speaking in Parliament), and Mathias took the view that there was no point trying to force the issue. But Neil Kinnock, David Steel and David Owen were happy to be quoted on occasion. In January 1985 the lobby committee released a two-page report proposing a 'permissive' change that would allow elected politicians to brief the lobby on the record if they wanted to. The lobby backed the new system by sixty-seven votes to fourteen. The opposition leaders and some ministers, including Nigel Lawson, the Chancellor, all agreed to speak on the record. But the arrangements were discretionary and, with some members of the lobby still in favour of the old system, there was no permanent change in the lobby's culture. The Government's main dealings with the lobby remained unattributable.

'Two Old Dinosaurs': Parliament and the Press

Two centuries after Parliament gave up trying to stop reporters covering debates, and almost a decade after MPs got round to passing a resolution admitting that the ban had lapsed, the Commons put on a minor display of reaction that would have done credit to Colonel Onslow himself. It happened in 1980 when Norman St John-Stevas, leader of the House, declared that people listening to a debate from the public gallery should not take notes. In the long catalogue of parliamentary restrictions on newsgathering, it was a largely irrelevant intervention. But it shows that the Commons was still acutely sensitive about the reporting of its proceedings, as the press was to discover in a much more serious case later in the decade.

There was nothing new about the ban on people in the public gallery taking notes. The rule had survived as a hangover from the days when all reporting was outlawed. What was remarkable was that St John-Stevas thought it was a good idea. As leader of the Commons, he was also chairman of the services committee. The committee considered the matter early in 1980 and came out in favour of the status quo. A few weeks later St John-Stevas told the Commons why the ban on note-taking in the public gallery should continue. 'This is a facility available only to *Hansard* and to those representatives of the press with authorised access to the press gallery. I think that if this rule were changed there would be the danger that it could lead to unofficial reporting by people who had failed to gain membership of the press gallery.'[11]

The rule was no mere formality. As John Hunt, a Conservative MP, told the *Sunday Times* a few days later, it was actually enforced by the Commons authorities. 'I have noticed people sitting in the public gallery earnestly taking notes and they look ashamed and very surprised when they are pounced upon by attendants and told they are not allowed to do it,' he said.[12] The issue was relevant to campaigners dealing with subjects like abortion who wanted to take notes during debates so they could issue instant press releases. They could not understand why they were allowed to scribble away during committee stage debates (held outside the main chamber) but not at second reading, report stage or third reading. In his announcement in the Commons, St John-Stevas implied that the press gallery journalists were opposed to change. It turned out that this was based on a misunderstanding. William Russell, the press gallery secretary, explained later that he could not care less either way. It was not until March 1994 that the ban on note-taking from the public gallery was permanently lifted.

In 1982 the press gallery did request a minor change in Commons regulations. With the proceedings in the chamber now being broadcast, Russell wrote to Peter Jennings, the Deputy Serjeant at Arms, asking if reporters could be allowed to use tape recorders in the gallery. As the rules stood, a journalist (and indeed anyone else) could tape an exchange in the Commons from a radio outside the chamber, but not from his or her seat on the inside. The proposal seemed innocuous, particularly since the *Hansard* reporters were already allowed to use tape recorders. It would not have altered newspaper coverage. It would just have made it slightly easier for a few people to check their quotes. But the Commons authorities were suspicious. Jennings wrote back to say that he doubted very much the idea would find favour with Members 'as it seems to me it would open up a Pandora's Box'.[13] Tape recorders remained banned for another eighteen years.

As in the 1970s, the most contentious disputes affecting Parliament and the press revolved around leaks from select committees. St John-Stevas had more enlightened views about these bodies than he had about note-takers in the public gallery and, in one of the most significant pieces of parliamentary reform of the Thatcher years, he overhauled the system soon after the Conservatives came to power. The existing committees were replaced with fully fledged departmental ones that were given the job of holding ministers to account. Consequently their work became more interesting to journalists and leaks became more common. In March 1985 the committee of privileges investigated a complaint against *The Times* after it published in its diary material from a draft home affairs committee report on Special Branch. The committee recommended no action, even though it decided that the leak was 'a serious contempt of the House'.[14] But it called for a review of the privilege rules covering these matters and agreed to undertake the inquiry itself.

Although the Commons rule banning the publication of draft select committee reports was still in place, the committee found that the days when a reporter like Gordon Greig was prepared to acknowledge the rule's importance (and even offer a 'whole-hearted and unqualified' apology for apparently breaking it) were over. James Naughtie, a *Guardian* lobby correspondent, told the committee that the privilege rule had been shown to be 'unworkable'.[15] Other journalists also made it clear that the rule would not stop them looking for a select committee exclusive. The committee concluded regretfully that,

> Despite the acceptance in the Notes on the Practice of Lobby Journalism . . . that the rules of privilege prohibited the publication of unreported proceedings, the lobby journalists themselves did not feel bound by those rules; indeed, they openly ignore them on the grounds that the case law on privilege has changed over the years, and that the rules were no longer enforced.[16]

In its report, the committee admitted that only six leak complaints had been referred to it in the preceding twenty-five years (and of these, the *Economist* case was the only one leading to a recommendation that a journalist be suspended). But the number of informal complaints was growing, and the committee decided that Parliament's censorship rule was worth preserving in some form. It recommended that the Commons should take action only in 'really serious cases', such as those where a leak was likely to cause 'substantial interference' with the work of the House.[17] In those circumstances, editors and journalists should be liable for an appropriate penalty, including the possible withdrawal of lobby or press gallery passes for a specified period.

The new system was put to the test before the year was out. Richard Evans was a *Times* reporter assigned to cover the select committees. He had already written quite a number of stories based on committee leaks when, in December 1985, he obtained a draft of the environment committee's report on the nuclear industry. It was, according to the story he wrote, 'devastating'. It concluded that facilities for the disposal of nuclear waste in Britain were 'primitive in the extreme' and that the condition of the industry had left the committee with a feeling 'almost of shame'.[18] Evans's story appeared in *The Times* on 16 December. Sir Hugh Rossi, the environment committee chairman, at once retaliated by launching an inquiry intended to lead to disciplinary action. He first wrote to all members of his committee to ask if any of them was responsible for briefing *The Times*. They all assured him that they were not. The committee then considered the damage done, and it concluded that Evans had passed the 'substantial interference' test. 'Despite the assurances we received, the suspicion that a member of the committee did, in fact, leak the report is bound to be there and to damage the trust that needs to exist between members of a group if they are to carry out their work effectively,' it said. The leak was also 'bound to influence discussion' of the controversial sections in the draft report, and the impact was so serious that the committee claimed even to have considered giving up the radioactive waste inquiry.[19] At that stage the matter was passed to the privileges committee. Evans and his editor, Charles Wilson, were summoned to explain why they had broken the rules. Their performance illustrated the extent to which journalistic attitudes had changed since the 1970s. Unlike Gordon Greig, who claimed that he would not knowingly have committed a contempt, and Mark Schreiber and Andrew Knight, who did so only because there was some doubt in their minds as to whether they were flouting Commons regulations, Wilson said that when he put the story in the paper he knew full well it was a breach of privilege. He said that the rules were 'out of date, and acknowledged as being out of date',[20] and that public interest justified publication. Evans said that it was becoming routine for journalists to publish select committee leaks and that he himself had done so several times before. Neither of the two men offered even a token apology.

This was a serious challenge to the authority of the body charged with enforcing discipline in the House of Commons. As the privileges committee said in its report: '*The Times* decision to commit a contempt in this case was taken in open defiance of a very recent, considered warning and not just of some obsolete rule.'[21] It claimed that the journalists had shown no interest in the damage they had done to the work of the environment committee. Evans had shown 'scant respect for the traditions and rules of the House',[22] and *The Times* had decided as a matter of policy that leaks should be published. As punishment, it recommended that Evans should be suspended from the lobby for six months and not allowed to work in the Commons during that period, and that while the exclusion was in force, *The Times* should lose one of its lobby passes.

The report was debated on 20 May 1986. It pitted press freedom against the authority of the House, and MPs could not uphold them both. John Biffen, leader of the House and chairman of the privileges committee, moved the motion to ban Evans for six months and penalise *The Times*. He pointed out that the House had already voted by a large majority to approve the new rules for dealing with select committee leaks, and he urged MPs to take this first opportunity to enforce them. Otherwise, he pointed out, there would be no point in the privileges committee investigating these complaints. Peter Shore, the shadow leader of the House and a fellow privileges committee member, supported him. He argued that the *Times* report gave a 'seriously misleading' impression of the select committee's conclusions.

> It made it more difficult for Members to approach the evidence impartially, it damaged trust between members of the committee, and it delayed for some weeks the completion of its report. Both the journalists and the editor insisted . . . that they were acting in the public interest, and it was made plain that it was the settled policy of *The Times* newspaper to seek such information from select committees and to publish it.
>
> When asked: 'If you say it is in the public interest to publish it when you did, why is it less in the public interest to let it wait a fortnight until it has been properly discussed and publish it then?' Mr Evans replied: 'Perhaps I could take up one point. If we waited two weeks another newspaper might get hold of it.' I do not automatically equate the commercial interest of *The Times* with the public interest, nor should the House.

Shore said that it was 'ludicrous' to present the argument as a clash between advocates of open government and advocates of closed government, because the privileges committee was concerned only with protecting the confidentiality of another committee's work during the 'closing and deliberative stage'.[23]

There was some support for the committee's recommendation. Ian Mikardo, a Labour backbencher, dismissed the idea that the leak had increased public interest in radioactive waste. 'As we know, if one newspaper gets a scoop the others will not touch it with a barge pole. There is publicity in only one newspaper, whereas if the matter is dealt with properly, with a press conference when the report is published, there is publicity in all the newspapers.'[24] Some Members favoured a compromise. Rossi, the environment committee chairman who had initiated the anti-Evans inquiry in the first place, called for *The Times* to be punished, but not Evans personally. 'It goes against the inherent sense of fair play of the House that a young, well-liked journalist should be punished while the real villain, possibly a Member of the House, escapes censure.'[25] David Harris, a Tory who described himself as perhaps the only former chairman of the lobby ever to become an MP,[26] called for a six-week suspension, which he said would be a more reasonable punishment. Michael Cocks, the Labour former Chief Whip, recommended just five days.

Douglas Hogg, whose father Quintin had secured the expulsion of Garry Allighan in 1947, was among those leading the opposition to Biffen. The Tory MP had tabled an amendment saying that it would be right to punish an MP for leaking a select committee report, but not a journalist for publishing it. Declaring an interest (his wife, Sarah, worked for *The Times*), he said: 'I hold a passionate belief in the right of newspapers to publish the news. I also have a healthy distrust of those who seek to stop that.'[27] Sir Ian Gilmour, a former member of the Thatcher Cabinet, said it was 'absurd' to censor the deliberations of select committees, and he dismissed the idea that members could not operate properly if there were leaks. 'They are grown-up people and if they are not able to withstand these pressures, they should not be Members of this House.'[28] Tony Benn managed to condemn the protagonists on both sides. 'When I heard what the lobby journalists said about the report of the committee of privileges, I was reminded of two old dinosaurs locked in combat. The misuse of privileges and the lobby system are both designed to deny the public the information it should have.'[29] Perhaps the most powerful reason given for rejecting Biffen's recommendation was that his proposal would create an absurd distinction between committee leaks and government leaks. Michael Foot was among those who used this argument:

> If it is right for members of the lobby and other journalists working in the House of Commons or its environs to try to search out what is happening in the Cabinet and to publish that, why should it be wrong for them to try to search out what is happening in select committees and to publish that?

> If we are told . . . that it interferes with the process of discussion in the
> select committee, then we must accept that there is a whole range of cabinet
> committees, including the Cabinet itself, which could make exactly the same
> claim.[30]

As the debate carried on, Evans and Wilson watched from the gallery. 'Laddie, things do not appear to be going very well for you,' muttered Wilson at one point.[31] Evans was asked if he would like to spend six months in Belfast or New York. But he was quietly confident, having been assured beforehand that the Government was running an unofficial whip in his favour. At 1.00 a.m. the House divided and Hogg's amendment, saying that 'it would be wrong to punish a journalist merely for doing his job', was carried by 158 votes to 124, a majority of thirty-four. Six cabinet ministers, including Margaret Thatcher, were among those voting with Hogg and against the leader of the House. As Biffen predicted, the decision destroyed any prospect of his committee ever being able to use its new anti-leak disciplinary powers. Since 1986 there have been no further attempts to remove journalists from the Commons for offences of this nature. Without having to suffer martyrdom in Northern Ireland, Evans ensured that another area of parliamentary life was open to the press.

Bevins and Bernard: The Lobby in the Late 1980s

One person not intended as a target when Hennessy et al. fired their broadside against 'spaniel journalism' was Anthony Bevins. A lifelong member of the 'awkward squad', Bevins had been in the lobby since 1970, when he joined as the Liverpool Daily Post's political correspondent, but he had never been comfortable with the collegiate aspects of life in the press gallery. Preferring to operate outside the pack, he specialised in trawling through the bulky Commons documents most journalists ignored. His father, Reginald Bevins, had been Postmaster General under Macmillan; as a working-class Tory, he was patronised by the party's establishment, and it was widely assumed that this coloured his son's attitude towards the political elite. Bevins certainly relished confrontations with authority. Peter Hennessy was a fan, and he captured the essential Bevins when he described how they used to share a 'cramped, tatty office' off the press gallery corridor. 'I'd arrive just before lunch and he'd look up with a mad gleam in his eye, wave some obscure public accounts committee report on MoD overspending on frigates and roar "I've got the bastards this time."'[32] By 1986 Bevins had worked his way through jobs on the Sunday Express, the Sun and the

Daily Mail. He was political correspondent on *The Times* but had been offered the political editorship of the paper that was to be launched that autumn as the *Independent*. Bevins and the paper's editor, Andreas Whittam Smith, were both keen for the new paper to live up to its name by pulling out of the lobby system. Their initiative was to infuriate Downing Street, panic their commercial rivals and propel the lobby into the most public and prolonged bout of soul-searching in its history.

Most of the arguments against the lobby system were well rehearsed: that government should be open; that the public had the right to know who was saying what; and that on-the-record statements were more reliable because they could not be denied. The counter-argument – that journalists got more information and better stories 'on lobby terms' – was also well known. But by 1986 there was a new factor, which was cited by the *Independent*, the *Guardian* and the *Scotsman*, the three papers that did eventually withdraw from the lobby briefings. This was the suggestion that the system was being 'abused' by Downing Street and in particular by Bernard Ingham, Margaret Thatcher's press secretary. On two occasions there were particular objections to what he said during lobby briefings. In February 1982, when Francis Pym, the leader of the Commons, gave a speech predicting prolonged high levels of unemployment, Thatcher defended him on the floor of the Commons but Ingham told the lobby he was sounding like 'Mrs Mopp', the wartime radio Victor Meldrew character with the catchphrase 'It's being so cheerful as keeps me going.'[33] A similar episode occurred in May 1986 when Biffen, then leader of the Commons, suggested in a television interview that Thatcher was an electoral liability. The following day Ingham told the lobby not to take his remarks too seriously because he was 'a well-known semi-detached member of the Government'.[34] (This occurred only a week before the vote on expelling Richard Evans showed just how 'semi-detached' Biffen had become.) The two remarks meant that by the time the *Independent* was being conceived, Ingham had acquired a reputation as a character assassin who employed the lobby as his accomplice.[35]

Ingham might have been able to live down those two remarks had he not also been implicated in one of the murkier aspects of the Westland affair, the row about the fate of a helicopter company that led to Michael Heseltine's resignation as Defence Secretary in January 1986. The key event came when the Government leaked a letter from the Solicitor General in an attempt to undermine the case Heseltine was arguing in Cabinet. Ingham was involved in that he spoke to Colette Bowe, the head of press at the Department of Trade and Industry, on the afternoon that she broke government protocol by giving the information about the contents of the letter to the Press Association's Chris Moncrieff. There are conflicting accounts as to precisely what happened. According to accounts attributed to 'friends' of Bowe at the time, Ingham ordered the rubbishing operation himself. Ingham insists that at most he gave 'tacit acceptance', in that he did not actively object to the plan to leak the letter.[36] (He says that he should have told Bowe to have nothing to do with the idea.) Westland was more important than the incidents with Pym and Biffen. Although ostensibly about the rival merits of Sikorsky and a European consortium as potential purchasers of Westland, it was really a personal and ideological clash of the most poisonous kind. Bevins was firmly in the Heseltine camp. A Liverpudlian, he admired what Heseltine had done as Environment Secretary to regenerate the city after the Toxteth riots in 1981. Heseltine was as close as anyone got to being a political hero to Bevins, and one way to view what happened subsequently in the lobby is to see it as a rerun of Westland, fought through proxies.

In July 1986 Bevins arranged to speak to Ingham at the end of one of the regular 11.00 a.m. briefings. He told him that he was joining the *Independent*, and that the policy of the new paper would be to boycott the lobby briefings. According to Bevins, Ingham was 'absolutely incensed'; he went bright red and he dismissed the idea as 'silly' and 'childish'.[37] Bevins is the journalist who is even more vilified than Hennessy in Ingham's memoirs, and Ingham's account of the meeting focuses on Bevins making sure that the *Independent* would still be able to collect advance copies of government reports. 'Not the stuff that martyrs are made of,' Ingham writes.[38] Ingham said that, since the *Independent* journalists would remain accredited members of the lobby, they would still get access to embargoed documents. Bevins went away satisfied.

As word got out what was being planned, the *Guardian* realised that it was in danger of being outflanked by a commercial rival. As an anti-Thatcherite paper with a commitment to open government, pulling out of the lobby was exactly the sort of move its readers would admire. Peter Preston, the paper's editor, had been sceptical about the lobby system for a long time. Ian Aitken, its political editor, was opposed to following the *Independent*, but Preston, after failing to persuade the editors of *The Times* and the *Daily Telegraph* to support him, announced in September that his paper would not observe lobby rules. (Like the *Independent*, the *Guardian* was opposed only to collective unattributable briefing; both papers continued to speak to individuals on lobby terms.) The *Independent* was duly launched on 7 October (carrying, among other things, a Bevins interview with Heseltine). Technically the *Guardian* was in a different position from the

Independent. Bevins and his colleagues had decided voluntarily to stay away from the lobby briefings. Preston wanted his reporters to attend but to attribute Ingham's remarks to a spokesman. Other members of the lobby had to decide whether to make a similar stand or whether to ask the *Guardian* to stay away. They decided that the latter was preferable and so, when the first briefing after the summer recess took place on 20 October, the *Guardian* was banned. (It was all very civilised. None of the *Guardian* journalists tried to force their way in.) Nine days later the lobby held a formal vote to decide the way forward. By sixty-seven votes to fifty-five, members rejected the idea of changing the rules of non-attribution. But they did support the setting up of an internal inquiry into lobby practice.

The *Guardian* submitted evidence and stressed that the leaders of the main opposition parties, Neil Kinnock, David Steel and David Owen, all believed that the system should be changed. All three already gave briefings that were largely or totally on the record, and they pledged that if they got to Downing Street, they would continue the practice. 'In such circumstances – with powerful additional support from the Conservative backbenches for change – it is surely time for the journalists at Westminster to raise their eyes to what politicians of all parties are saying,' wrote Preston in his letter to the inquiry team. 'A situation in which many powerful politicians wanted attribution whilst the journalists resisted it would be one to set logic on its head.'[39] Among those supporting the case for reform was Joe Haines. 'It is basic to my objection to non-attribution at institutionalised mass lobby briefings that the source of information is an integral part of the story,' he wrote. 'Sometimes, in fact, it is the story. If a Labour backbencher says a cabinet minister is a semi-detached member of the Government, no one cares a damn . . . If the Prime Minister's press secretary says it, it is a major story.'[40]

From today's perspective, the reaction to Ingham's briefings against Pym and Biffen seems peculiar. Bevins, for example, thought it was 'despicable for a servant of the Crown to be backstabbing colleagues of the Prime Minister'.[41] In his biography of Ingham, *Good and Faithful Servant*, Robert Harris describes the anti-Pym briefing as 'significantly different, and in some respects, worse' than any previous act of mud-slinging by a Downing Street spokesman. 'Never before had the Government's official spokesman, a civil servant, deliberately disparaged a minister for speaking what he saw as the truth – and done it, moreover, to the entire lobby only moments after the Prime Minister had given an entirely different version of events.'[42] Yet after several years of New Labour, when the complaints have been about the accuracy, not the propriety, of what has been said to the lobby, Ingham's two most controversial briefings stand out as rare examples of civil service candour. He was asked what Thatcher thought of the two ministers and, to the amazement of the assembled journalists, he actually told them. This was remarkable, because ministers and spokesmen normally shelter behind the convention that political colleagues always agree with one another (which is often a lie, and arguably a much greater 'abuse' of the briefing system than anything said by Ingham). The argument put by those wanting to reform the lobby system was that, if official 'sources' were disparaging government ministers, the public had a right to know who those sources were. The counter-argument was that if lobby briefings were on the record, then Ingham and his successors would be less honest. It was a classic journalistic dilemma. Both sides could agree that their duty was to tell the public the truth, but that did not solve the problem as to which approach to truth-telling was preferable.

That, at least, was how the debate ran at a theoretical level. But for those members of the lobby occasionally distracted from the pursuit of absolute truth, the existing system had other advantages. As Nicholas Jones politely phrases it, unattributable guidance suits the press because it allows for 'a wider interpretation of the facts' than would otherwise be the case.[43] Put more bluntly, the system has let lobby correspondents exaggerate wildly. This has been a complaint ever since the days when MacDonagh's anonymous reporter concocted a whole article on the basis of a one-sentence exchange with Gladstone, and in part it has been a direct consequence of the reliance on unattributable briefing. Tom Utley was a lobby correspondent on the *Liverpool Echo* and the *Sunday Express* and he later wrote a brutal caricature of the way the lobby operated.

> The system suited us journalists too – or at least, it suited the lazy amongst us. At 11 o'clock every morning, we were spoon-fed the main course of our work for the day by the Prime Minister's press secretary. We would make ourselves sound terribly well informed, by writing of 'insiders' and 'sources close to Downing Street', when all we were doing was spewing out the Government's thoughts as they were dictated to us by good old Bernard Ingham, or whoever happened to be taking the lobby briefing that day.
>
> The competition between the papers was not to get the story, but to put the most melodramatic spin on it that the facts would bear. This often led us to write very stupidly. But just as the Government could hide behind the confidentiality of the system, so could we. 'What evidence have you, Tom, for writing that "Premier Maggie Thatcher is set to storm into a furious Commons row over benefits reform"?' "Couldn't possibly tell you old boy. Lobby rules, and all that. But I have very senior sources, believe me."[44]

Harris, who worked in the lobby for the *Observer* in the late 1980s, made a similar point after he left. He complained that unattributable briefings forced journalists into conjecture, and that when Ingham said the occupational hazard of public figures was to be 'misrepresented by misinterpretation', he had a point. 'The flaw in Mr Ingham's analysis is not to see that it is the lobby system, of which he is such a stout defender, that does more than anything else to pollute British journalism with clouds of speculation.'[45]

Although the lobby had voted against changing its rules, this did not necessarily mean that a majority actually wanted the status quo. Many of the younger correspondents who had arrived in the 1980s were sympathetic to reform. But Ingham had made it clear privately that he would not brief on the record, and so the choice for the lobby as a whole was between unattributable briefings and no briefings at all. Some journalists resented being made to appear reactionary by the two rebel newspapers. 'I must confess to a certain irritation at the hypocrisy displayed by the *Guardian* and the *Independent*, who give the impression in their public statements that they are breaking free from an archaic system yet whose columns are littered with references to anonymous government sources,' wrote Jon Hibbs, the chief political correspondent for Thomson Regional Newspapers, in his submission to the inquiry.[46] In his contribution, Ian Aitken proposed, as a minimalist reform, that the lobby should legitimise the practice of referring to 'Downing Street sources' when reporting Ingham's briefings. Technically this was still against the rules, but at the time journalists were using the formula without Ingham complaining. 'A change such as I propose would scarcely ruffle the surface of the relationship between us, MPs and ministers . . . What it would do, however, is put an end to the infuriating and humiliating fulminations and fabrications of people like Peter Hennessy.'[47]

The inquiry team published its report on 8 December. The authors, Peter Riddell (*Financial Times*), Chris Moncrieff (Press Association), Gordon Jackson (Thomson Regional Newspapers) and David Hughes (*Sunday Times*, and lobby secretary), concluded that the lobby system represented an acceptable trade-off between the desires for as much information as possible and as great a degree of attribution as possible. They put forward four recommendations that were the subject of a ballot on 13 February 1987. Two of them were carried overwhelmingly: that lobby rules should be simplified (eighty votes to five); and that the lobby should reaffirm its 'long-standing commitment to pressing for on-the-record information wherever and whenever practicable [*sic*] – but not where it inhibits the flow of information from the Government to the public' (seventy-six votes to eight). A proposal that people attending lobby meetings should have to give a written undertaking to obey the rules was rejected (fifty-four votes to thirty-one). On the fourth recommendation, that members who broke lobby rules should be excluded from future meetings, there was a tie (forty-two to forty-two). On 27 March there was another ballot on two aspects of the revised rules. In what was essentially a rerun of the decision to keep briefings unattributable, members voted to attribute stories to 'government' or 'Whitehall sources' rather than to a Downing Street spokesman. They also voted in favour of expelling reporters who ignored the rules until they were prepared to promise to respect them.

While the lobby committee was trying to patch up the existing system, the *Independent* and the *Guardian* were doing their best to tear it apart. Generally they were able to find out what was being said at the briefings and, when they did, they could attribute quotes directly. The result was that Ingham could not speak to the lobby collectively without knowing that, if he came out with anything interesting, he would probably be identified as the source. An early example came in November 1986 when Jim Coe, Ingham's deputy, told the lobby that it was difficult to believe that somebody who was looking to be a potential Prime Minister would behave the way Neil Kinnock was behaving over the Peter Wright affair. (Wright was an ex-MI5 spy trying to publish his memoirs.) The following day the *Independent* named Coe, and the *Guardian* attributed the remarks to Thatcher's spokesman. Ingham reasoned that the two papers must have got their information from someone at the briefing. 'There could not be a more blatant case of defiance of the lobby's rules and of a specific undertaking freely given by its members,' Ingham said in a letter to Hughes.[48] Coe's remarks were controversial because they were deemed too partisan for a civil servant, but this notion prompted Ingham to erupt again in a further letter.

> I am lost in wonderment at a lobby which, having asked a question about the attitudes of ministers who are at the heart of politics, then complains about getting an answer which has 'political overtones'. What do they want? A misleading answer? An 'acceptable' answer? A lie? Or no answer at all?

If the lobby did not like the answers it got, then it had better stop asking the questions that produced them, Ingham said.[49]

In another letter the following month, Ingham complained that the situation was becoming 'ever more Gilbertian' in that Bevins and his colleagues were calling Downing Street for information. 'Some journalists are unwilling to receive briefing from No. 10 when we speak to the lobby collectively; but only too anxious to receive it from us one to one; and apparently only too delighted to receive it second hand, unattributably, from members of the lobby they affect to despise.'[50] Ingham did not assume that Bevins and his colleagues received all their information from leaks. 'It is far from clear whether this constitutes a breach of our rules or simply Bevins putting my name on top of PA or *Evening Standard* copy,' he wrote in yet another protest letter to the lobby secretary.[51] However, some members definitely were feeding information to the dissidents, and the lobby's decision to revise its rules, and to threaten offenders with expulsion, did not make much difference. The situation continued for the rest of the decade, and in 1989 the *Scotsman* joined the *Independent* and the *Guardian* and pulled out of the lobby briefings too. Progressive readers liked the anti-lobby stance, although within the profession views were mixed.

In his memoirs Ingham describes the uprising as 'the Great Lobby Revolt that flopped'.[52] Although he did not deny Bevins and his colleagues access to embargoed documents, he made their life difficult in other ways. The rebel newspapers received only limited help from the Downing Street press office when they phoned up with enquiries, and Ingham took delighted in excluding them from the RAF VC10 taking Thatcher on overseas trips. But the affair did change the way in which the lobby system operated. As a result of the lobby inquiry, Ingham agreed that he could be referred to as a 'government source'. Ingham plays down the significance of this in his autobiography, and in one sense he was just sanctioning what was already an increasingly common practice. Yet this concession can also be seen as a step towards the abolition of collective unattributable briefings. In 1982, when *The Times* started one report based on what was said at a lobby briefing with the words 'Official Whitehall sources yesterday stated . . .', Ingham complained about a possible breach of lobby rules.[53] Four years later, a similar formula had become acceptable. The briefings were still unattributable in the sense that they were not explicitly linked to Downing Street. However, the publicity surrounding the 'lobby revolt' meant that by the end of 1986 anyone with the faintest knowledge of Westminster politics was able to read a story written by a lobby correspondent and have a good guess who the 'government source' might be. (As in the past, anyone prepared to buy at least two newspapers would have been able to work out what was coming out of the collective briefing with a fair degree of certainty.) Ministers also continued to brief on lobby terms. But, like Ingham, they found it increasingly likely that if they said anything controversial, their cover would be blown. In November 1988 Nigel Lawson gave a briefing to Sunday lobby correspondents that caused them to write stories saying that pensioners could lose benefits. Lawson had to admit that he had spoken to the journalists, although he insisted vehemently that his remarks had been misinterpreted. In March the following year Paul Channon, the Transport Secretary, claimed to have no idea why various papers were reporting a breakthrough in the investigation into the Lockerbie bomb. It later turned out he had had lunch with the journalists involved at the Garrick.

The *Independent*, the *Guardian* and the *Scotsman* maintained their boycott of the Downing Street briefings until Heseltine (finally getting his revenge for Westland) launched the leadership challenge that brought down Thatcher. Ingham left Downing Street at the same time. The new Prime Minister, John Major, appointed Gus O'Donnell his chief press secretary. O'Donnell, a career civil servant who had done the same job for Major when he was Chancellor, was less wary of the press than his predecessor and in 1991 he agreed that his briefings could be attributed to 'Downing Street sources'. The *Guardian* rejoined the system in July, and the *Independent* and the *Scotsman* followed in the autumn. By then, the Government's main press spokesman was practically on the record.

Labour and the 'Media Class'

One of the weaknesses of *Sources Close to the Prime Minister* is that it makes little allowance for party politics. If Labour had been in power in 1984, would the lobby's relationship with the Government been the same as it was under Margaret Thatcher and Bernard Ingham? Would Michael Cockerell, Peter Hennessy and David Walker have been able to write about the 'credulity' of the correspondents and their 'spaniel journalism'? Their core arguments about unattributable briefings might have been just as valid, but relations between the press and Downing Street would certainly have been very different. It is very hard to imagine the same book appearing with Michael Foot or Neil Kinnock's picture on the cover.

For the first half of the 1980s the Labour Party conducted its own regular lobby briefings in the lobby room and, like other the opposition leaders, Neil Kinnock took advantage of the 1985 rule change allowing them to be sometimes on the record. The system broke down when Rupert Murdoch routed the print unions with his move to Wapping in January 1986. Labour's national executive committee voted unanimously in favour of a boycott that was supposed to stop the party's MPs and staff cooperating with journalists from *The Times*, the *Sun*, the *Sunday Times* and the *News of the World*. Anthony Bevins, then on *The Times*, and Christopher Potter, from the *Sun*, were asked to leave the post-NEC briefing at which the ban was announced, although they were both assured that 'no personal discourtesy' was intended.[54] Neil Kinnock was due to meet the lobby correspondents the next day for their regular weekly briefing, and following the NEC meeting he wrote to Chris Moncrieff, the lobby chairman, saying that he would not accept questions from News International journalists. Moncrieff wrote back cancelling the meeting, saying the lobby could not allow the Labour leader to impose conditions.[55] Kinnock later got round the problem by inviting non-Murdoch journalists to on-the-record briefings held in the shadow cabinet room in the Commons.

The boycott did nothing to help relations with papers that were already hostile to Labour. The party had always complained that the press as a whole was biased against it, and for much of the 1980s the coverage it received, particularly in the tabloids, was as ghastly as ever.[56] Anti-Labour papers wanted stories that presented Kinnock as a gaffe-prone incompetent, and this was particularly apparent when he went abroad. One of Alastair Campbell's earliest polemics against Westminster political journalists was written after he accompanied Kinnock to Washington in March 1987. At the time Campbell was political editor of the *Sunday Mirror* and a fervent cheerleader for Kinnock. He was so appalled by the behaviour of his lobby colleagues that he took the unusual step of writing an article afterwards in the *New Statesman* denouncing them. Under the headline 'You guys are the pits', it claimed that the 'cynical, cowardly and corrupt Tory press' had conspired with the White House in making it look as though Ronald Reagan had humiliated Kinnock. The problem with Campbell's argument was that on this occasion the White House *had* humiliated Kinnock.[57] Campbell could have chosen much better examples of anti-Labour bias. But his article nevertheless accurately reflected the despair Kinnock felt about ever getting a fair hearing. When Labour came to power in 1997, its handling of the lobby was to a large extent shaped by the party's experiences a decade earlier.

One of Kinnock's misfortunes was that he became party leader at a time when the press appeared to be growing more influential. The balance of power between politicians and journalists seemed to be shifting, and this affected relations at Westminster. In his biography of Campbell, Peter Oborne explains this in terms of the development of a 'Media Class'. His argument is that within little more than a generation, journalists were transformed from being members of a 'dishonourable and poorly esteemed profession' into potential celebrities with the ability to wield 'immense social, economic and political power'. In political journalism, this coincided with the collapse of deference. Oborne mentions Oliver Poole, the Conservative Party chairman under Macmillan, who once said that lobby correspondents were not quite the sort of people one would invite into one's own home. By the 1980s that had all changed, he says.

> The Media Class became an elite at Westminster. It suddenly became the case that journalists, now for the most part graduates, were cleverer, more self-assured, far better paid and very much more influential than most of the people they were writing about. The brightest and the best were going into the media; by contrast it seemed the dunderheads who went into politics.

Parliamentary correspondents, representatives of the old order, were being phased out and replaced with lobby correspondents, paid-up members of Oborne's Media Class. According to Oborne, by the 1980s this group had established itself as 'the most powerful force in British national life, comparable in a number of ways to the over-mighty trade unions in the 1970s'.[58]

Oborne over-states his case. The idea that columnists and television pundits run the country is a seductive one (particularly if, like Oborne, you happen to be a columnist and a pundit) but most political analysts do not believe it is true. Equally, although the postwar press gallery clearly was deferential, the Poole anecdote probably says more about the Conservative Party than it does about the House of Commons as a whole. In 1950 a quarter of Tory MPs were Old Etonians, and if Poole was fussy about whom he invited home, it might have had something to do with the fact that he became a hereditary peer and chairman of Lazards. Most journalists are not 'far better paid' and 'very much more influential' than MPs. But some are, and the trend Oborne identifies is a real one. After the 1970s journalists did get more assertive, aggressive, swaggering and self-confident. More of them became famous.

In politics this showed particularly in the development of the political column, a vehicle that enabled newspapers to project particular writers as authority figures and quasi-celebrities. Sketch-writers already enjoyed this status; columnists were really sketch-writers with a wider remit. The two journalists who are credited with creating the modern political column are Hugh Massingham and Henry Fairlie. 'Between them, they changed political journalism in this country,' says Alan Watkins, a columnist who has followed in their tradition.[59] They showed that it was possible to write about political developments, and not just what happened in the chamber, in a way that combined original insight with wit and literary panache. Massingham, whose father Henry was the distinguished Liberal editor and sketch-writer, joined the *Observer* as a political correspondent after the war. 'He saw in politicians not walking issues or embodied problems but living men, fallible, laughable, admirable, contemptible, lovable, human, all too human,' said one of his obituaries. 'Those he liked best were not necessarily the most successful but those with the most fire, wit, honour, with the most personality and panache.'[60] Massingham doubled up as a novelist, but it was not just his grasp of character and narrative that made his columns stand out. When Attlee was Prime Minister, Massingham's accounts of what was said at cabinet meetings were so accurate that security experts were called in to conduct a leak inquiry. (It later transpired that he got his information by having tea every week with the wife of Sir Stafford Cripps.) Fairlie, 'a charmer, an adulterer, a drinker, often a beggar man, even (it must be said) on occasion a thief',[61] worked in the lobby for the *Manchester Evening News* in 1945 but made his name as a columnist on the *Spectator* in the 1950s. Later journalists like David Watt of the *Financial Times* and Peter Jenkins of the *Guardian* adapted the format by writing columns concentrating more on policy and heavyweight analysis. By the 1980s political columns based on these models were becoming increasingly common. Columnists did – and do – often perform on the broadcast media as pundits and, as the number of television and radio programmes expanded, the political columnists found themselves in increasing demand.

Some Westminster lobby correspondents have achieved fame as commentators. But many political columnists do not work at the Commons, and the emergence of a new tribe of influential media opinion-formers has not necessarily enhanced the status of the press gallery. There is one fairly easy way of measuring the relative importance of journalists and, by this measure – the honours list – political correspondents have done rather badly in recent years. It used to be not unheard-of for the most distinguished Westminster journalists to get knighthoods. Henry Lucy, the pioneering lobby correspondent and sketchwriter, was knighted in 1909. At least six knighthoods were given out to journalists associated with the press gallery towards the end of the First World War (which, admittedly, might say more about Lloyd George's approach to honours than about the relative merits of the recipients). Alexander Mackintosh, a long-serving political correspondent, was knighted in 1932 – even though he worked for the *Aberdeen Free Press* and the *Liverpool Daily Post* rather than any of the London papers. Harry Boardman, sketch-writer on the *Manchester Guardian* and the one parliamentary writer whose judgement Churchill valued, was rumoured to have been offered a knighthood after the Second World War. Harold Wilson was the last Prime Minister prepared to distribute such honours around the gallery and in 1976 he arranged knighthoods for the *Guardian*'s

Francis Boyd and the *Daily Telegraph*'s Harry Boyne, two political editors at the
end of their careers. Since then lobby correspondents appear to have slipped
down the pecking order. When Robin Oakley left the BBC, despite having been
political editor of both *The Times* and the corporation, he had to make do with
an OBE. This is not a precise system for measuring esteem, because the granting
of honours can be pretty arbitrary. But it does suggest that, although there may
be a new Media Class, lobby correspondents are not necessarily members.

Television and 24-hour News

At Prime Minister's Questions on 9 February 1988, Neil Kinnock took
something of a gamble and asked Margaret Thatcher if she was in favour of televising the House of Commons. MPs were due to debate the subject later that day
and Mrs Thatcher's views were likely to be influential. In the past, when MPs
considered the broadcasting of their proceedings, opinion was split in a relatively
non-partisan way. But by the 1980s letting the cameras in was becoming identified as a Labour cause. Mr Kinnock sought to capitalise on this when he asked
Mrs Thatcher why she was so opposed to letting the British people 'see her on
television in this House'. The Prime Minister replied:

> My concern is quite simply this: my concern is very much for the good repu-
> tation of this House. (Hon Members 'Frit.') I do not think that television will
> ever televise this House. If it does televise it, it will televise only a televised
> House, which would be quite different from the House of Commons as we
> know it.

When Kinnock pointed out that the Commons was already broadcast on radio,
and had been for ten years, Thatcher claimed that he was making her case for
her. 'The reputation of this House has not been enhanced by sound broadcasting.'[62] When the House had rejected television by twelve votes in 1985, those
in favour blamed their defeat on a last-minute swing by Tory MPs anxious to
ingratiate themselves with their leader. Three years later it looked to some as
though Kinnock might be encouraging them to do just the same again.

The debate that finished a few hours later was decisive. MPs backed a motion
calling for the House to be televised on an experimental basis by 318 votes to
264, a majority of fifty-four. One hundred and thirteen Tory MPs were willing
to go into a division lobby against Thatcher. Kinnock's intervention obviously
did not do his cause that much harm. By this stage almost all other countries in

the developed world allowed television coverage of their parliamentary proceedings, and cameras had been in the House of Lords since 1985.[63] But that did not mean implementing the Commons vote was going to be easy. There were arguments about who should sit on the select committee dealing with the practical arrangements, and there had to be another debate in March to fix its membership. The BBC wanted to bring dozens of extra journalists into Westminster to run the experiment, and the journalists already in the building complained that this would lead to overcrowding. At the time there were around 350 accredited members of the press gallery, of whom around 180 attended every day. The press gallery committee passed a resolution saying it was 'extremely concerned about the already mounting pressure on the press gallery facilities' and that the 'extra numbers proposed should be strictly limited'. In a submission to the MPs dealing with the arrangements, John Deans, the press gallery secretary, urged them not to be too indulgent towards the BBC. 'In private conversations with BBC staffers, I have been told that the existing staff number is too high, with too little to do and often duplicating on jobs which are unnecessary.'[64] The committee dealing with the broadcasting arrangements did not report to the House until May 1989, and the experimental televising of the Commons did not start until the state opening of Parliament on 21 November that year.

The first MP to deliver a speech on camera was the Tory backbencher Ian Gow. Proposing the loyal address to the Queen, Gow (an opponent of televising the Commons) said that he had recently received a letter from some consultants making the following 'preposterous' assertion: 'The impression you make on television depends mainly on your image (55 per cent) with your voice and body language accounting for 38 per cent of your impact. Only seven per cent depends on what you are actually saying.'[65] MPs did not want to believe that the consultants could be right; but at least one sketch-writer conceded that they had a point. 'It's true,' wrote Andrew Rawnsley in the *Guardian*. 'All I can remember of the rest of Mr Gow's speech is a bald, bespectacled man in a dark suit peering at his notes.'[66] Initially the broadcasters could show only the head and shoulders of the MP speaking or a wide angle. After a few weeks the rules were relaxed slightly to allow reaction shots. Even though adventurous filming was banned, the decision to admit the cameras led to a substantial increase in the number of television news reports featuring the Commons, and in July 1990 the House agreed to make the experiment permanent.

The arrival of the cameras roughly coincided with another development that probably had an even greater effect on the way politics is reported in Britain: the start of 24-hour television news. Rupert Murdoch's Sky News took to the airwaves in February 1989 and, according to Adam Boulton, Sky's political editor, it was 'no accident' that the two events happened in the same year. For a news service with a lot of airtime to fill, a live feed from the Commons was a godsend, and in the early years Sky used more than an hour a day from Parliament (much more than it does now). 'Parliamentary coverage was a significant safety net for us,' says Boulton. It was also, he points out, 'very cheap telly'.[67] When Sky was launched, it was not clear whether there was any real public demand for 24-hour news. A decade later, following the launch of Radio Five Live, the BBC's News 24 and countless news services on the internet, it was obvious that Murdoch was ahead of his time. 'Live media is where the future is at,' Alastair Campbell told a Fabian Society seminar in 1999.[68] Even though the audiences for 24-hour news services are still relatively small, Sky and its competitors have changed the way all political reporters operate. First, 24-hour news has made it clearer than ever that television, and not Parliament, is now the nation's principal noticeboard. One of the reasons why ministers make their policy announcements in Parliament is that that used to be the most effective way of getting information out to the public. Now it is much quicker and easier to do a live television interview which, unlike a parliamentary statement, will at least be seen by all the newsdesks that matter. Second, the pressure on newspapers to provide something different (analysis, conjecture etc.) has increased. And third, the availability of instant news has accelerated the news cycle. Stories develop more quickly, and immediate reaction has become more important. This is particularly noticeable in politics, and it has not made life easier for the politicians.

In 1995 Steve Richards provided a detailed explanation of how contemporary political news works in an essay for the Reuter Foundation. He compared Harold Wilson's situation in the spring of 1968 with John Major's in the autumn of 1993. At the time the 'John Major leadership crisis' was already a familiar media occurrence. As Richards writes, the story would unfold along familiar lines.

> Newspapers run a story about Major's leadership crisis sparked off by an outburst from a critic – often his former Chancellor, Norman Lamont, who he sacked in the spring of 1993. This may be in the form of a newspaper article. Radio 4's *Today* programme team obtain the article when the first editions of the newspapers are distributed in London and get a reaction from another malcontent on the Conservative backbenches. That is enough for the *World at One* to justify a sequence which will include another Conservative

rebel MP and a defence of John Major from a senior minister or the party chairman. The rush to defend the Prime Minister only heightens the air of crisis, though by this stage no one is quite sure what he is being defended from. The original spark will have been forgotten about . . . At this point there is another important new element: newspaper correspondents wanting to 'move the story on' for the next day now have plenty of fresh on-the-record quotes from the current affairs programmes to give their reports some substance . . . These new front page stories inspire the overnight team on the *Today* programme to invite other MPs on their programme and the whole routine starts again.

Wilson's position in 1968 was in some ways even worse than Major's. As well as being twenty-odd points behind in the polls, he had lost the support of a significant section of his parliamentary party and some of the most powerful figures in his Cabinet. Yet, says Richards , 'given a recognised widespread unhappiness with Wilson amongst cabinet ministers, Labour MPs and senior lobby correspondents, it is remarkable how little attention was devoted to it in the form of front page news stories.'[69] At the time there were far fewer current affairs programmes and the political interview was still something of a rarity. Newspapers reported the threats to Wilson but, without the constant supply of fresh, on-the-record quotes to keep the story going, the 'leadership crisis' never developed momentum in the media in the way that it did for Major.

In his memoirs Robin Oakley, the former BBC political editor, writes dolefully about being caught up in some of these Major leadership stories. According to his account, they would typically start with predictable comments from rent-a-quote Tory rebels that he would tell his programme editors to ignore. The tabloids would build the story up, the broadsheets would make some reference to the row to cover themselves, the *Today* programme would pick the story up (on the grounds that it was in the 'heavies') and interview some new insignificant rebel, Downing Street would comment and eventually the BBC would have to run something on its bulletins. 'Shortly afterwards, a reproachful *PM* programme editor or producer would say to me: "Hey, I thought you told me yesterday that this was a non-story." And next time I would probably be more reluctant to insist that was so.' Oakley deprecates this form of self-fulfilling journalism because he believes that it allows the media to create a story out of nothing. 'Momentum in itself becomes a story. Denial merely increases coverage. Once again, it's a case of strong media, weak politicians.'[70] Many reporters share his qualms. But journalists have always been open to the charge of making the news as well as reporting it, and even if some of the stories about Major's position were over the top, that does not necessarily mean that readers and viewers received a more accurate account of Wilson's predicament in 1968. By not reporting developments in the way that they would today, it could be said that newspapers and television at the time were also playing a self-fulfilling role because they were helping Wilson cling on.

Even before the launch of 24-hour news and the arrival of cameras in the Commons, television had already made a difference to the way politics was reported because it changed the way people perceived politicians. As Andrew Marr explains in *Ruling Britannia*:

> Television is very good at telling the voter certain things about a politician or an interviewee. One can read the facial tics and expressions that suggest tension, lying, anger and so forth. One can make a personal judgement about an individual minister or leader in a way that earlier generations never could, unless they were part of the privileged political elite. If before, one could read X's speech given verbatim in *The Times*, and treat X solely on the basis of his language and arguments, now one can conclude that X's grandson, the new minister, is a sanctimonious creep. And in the real world, the fact that 'X is a creep' is a valid personal assessment and matters to most of us just as much as his speechifying.[71]

It goes further than that. Television does not just allow the public to make a personal judgement about ministers; it actively encourages it to do so, by turning them into celebrities. This is apparent whenever politicians stage a walkabout. People gawp not because they particularly admire MPs for their contribution to the democratic process, but because they are intrigued when they recognise someone they have seen on television. As a result, television has increased the demand for personality stories in politics.

It is conventional to dismiss this as dumbing down or tabloidisation. 'What makes Britain unique is that our broadsheet press now faithfully tracks the agenda of the tabloid press,' Robin Cook said in a speech in May 2002. 'Politics is reported as a soap opera of personality conflict, which puts the spotlight on the process of decision-making rather than the outcome of policies.'[72] A month later Cook, the leader of the Commons, was banging away at the same theme. 'Westminster spawns more village gossip than Ambridge. But we should not kid ourselves that anybody else out there shares our preoccupation with our gossip,' he told a press gallery lunch.[73] Given that Cook's own career would have been very different had it not been for some ancient and obscure feud with Gordon Brown, he is probably one of the last people who should be arguing against personality journalism. He is also wrong. The readers and viewers 'out there' tend to lap the gossip up. Politicians as a class may complain about the reporting of incidental trivia, but when they come to sell the serialisation rights to their own memoirs, they are often not shy about dishing it out themselves. The personal has always been a factor in politics. Television has made it more visible.

SEVEN

Sleaze, Spin and Cynicism

I stopped it [*The Times* parliamentary page] because I couldn't find anyone who read it apart from MPs. We are not there to provide a public service for a particular profession.

Simon Jenkins, former Times *editor, 17 January 1995*

You just have to be economical with the truth. You have to say things. You should never lie, but it's very difficult. They understand. They will certainly understand tomorrow and forgive me.

Charlie Whelan, Labour spin doctor, 1997

We have got to be less buttoned-up, far more open, far less worried about what you guys are going to write.

Alastair Campbell, 2 May 2002

The Collapse of Gallery Reporting

As the Second World War was coming to an end, Winston Churchill made a prediction. Speaking at a press gallery lunch, he told journalists: 'The long fight which the House had against being reported is succeeded by the long fight which it is having and going to have over being reported at all.'[1] Although it was not an original comment (MPs had been saying much the same thing for at least seventy years) it was, in the long term at least, a fair one. Parliamentary reporting became less and less of a priority. MPs often complained about this when they were discussing broadcasting in the 1960s, 1970s and 1980s, and normally the fact that newspaper debate reports were vanishing was presented as an argument in favour of admitting radio and television. The decline was a gradual one. Then, relatively suddenly, the tradition collapsed. In 1990 *The Times* gave up devoting a whole page to Commons and Lords debates, and within a few years all the other papers still engaged in old-fashioned parliamentary reporting had done the same thing. They continued to carry sketches and to report the interesting debates, statements and questions taking place in the chamber. But national newspapers abandoned the custom of employing gallery reporters to provide a straightforward record of what was said in the House, a form of journalism that had survived more or less unchanged since the 1770s.

Jack Straw was one of the politicians to complain most vigorously about this development. 'Argument lies at the heart of the democratic system. It is the only alternative to violence . . . If people are to have confidence in the democratic system, they must be able to see it in operation,' he wrote in 1993 as he published a study showing in detail how newspapers had cut the amount of space devoted to parliamentary affairs over a sixty-year period.[2] He found that between 1933 and 1988, debate coverage in *The Times* filled between four hundred and eight hundred lines on an average day and in the *Guardian* between three hundred and seven hundred lines, and that by 1992 the average in both papers was below one hundred. Similar studies produced similar conclusions. In 1996, under the title, 'Keeping it "Bright, Light and Trite": Changing Newspaper Reporting of Parliament', Bob Franklin, an academic, published a survey which said that not only was the amount of coverage declining, its quality was changing too. Parliamentary stories were becoming 'more polarised, less measured and less willing to be neutral'.[3] Three years later the Hansard Society weighed in with its own report on the subject, written by David McKie. He had also been going through the cuttings with a ruler and his study highlighted the fact that, proportionally, the decline in space allocated to debate reporting was even bigger than the raw figures suggested. In a typical week in 1946 *The Times* devoted 4,148 lines of newsprint to reports about what was said or done in the Lords or the Commons. The paper normally had only ten pages and, excluding the Monday edition (because Parliament does not sit on Sundays), those 4,148 lines were squeezed into forty-eight pages. Over a single week forty years later there were 3,425 lines of parliamentary coverage in 160 pages. By 1996 most of the stories on the 'Politics and Government' page were political, rather than debate-orientated, and there were just 290 lines of parliamentary coverage in the week's 228 pages of newsprint.

Although the abandonment of debate reporting was a recognisable fact, there was surprisingly little agreement as to why it happened. Simon Jenkins, editor of *The Times* from 1990 to 1992, explained why he got rid of the parliamentary page when he gave evidence to the Nolan committee. 'I stopped it because I couldn't find anyone who read it apart from MPs. We are not there to provide a public service for a particular profession.'⁴ In other words, it was boring. But that does not explain why a feature that had been sufficiently interesting to survive in some newspapers for over two hundred years suddenly became tedious. There was more to it than that.

One common explanation was that the parliamentary page was the victim of intense competition in the newspaper industry, a process which is always assumed to drive standards down rather than up and for which the blame is conventionally attached to Rupert Murdoch. But this does not really work; competition was the same force that encouraged James Perry to pioneer team debate reporting in the 1780s. Jack Straw, in his study, said one of the reasons was the arrival of a new generation of broadsheet political editors, for whom stories from the lobby were more important than debate reporting. That may be true, but it does not explain why they thought that. In a follow-up article, he offered another theory: that new technology put more power in the hands of newspaper news editors, and that they were less likely to use stories from Parliament. That also fails to explain why the Commons was losing its appeal.

Another of Straw's ideas was that the televising of Parliament meant that newspapers no longer felt the need to cover what was going on in the chamber. Max Hastings has given this as the reason for his decision to end parliamentary reporting when he was editor of the *Daily Telegraph*,⁵ and it does explain best why debate coverage was abandoned at the time it was. But, probably more importantly, the shift of focus away from the chamber occurred because political journalists were finding better stories elsewhere. Politicians were becoming more adept at putting out press notices or holding press conferences (something that was happening partly because they thought that what they said in a debate would no longer be reported). The select committees were also becoming more newsworthy and there was a growing interest in the behind-the-scenes stories coming out of Whitehall. Television contributed to this process because the launch of 24-hour news, and the vast expansion in the number of programmes carrying political interviews, meant that journalists had a wider choice of story material than ever before.

The final set of explanations related to what was happening to the Commons itself. One theory was that the chamber was not as interesting because the quality of debate was not as high as in the past, a questionable assumption based on the myth that there was some supposed golden age of parliamentary oratory. Another, offered by Straw, was that parliamentary coverage was abandoned as a delayed reaction to the large majorities of the 1980s that made voting in the chamber predictable. The problem with that was that Straw was writing in the year that saw John Major almost brought down trying to get the Maastricht Bill through the Commons on a slender majority. Parliamentary reformers tended to highlight some of the practical aspects of Commons life that made newspapers less likely to report its proceedings. MPs were still debating and voting late into the night, which meant that key events often took place after the newspapers had printed their first editions. Commons rules stipulated that, during ministerial question time sessions, ministers had to respond to questions tabled two weeks beforehand. MPs could ask about anything topical only if it fitted in with one of the questions already on the order paper. It was as if the Commons, having given up using the fourteen-day rule to stop broadcasters discussing the subjects it was debating, had imposed the same rule on itself, restricting MPs from talking about the subjects that might be of interest to the public at large on any given day.[6] It was hardly surprising that reporters found it more useful to watch ministers being interviewed on BBC, ITN or Sky than to listen to them answering questions in the chamber.

The absence of topical questions illustrated a much larger problem: Parliament was seen as less important. There was nothing particularly new about this. 'Never in my long experience as a journalist has Parliament been so lacking in forcible and picturesque personalities, or so out of touch with the feeling of the nation, as at the present time,' wrote Ralph Blumenfeld in 1933.[7] For much of the twentieth century Parliament was seen as an institution in decline, and by the 1990s concern about its status was particularly acute. The reasons were well documented: the executive had become stronger relative to the legislature, and government itself had found its power constrained by the courts, the European Union and economic globalisation. One factor was particularly relevant to the press. Parliament's role had been not just to pass laws, but also to act as a forum for national debate. In his classic guide to parliamentary government, *The English Constitution* (1867), Walter Bagehot identified the various functions of the House of Commons. As well as the 'elective' one (sustaining the Government of the day) and the legislative one, he said there were three others: an 'expressive' one ('to express the mind of the English people on all matters which come before it'); a 'teaching' one ('a great and open council of considerable men cannot be placed in the middle of a society without altering that society'); and an 'informing' one.

In old times one office of the House of Commons was to inform the Sovereign what was wrong. It laid before the Crown the grievances and complaints of particular interests. Since the publication of the parliamentary debates a corresponding office of Parliament is to lay these same grievances, these same complaints, before the nation, which is the present sovereign.[8]

Bagehot suggested that newspapers were not particularly good at the 'informing' job, because they were biased in favour of one side of the argument (although he thought the 'higher part of the press' could perform the 'teaching' role with 'a greater vigour and a higher meaning' than Parliament).[9] Within a hundred years, this had changed. Journalists had appropriated all three of these functions, leaving MPs occasionally wondering what they were there for. Mass readership newspapers, and in particular television, allowed journalists to hold ministers to account at least as effectively as the House of Commons.[10] This is exactly what Churchill and other party leaders feared, and why they were so keen to preserve the fourteen-day rule. After 1956, as Churchill predicted, debates in the House were forestalled 'time after time by expressions of opinions by persons who had not the status or responsibility of MPs', and that to a large extent explained why parliamentary reporting was dying out. At the risk of simplifying grotesquely, debate coverage started when matters of national importance were debated in the Commons and then reported in the newspapers. By the time it faded out, matters of national importance were being discussed first on television and only later picked up in Parliament.

The Sleaze Effect

Besides setting Anthony Bevins on collision course with Bernard Ingham, the launch of the *Independent* in 1986 was to have another important effect on Westminster journalism. David Hencke, the social services correspondent on the *Guardian*, was offered a post as Whitehall correspondent on the new paper. Peter Preston, the *Guardian*'s editor, did not want to lose him and came back with a counter-offer. Hencke could do the same job for the *Guardian*, but as a member of the political team, working in the Commons with a lobby pass and all the access that entailed. (The *Independent* was proposing that he cover Whitehall from outside the lobby.) Hencke accepted. In doing so he helped to develop a new style of lobby journalism, becoming almost a counter-lobby lobby journalist.

According to Hencke, Preston wanted him to do the job because he was convinced that there were plenty of stories waiting to be written in Parliament that were being ignored by the lobby because it inevitably concentrated on the

SLEAZE, SPIN AND CYNICISM

main political stories of the day. Anthony Howard had had a similar idea at the start of his short and ill-fated spell as the *Sunday Times*'s Whitehall correspondent in 1965. Since then Peter Hennessy, who left the *Financial Times*'s lobby team for a job covering Whitehall on *The Times*, had shown that the civil service was a good subject for journalistic enquiry. What was different about Hencke's job was that he was proposing to do the same kind of work from the *Guardian*'s office in the Commons. He thought it would be essential to be able to enjoy the kind of informal contact with politicians that lobby correspondents get because they can track down MPs and peers in the building.

At first Hencke found it difficult to make an impact. But then he realised that the lobby was not covering the public accounts committee properly. Specialists would cover PAC reports and National Audit Office reports but only if the subject related to their area of expertise. Other material was slipping through the net. 'I realised that if I wanted to combine Whitehall and Westminster and big stories, the clever thing to do was to alight on the National Audit Office, because they were monitoring Whitehall anyway,' Hencke recalls. His big breakthrough came in November 1989 when he was following an NAO inquiry into the sale of Rover to British Aerospace. He received a telephone call, fixed up a meeting with his source and was shown a confidential report from the NAO to the PAC showing that the Government used a secret £38 million package of 'sweeteners' to persuade BAe to buy Rover. Nicholas Ridley, the Trade Secretary, had to make a statement in the Commons and the revelation forced the European Commission to reconsider its decision to approve the sale. 'After that, all sorts of things started coming my way,' says Hencke.[11] The incident also showed how important the Richard Evans case had been. Hencke was called to give evidence to the privileges committee and he made it clear in advance that he would not reveal his source. Although his leak had been far more serious than Evans's, the committee decided to avoid a confrontation and he was not asked anything about where the story came from.

For journalists who specialised in investigating Westminster scandal, the next decade was a golden era. Newspapers described what they discovered as sleaze, a useful catch-all term that covered sexual impropriety as well as financial and professional misconduct. John Major's administration was mired in both and Labour exploited this mercilessly, only to discover when it got into power that its own MPs and ministers were just as likely to misbehave. Many of the reporters who broke 1990s sleaze stories (particularly the sex ones) were not based in Parliament. The 'cash for questions' scandal, centred on the revelation that two Tory MPs were willing to ask parliamentary questions for £1,000 a time, was published by the *Sunday Times* in July 1994 after an investigation by its Insight team. But some of the best revelations came from Hencke. In October 1994 he wrote the story that forced Neil Hamilton and Tim Smith to resign as ministers and led to the setting up of the committee on standards in public life. Four years later he was one of the team that ousted Peter Mandelson from his post as Trade Secretary with the story about the secret £373,000 loan from Geoffrey Robinson. Hencke's success encouraged some other papers to try appointing Whitehall correspondents within the lobby and it vindicated the case made by Anthony Howard more than twenty years earlier.

Many of the sleaze allegations levelled against MPs involved their failure to comply with the register of Members' interests and, for long-serving members of the press gallery, there was a rich irony in this. In December 1985 the Commons voted to introduce a compulsory register of outside commercial interests for journalists working in the building. The requirement, introduced amid allegations that some journalists were passing on embargoed copies of documents to private firms, did not impose much of a burden. Most reporters had nothing to declare other than occasional freelance work. But what was galling was that on the same night MPs tightened the rules for the press, they also rejected a motion that would have made it compulsory for Members to fill in their own register of interests. The vote was condemned at the time as a clear example of double standards.

The 1990s sleaze cases confirmed that the House had lost the will to punish journalists for breaches of privilege. The *Sunday Times* obtained its cash for questions story by entrapment: an undercover reporter approached MPs and offered them money for tabling a parliamentary question. When the privileges committee published its report about the affair, it condemned the *Sunday Times* for falling below the standards of legitimate investigative journalism but recommended no further action. As part of the *Guardian*'s investigation into Jonathan Aitken and the lies he told about his stay at the Ritz in Paris, the paper sent a forged letter to the hotel purporting to come from Aitken himself. In a report published in January 1996, the privileges committee said that what the paper did was improper, but again it recommended no further action. The conduct of both papers was open to question, and arguably harder to justify than the practice of paying MPs for information that the Commons condemned so severely in the late 1940s. But at a time when MPs had lost the trust of the public, the committee recognised that it was not in a position to punish the journalists who were exposing corruption with some success.

MPs showed their animosity towards the press in other ways. For years there had been mutterings about the amount of space in the building allocated to the press. Members often had to share offices and many resented the fact that journalists had desks only a few hundred yards away from the chamber. This discontent came to a head in the early 1990s when members of the accommodation committee and the administration committee started actively canvassing the idea of forcing the journalists out. 'They had the impression that we had big rooms and a huge amount of space,' says John Deans, the press gallery secretary, who sought to persuade the political parties that it would not be in their interests to have the press dispersed.[12] The idea eventually fizzled out, and with the opening of the new £235 million Portcullis House as office accommodation for MPs, the likelihood of their annexing the press gallery seemed ever more remote. But MPs did win one significant territorial battle during this period when the lobby journalists were stripped of their right to use the terrace. In the summer the terrace is the most attractive drinking spot in the building, and journalists had been allowed to use it on the understanding that lobby terms prevailed and that they would respect the privacy of MPs at adjoining tables. During the Maastricht rebellion stories started appearing about the anti-Major plotting being conducted on the terrace, including eyewitness accounts of who was talking to whom. MPs finally lost their patience, and the lobby was told it would have to find somewhere else to get a drink on a warm summer evening.

That episode illustrated the extent to which the lobby was becoming increasingly indiscreet. This had been a complaint (or, more properly, a virtue) since at least the 1970s, but with the lobby continuing to expand, the temptation to tell all grew ever stronger. Fellow journalists were just as likely to be exposed as MPs. Under the old 'Notes on the Practice of Lobby Journalism', the lobby activities of colleagues were not supposed to be the subject of published comment. Journalists flouted this convention on some occasions in the 1970s and 1980s, although many members of the lobby felt at the time that this was bad form. By the 1990s these reservations had largely disappeared, and if one group of journalists were given an important story in private on lobby terms, rival reporters felt happy to identify the source (if they could) in their follow-up pieces a day later. Lunch or dinner was normally involved, and the story behind the story (complete with reference to who was there, the name of the restaurant, and what was consumed) became a familiar subgenre in lobby journalism. In January 1992 Neil Kinnock threw Labour's tax and spending plans into disarray when he told a group of six journalists (at Luigi's in Covent Garden) that the party's plans to increase taxes might be phased in, rather than introduced immediately as everyone assumed. In September 1996 four lobby correspondents covering the TUC reported that Labour was considering breaking its link with the trade unions. Stephen Byers, then a Labour employment spokesman, said the stories deserved 'the Booker prize for fiction', even though he was the person who had had dinner with the four (at the Seafood Restaurant).[13] Three months later Kenneth Clarke, the Chancellor, told two BBC journalists (at Chez Nico in Park Lane) that he would resign if John Major changed the 'wait and see' policy on the single currency. Labour's Frank Dobson was having lunch in the same restaurant and when Jon Sopel reported Clarke's thinking on the *World at One*, Labour was able to name Clarke as the source. In May 2002 Byers (by now Transport Secretary) went through the whole process again when he talked to women journalists (at Shepherd's) about the possible timing of a referendum on the euro. With around twenty reporters at the lunch, news of his comments leaked almost immediately, and Byers was identified on television as the source before newspapers had even had the chance to print the original stories. On a one-to-one basis, modern journalists are just as willing to protect their sources as any of their predecessors. But they no longer feel any obligation to protect anyone else's. It is as if the Bevins approach to No. 10 briefings is now being applied wholesale to other encounters conducted on lobby terms.

While the press gallery became more open with information, it did not become much easier for outsiders to join. The Commons authorities have always restricted the number of passes available to broadcasters, newspapers and other magazines because there is only a limited amount of office space available. Many publications have been refused. In 1994 Charter 88 devoted one of the papers published in its 'Violations of Rights in Britain' series to the subject. The author, Lesley Abdela, explained that she had applied for a pass after being appointed the first political editor of a major women's magazine, *Cosmopolitan*. As a serious journalist with a long involvement in politics, she expected to be admitted. In fact, she got the same response as the *Women's Penny Paper* did in 1890. What really infuriated her was that she spent almost a year trying to get the administration committee to explain why her application had been refused. Eventually she was told there were 'measures and constraints' affecting decisions of this nature. 'Parliament is still allowed to be run in outrageously undemocratic and secretive ways,' she concluded.[14] Abdela was right to point out that the arrangements were restrictive. There were increasing numbers of women working in the press gallery in the 1990s, but (in common with the newspaper industry in general) relatively few journalists who were not white. Specialist magazines and publications that might have brought a different perspective continued to find themselves kept out.

In her paper Abdela identified one of the culprits as Michael Martin, the Labour MP who chaired the administration committee at the time. In the same capacity, Martin was also held responsible for the decision to stop journalists using the terrace. This subject resurfaced when the Commons came to decide in October 2000 who should be the next Speaker. Peter Snape, the Labour MP who proposed Martin, said that Martin had been described as the man who prevented journalists from buying Members a drink. 'If that were true, it would be a very serious matter,' Snape joked. 'My hon Friend's actions actually prevented them from buying each other drinks. He perhaps also inadvertently prevented them from putting the wrong name on their expense accounts when they got back to the office.'[15] Martin was duly elected Speaker and for his first year or two in the post he had to endure abuse by the bucketload from some of the sketch-writers. Quentin Letts of the *Daily Mail* and Simon Carr of the *Independent* were particularly severe. To Letts, he was 'Gorbals Mick', an 'old booby' or 'Parliament's answer to Rab C. Nesbitt'.[16] Carr was just as dismissive and on one occasion described the Speaker as a 'slumped old todger' who sat up when 'a rush of blood jerked him erect'.[17] It would be easy to describe this as belated revenge for Martin's anti-press activities on the administration committee, but that would be wrong. Letts and Carr just thought he was incompetent. What was significant, though, was that it had become possible, and even commendable, to write about the Speaker of the House of Commons in those terms. It was a sign of the way sketch-writing had become more caustic since the days of Andrew Alexander and the Denning ruling about 'fairness'. But the treatment of Martin also revealed something about how the balance of power between Parliament and the press had shifted. In 1957 John Junor was deemed guilty of a serious contempt and censured at the Bar for publishing a relatively tame editorial criticising MPs over petrol allowances. Forty-five years later a national broadsheet could publish an article comparing the Speaker to a penis and no one took very much notice.[18] After a decade of intensive media sleaze-busting, the reputation of all MPs had been damaged. Newspapers found it easier and more tempting to denigrate them, and Parliament had in practice lost the ability to do very much about it.

Spin and Cynicism: 1997 Onwards

One of the theories advanced by those leading the lobby 'rebellion' in the 1980s was that if political reporting were more open, there would be less manipulation. 'Our sole purpose has been to create a structure of journalism within which we could give our readers the best possible service of political coverage, without political bias or spin,' Anthony Bevins said at the time.[19] After Tony Blair took

Labour into government in 1997, the lobby was to become more open than ever before. In fact, before the year was out, the lobby system as Guy Eden would have recognised it, meaning collective briefings that were not on the record, was to be abolished. Yet if anyone thought this would put an end to complaints that the press was being manipulated, they were to suffer a mighty disappointment. With the pejorative label 'spin' being applied at one stage to almost everything the Government said, Labour was to end up being accused of abusing the communications process more shamelessly than any other government in modern times.

The key figure, in terms of relations with the lobby, was Alastair Campbell. A former *Daily Mirror* political editor, Campbell became Blair's press secretary in 1994 and thereafter exerted a mesmerising influence over his former colleagues. Bernard Ingham spent more than ten years working in Downing Street before a sceptical journalist got round to publishing his biography. Campbell had been in government for only two by the time Peter Oborne immortalised him between hard covers. The book's dustjacket describes Campbell as 'the second most powerful man in Britain'. That is going too far; the jibe that Campbell is the real deputy Prime Minister is true only to the extent that, in the British political system, being deputy Prime Minister is not the second most important job. Campbell has said that the media exaggerates his status because it is self-obsessed. 'Most political journalists probably see me more than anybody else and I think they elevate my significance because of that. It makes them feel important,' he told an interviewer.[20] Yet, as Downing Street press secretary, he was undoubtedly more influential than any previous person appointed to that role and, when Labour came to power, most lobby journalists were delighted to have one of the Government's key power-brokers briefing twice a day.

Campbell's politics are tabloid and anti-elitist, *Daily Mirror* rather than *Guardian*. One of his lobby party pieces in the early days was to sneer at the freedom of information agenda, which had rather half-heartedly been adopted as Government policy. Yet ironically, within months of coming into office, he was to champion one of the *Guardian*'s great liberal causes. He put the lobby on the record. Robin Mountfield, second permanent secretary at the Office of Public Service, was commissioned to produce a report on the Government Information Service and in the course of his inquiry he considered the question lobby reformers had been grappling with since the 1970s. 'The pros and cons of non-attribution have been the subject of continuing debate,' he concluded.

> We do not intend to rehearse that debate in this report save to note that it is anonymous sources which increasingly dominate political journalism, both

news and commentary. A lobby system which relies on non-attribution tends to give an unwarranted credibility to those unnamed sources who are always 'senior' and invariably 'close' to whichever minister is the prime subject of the story. In these circumstances, it becomes ever more important to ensure that authentic government statements, especially from the centre, carry due authority.[21]

Mountfield recommended that Downing Street's twice-daily briefings should go on the record, with remarks from the chief press secretary (Campbell) attributed to the Prime Minister's official spokesman, or PMOS. Other press officers would just be Downing Street spokesmen. Mountfield rejected the idea of attributing comments to Campbell by name on the grounds that this would 'build up an official, appointed to represent the position of his elected masters, too much into a figure in his own right'.[22] Televising the lobby was ruled out for the same reason. Blair accepted the proposal and at 4.00 p.m. on Thursday 27 November 1997 Campbell officially went on the record. He turned up in the lobby room with a tape recorder, and before long, at subsequent briefings, reporters were bringing theirs. In the past, the lobby had been strongly opposed to giving up its secrecy; in 1997 it let go without a murmur of protest. (This was largely because, with information already sourced to Downing Street, the briefings were virtually on the record anyway.) The only slight worry was that Campbell's rebuttal strategies might get more anodyne, and that journalists would no longer be able to enjoy hearing him showering vulgar abuse on whoever might have written something offending against New Labour orthodoxy. Happily, this fear was not realised.

Three years later, openness was taken even further. Downing Street relaunched its website and the new version included, for the first time, an account of what was said at the twice-daily briefings. The service started with the morning lobby on Thursday 10 February 2000. The following month Campbell put himself even more on the record and 'agreed' that journalists could abandon the PMOS formula and attribute quotes to him by name. They jumped at the chance, and on Tuesday 14 March his name appeared widely in press reports. The BBC named him too. The *Guardian* even published a full, verbatim transcript of an afternoon lobby briefing, although as Michael White, the paper's political editor, admitted, the exchanges were 'pretty routine'.[23]

This time, however, Campbell's display of lobby *glasnost* was a mistake, and the story behind it goes some way towards explaining why Labour's openness coincided with growing discontent about the culture of spin. Like other

Downing Street press secretaries, Campbell had spent much of his time complaining about the quality of the media. Bernard Ingham wrote off stories he did not like as 'bunkum and balderdash'. Campbell's equivalent catchphrase was 'bollocks', or 'garbage'. (Or 'garbagic', in the adjectival. Under Campbell, Labour's modernisation programme extended to the English language. 'Processology' was another of his coinages.) Campbell's complaints were many, but they included journalists getting things wrong, being obsessed with trivia, being obsessed with process (another type of trivia, in his book) and being hypocritical about spin, because journalists were liable to spin facts just as much as spin doctors were. In the hope that he could make some of this apparent to the public, Campbell had agreed to let Michael Cockerell make a fly-on-the-wall documentary about the Downing Street press operation. Cockerell is an accomplished television journalist. But he was also one of the authors of *Sources Close to the Prime Minister*, the anti-lobby polemic that caused so much offence in 1984. When Campbell told the lobby that he was letting Cockerell bring his camera into their briefings to gather material for his project, the journalists suspected they were about to be stitched up, and that if Campbell wanted them on film, it was not because he wanted them to emerge as honest, fearless seekers after the truth.

A few days later, at the Monday morning briefing, the journalists arrived to find Cockerell was starting work. At this point George Jones, the *Daily Telegraph*'s political editor, and Trevor Kavanagh, the *Sun*'s political editor, pointed out that if Campbell was going to talk on camera, it would be absurd for newspapers not to identify him by name. In a display of nonchalance that appeared to be staged for the cameras, Campbell insisted that he was not bothered what they did. 'Yes, you can call me what you want. I don't think it adds up to a row of beans. I speak as the Prime Minister's official spokesman, that is what I am,' he told them.[24]

Campbell later decided that the form of attribution used at lobby briefings did amount to more than 'a row of beans'. In a letter to the *Daily Telegraph*, he denied that he had agreed to be named and he said that 'Prime Minister's official spokesman' was still a 'perfectly adequate formulation for both government and media'.[25] In the 1990s political communications advisers became known as 'spin doctors' and, although paid to improve the reputation of their masters, they had themselves managed to acquire the most appalling image. Frank Dobson was fond of comparing them to poisoners and quoting an old maxim: you could be a successful poisoner, or a famous poisoner, but not both. Campbell's problem was that, by March 2000, he had become very famous indeed. Several newspapers ignored his pleas and continued to name him after the Cockerell episode, and that only made the problem worse. As a result, in June he announced that he would be cutting down on his personal appearances at the lobby and that more of the Downing Street briefings would be conducted by Godric Smith, his civil servant deputy.

Cockerell's programme was finally shown in July 2000 and, although it may not have delivered quite the knock-out blow to the reputation of the lobby that Campbell hoped, it did not show the journalists in a particularly flattering light either. 'The interaction between Mr Campbell (even on his best behaviour) and Her Majesty's Lobby appears close to what psychotherapists term an "abusive relationship" – one in which the partners feel trapped in a downward spiral of passive-aggressive behaviour,' wrote Alan Rusbridger, the *Guardian*'s editor, after seeing it.[26]

At the heart of the problem was spin. The political journalists did not trust Campbell because they thought he was out to manipulate them, and he did not respect them because he thought they were determined to spin whatever he said to suit their own political or journalistic agendas. Given that all governments have tried to secure favourable coverage in the press, Tony Blair must have wondered why spin became such an issue for Labour. Partly it was just technology. The expansion of broadcasting and the advent of 24-hour news meant there was more demand than ever for politics on the media and, as a result, government departments and political parties had to work harder to ensure that they always had the right thing to say. Mobile phones and pagers also made it possible for someone like Campbell to control the message being given out, hour by hour or even minute by minute, in a way that Joe Haines could only have dreamed of. But there was more to it than that. The creation of New Labour involved the transformation of a socialist party into something quite different, and image was part of that. 'Spin – or presentation – bought us the time and the space to change the underlying reality,' said Peter Mandelson, who, as Labour's director of communications in the late 1980s, started the process that was completed by Blair.[27]

Labour used spin brilliantly when it was in opposition but, in a textbook example of the way a political strength can become a political weakness, spin came to be seen as one of the most unattractive features of the Blair Government. Ministers invested more in their departmental press offices, and there was also an increase in the number of special advisers, some of whom specialised in briefing the media. These developments made it easier for political journalists to write stories. Yet, not surprisingly, there was not a word of gratitude in the press. Instead, New Labour, like Wilson in the 1960s, discovered that presentational tricks that were effective in opposition were less impressive when the party was in government. Political journalists increasingly complained that they were being manipulated. This became a political issue during Labour's first term (not least because the Tories could not find many other issues over which to attack the Government that resonated with the public) and the problem was exacerbated by the perception, widely held, that the Government was more willing to lie than its predecessors. In a documentary broadcast in September 1997, Charlie Whelan, Gordon Brown's spin doctor, admitted that he was willing to deceive the media. 'You just have to be economical with the truth. You have to say things. You should never lie, but it's very difficult. They understand. They will certainly understand tomorrow and forgive me.'[28] Whelan, who in some respects was the most cunning of all the Labour spin doctors, carried on working for Brown successfully for more than a year after the documentary was broadcast. But for the Labour spin machine, it was nevertheless a Gerald Ratner moment: a public admission that sometimes what they said was crap.

One of the particular complaints against Labour was that, in its eagerness to spin stories to the media, it was prepared to flout the convention that government policy announcements should be made first to Parliament. In one sense the complaints were justified. One of the conclusions of the Mountfield report was that government press offices should do more to trail announcements in advance (although it also warned press officers against breaching parliamentary protocol), and the special adviser spin doctors, who were given greater licence to leak than ordinary civil servants, embraced this task enthusiastically. MPs repeatedly complained to the Speaker about policies being unveiled in the press or on the *Today* programme before the ministerial statement at 3.30 p.m. and Betty Boothroyd formally rebuked ministers on six separate occasions.[29] The Opposition regularly attacked Blair for sidelining the Commons, and newspapers did too – although, curiously, they were quite happy to ignore parliamentary propriety when they received their own advance stories about government announcements. In her final address to the Commons, Boothroyd hit out again.

> It is in Parliament in the first instance that ministers must explain and justify their policies. Since becoming Speaker in 1992, I have made my views known about that, both publicly and behind the scenes, to both Governments. I have taken action to ensure that those who advise ministers should never overlook the primacy of Parliament. This is the chief forum of the nation – today, tomorrow and, I hope, for ever.[30]

The trouble with her analysis was Parliament had long since given up being the 'chief forum of the nation'. The practice of governments making announcements to the public via the media was an intelligent response to this. There was also something peculiar about MPs defending the traditional system because, actually, that still involved press gallery journalists being told first. Announcements were sometimes given to the press in advance under embargo, and in the press gallery the text of a ministerial statement would normally be handed out as the minister was speaking. In his diaries, Tony Benn recalls going to the press gallery to get hold a statement not yet available to MPs and being told by an attendant that he could not have one because he was not a journalist.[31] However, Blair was sensitive to the charge that he was downgrading Parliament and officially he remained committed to the idea that new policies should be announced first in Parliament. At the end of 2001 the Government even told the public administration committee that it would revise the ministerial code to make this clear, although in practice this did little to stop pre-briefing continuing.

Other, more significant attempts were made to reassert the primacy of Parliament. In the autumn of 1999 gallery reporting made a comeback. Charles Moore, editor of the *Daily Telegraph*, decided to revive the parliamentary page and to create a new post in his political team for a reporter covering the chamber. *The Times* and the *Independent* also went back to carrying extracts from debates on a daily basis (although they subsequently reverted to more occasional coverage), and the *Daily Mail* reintroduced its parliamentary sketch. Moore thought that even though Parliament had become less important, there was still a strong case for reporting what was said in the chamber. 'There is something weird about political journalism that constantly does the secondary thing without doing the primary thing, and about electing people to represent us and then not telling the voters what they are saying,' he explains. 'Obviously, once that happens, spin becomes more important and people are less well informed.'[32] Moore also believed that, in view of the Government's big majority in the Commons, debates in the Lords were becoming more interesting and that, without a parliamentary page, there was no satisfactory way of reporting them.

The Government made its own attempts to promote parliamentary coverage by changing some of the rules that inconvenienced reporters. A modernisation committee was set up, chaired by the leader of the Commons, and in Labour's first term it introduced a series of minor but media-friendly reforms. Journalists were allowed to use tape recorders in the gallery, camera crews were allowed to film in Members' offices, and the ban on using mobile phones in the committee corridor was lifted (which was supposed to help journalists covering committee hearings who did not have an office in the press gallery). The committee also considered changing the 'I spy strangers' rule that could be used to clear the galleries, but the only reform was a feeble one: MPs would still be allowed to use the procedure, but instead of saying 'I spy strangers', they would have to move that the House sat in private.[33] No one seems to have worried very much about Parliament maintaining an instrument of censorship because there was an assumption that the procedure would never be used successfully. But on 5 December 2001, nearly ninety years after Michael MacDonagh declared that the right of the press to report debates had become 'unconditional and superior to all other considerations', the press gallery was cleared. Paul Tyler, a Liberal Democrat, moved that the House should sit in private to make a protest about the time set aside for a debate on the anti-terrorism Bill. As in 1958, the motion was carried by acclamation because MPs on the Government benches did not realise what was happening. For the next fifty minutes the House sat in private. The episode demonstrated a great deal about the decline in parliamentary reporting. The 1958 'secret session' made front-page news. When the gallery was cleared in 2001, it happened after midnight and the event went virtually unreported.

After the 2001 election Robin Cook became leader of the Commons and (in an example of why he was wrong to downplay the importance of personality in politics) modernisation was pursued much more vigorously than under his predecessors. The low turnout on polling day triggered a public debate about voter apathy and, in a report published in the autumn of 2002, the committee said that the main reason why the Commons needed to modernise was to reverse its decline in public esteem. In part it blamed the media for the fact that MPs were perceived by the public as confrontational and unrepresentative. 'News reports of proceedings in Parliament tend to be fixated with moments of confrontation and conflict. The comparative neglect of the humdrum, serious business of Parliament, both in the chamber and in committee, leaves the public with an unbalanced perception of the work of MPs,' it said.[34] One of its main recommendations was that the Commons start work in the mornings on Tuesdays and Wednesdays (it already did so on Thursdays, and Fridays when it sat) so that statements would be reported on the lunchtime news bulletins and important votes would take place before newspaper deadlines. 'We are all professional communicators; no one in the chamber would plan a press conference for 4 p.m. If we are serious about the elected Parliament of the people setting the agenda for public debate, we need to start earlier in the day,' Cook told the Commons.[35]

The changed hours came into operation in January 2003. As expected, the new arrangements led to parliamentary exchanges being featured more often on the lunchtime news. Another consequence, which could perhaps alter the nature of political journalism more significantly, was that with the Commons sitting through the middle of the day, reporters found some MPs more reluctant to go out for lunch.

Labour's relations with the lobby did not improve after its second election victory. Campbell took on a new title, director of communications and strategy, and celebrated his promotion by doing even less direct communicating with the media than before, leaving two civil servants, Godric Smith and Tom Kelly, to conduct the lobby briefings. This was supposed to give the impression that the Government was being weaned off spin. But in the twelve months after polling day a series of events took place that actually made the Government appear even more manipulative and dishonest than in the past. The most crass incident took place on 11 September 2001 when Jo Moore, a special adviser to Stephen Byers at the Department for Transport, Local Government and the Regions, sent an e-mail to the press office shortly after the attack on the World Trade Center saying it was 'a very good day to get out anything we want to bury'.[36] It was probably the most damaging e-mail anyone had ever sent in British politics, and when it was leaked to the papers the following month, there was understandable outrage. Moore had learnt her spin doctoring working for the Labour Party before 1997 and the e-mail was significant not because it was written by a lone incompetent, but because it illustrated the way Labour's spin machine had learned to think.

Then, in early 2002, Downing Street got embroiled in slanging matches with newspapers over the accuracy of information it gave out in relation to stories about Lakshmi Mittal and Martin Sixsmith. In April Campbell lodged a formal complaint with the Press Complaints Commission about articles written by Peter Oborne in the *Spectator* and the *Evening Standard* and Simon Walters in the *Mail on Sunday* saying that Blair had tried to get a bigger role for himself in the ceremony at the start of the Queen Mother's lying-in-state in Westminster Hall. Downing Street had gone to the PCC before over privacy issues relating to the Blair children, but this time Campbell hoped he would be able to show that two political editors were lying about a story directly relevant to the Prime Minister. His strategy later backfired when it became clear that Black Rod, the parliamentary official dealing with the ceremonial arrangements, would not support Downing Street's story. Campbell had to withdraw the PCC complaint and Oborne and Walters were vindicated. But the row nevertheless reinforced Campbell's and Blair's view that there was something deeply wrong with the trivia-obsessed lobby, and the Government's relations with the press in general, and they resolved to do something about it.

The new approach was unveiled on 2 May. James Hardy, the lobby chairman, was called at short notice and asked to take a group of political editors to Downing Street for a briefing by Campbell. He told them that he wanted to replace the morning meetings at Downing Street with briefings at another, larger venue that would be open to specialists and foreign reporters as well as members of the lobby. In an attempt to focus attention more on elected politicians, ministers would conduct some of the briefings themselves. Policy officials would sometimes attend and the Prime Minister himself would give more press conferences. (This later became a commitment to hold monthly press conferences, which Blair started doing in June.) 'We have got to be less buttoned-up, far more open, far less worried about what you guys are going to write,' said Campbell, as he outlined the new strategy to reporters.[37] A few weeks later *The Times* explained Campbell's reasoning even more explicitly. 'Maintaining an exclusive, secret club is out of date. Other journalists have a right to know what the Government is thinking about real issues. The lobby's current focus on personality and lack of perspective does not serve anybody's interests. It is contributing to the disengagement of voters from the political process,' a 'Whitehall source' told the paper (speaking, without any sense of irony, on an unattributable basis).[38]

Campbell's plan was designed to enable the Government to cast off its reputation for spin. The idea was that if ministers, and particularly the Prime Minister, were seen answering questions more often, an element of trust might be restored. But Campbell's strategy was also widely seen as an attempt to weaken the power of the lobby. In particular, it was said that by opening the briefings to all-comers Campbell would make it harder for the lobby correspondents to pursue specific stories (like the Queen Mother affair) because as soon as the questioning got intense, the Downing Street spokesman would be able to dodge the issue by taking a question from a foreign journalist more interested in EU enlargement or whatever. Downing Street arranged to hold the new-style briefings at the Foreign Press Association in Carlton House Terrace. This presented another drawback because it took twice as long (fifteen minutes) to get there from the Commons as it did to get to Downing Street. (Those who complained were not all being idle; it was genuinely inconvenient for journalists with morning deadlines.) The afternoon briefings continued to be given in the lobby room in the Commons, as they had been for years. As the new arrangements came into force in October, Adam Boulton, Sky's political editor, declared that they demonstrated Downing Street's contempt for the lobby. 'Top figures in New Labour increasingly regard journalists as "scum". Now they are treating them as such,' he said.[39]

Campbell seemed to be under the impression that political journalism would be much better if only it were not written by political journalists. He thought that outsiders were more likely to report the Government's achievements fairly. Foreign journalists and specialist journalists did turn up to enjoy the grandeur of the Foreign Press Association (Gladstone's former residence), but the briefings were still dominated by the lobby and, in the short term at least, the tone of the exchanges with the Downing Street spokesman was much the same as it had been before. The first real test of the system came in December 2002, after the *Mail on Sunday* revealed that Cherie Blair had used a convicted fraudster to help her buy two flats in Bristol. Downing Street denied the story until the *Daily Mail* printed e-mails showing that it was not telling the truth. As the story about 'Cherie and the conman' ran on for days on end, it became obvious that the fears expressed in the spring about lobby journalists being sidelined were unfounded. There were some marathon morning briefings that were almost entirely taken up with questions about the affair. On one occasion the lobby correspondents were even joined by the parliamentary sketch-writers (who in the past had not been allowed to attend lobby briefings). As Westminster's arch-cynics, these were probably the last people Campbell wanted to invite when he planned the new arrangements. Yet, on the day the e-mails were published, they turned up in force to ridicule the spokesman given the task of explaining away the earlier lies. Like most political controversies, the affair eventually died down. It did not appear to diminish Downing Street's enthusiasm for the new arrangements. But it did show that one of the assumptions made by some of the lobby reformers in the 1980s was wrong, and that putting briefings on the record did not necessarily make them more honest.

CONCLUSION

'Mutual Suspicion and Constant Hostility'

> To perform its duties with entire independence, and consequently with the
> utmost public advantage, the press can enter into no close or binding alliances
> with the statesmen of the day, nor can it surrender its permanent interests to
> the convenience of the ephemeral power of any government.
>
> The Times, 6 February 1852

When Michael MacDonagh published his history of the press gallery in 1913, he
presented a portrait of an institution basking in self-confidence. Besides enjoying
all the 'comforts and conveniences of a well-equipped club', the reporters of his
day had a clear idea of what they were supposed to do (to record what was said in
the chamber) and the opportunity to do it properly. MacDonagh was brought up
with a Victorian's reverence for order and certainty, and he genuinely believed
that *Hansard* represented the highest form of parliamentary reporting.[1] He was
also in no doubt at all that, in doing what they did, he and his fellow reporters had
earned the right to be seen as respected contributors to the political process. The
reporters' gallery, he said, was now 'a complete and irrevocable part of
Parliament, a part that can never be lopped off and destroyed, so long as
Parliament is in existence. It will end only if and when Parliament itself is ever
brought to an end, and the powers of government are vested in a despotism.'[2]

Ninety years later, with gallery coverage virtually abandoned and lobby journalism (which MacDonagh treated largely as a frivolous distraction) the
standard form of reporting from Parliament, the reputation of the press gallery

was rather different. Instead of being seen as champions of parliamentary democracy, political journalists were just as likely to be depicted as presenting some kind of threat to it. The 59 per cent turnout in the 2001 general election prompted much agonising about the causes of electoral apathy, and many commentators decided that the media were partly to blame. 'To me the media is the absolutely central pillar and tenet of a free country and a democracy, and yet we have it spilling over in the way that it is now into not just simply providing a pillar for our freedoms and democracy, but actually creating an unhealthy relationship which is starting to erode those pillars,' Peter Mandelson said after Labour's re-election.[3] A common charge was that the lobby was just too cynical. The Government was often exasperated by the way it was reported in the press, and Alastair Campbell sometimes gave the impression that he would be only too happy for the press gallery to be 'lopped off and destroyed'.

A more realistic option for Campbell was to try to persuade the public not to take stories written by lobby journalists too seriously. When Bernard Ingham was Margaret Thatcher's press secretary, he was given to comparing government press officers to riflemen on the Somme, 'mowing down wave upon wave of distortion and taking out rank upon rank of supposition, deduction and gossip, while laying down a barrage of facts behind which something approximating to the truth might advance.'[4] He pined for the kind of objective reporting he associated with his time as a trainee on the *Hebden Bridge Times* in the late 1940s. 'The facts appear to matter less these days than what the so-called experts think of them . . . Time and again we need the still, small voice of the reporter to tell us where we started. But where do we start if fact attracts no premium over fiction; fairness over malice; and objectivity none over prejudice?'[5] A decade later Campbell was fulminating against the inadequacies of the media in near-identical terms. When he was a journalist, he used to lie awake at night worrying whether he had got a story wrong, he told a sympathetic interviewer. 'I am going to risk sounding like a middle-aged old fart, but I think standards have declined a lot. I don't get the sense that [today] journalists lie awake wondering whether they've got a story wrong.'[6] He claimed that journalists were working in a system that actually encouraged distortion.

I think there are still journalists who worry about getting things right. But I think the pressures on them are to get the story regardless; to get the story first, wrong, rather than get the story at the same time as everyone else, right . . . I believe journalists make up quotes, or maybe they get somebody, who's not very important, who says something as an aside at some do or other, and they turn that into a senior minister or a senior source or a senior aide and one quote becomes four and all the rest of it.

To cap it all, he went on, 'you never get a real sense that when newspapers get things wrong there's anybody getting bollocked for it.'[7]

Given Downing Street's own reputation for reliability under the Campbell regime, he is about the last person on the planet from whom any political journalist would be willing to take a lecture on media standards. Yet, nevertheless, he and Ingham had a point. When MacDonagh was working, it was easy for most political journalists to get it right. All they had to do was to take an accurate shorthand note and make sure they got the name of the speaker. Lobby journalism has always been more problematic. It involves interpretation, which is inevitably contentious. (Campbell often described lobby correspondents as spin doctors, possibly because by the end of the 1990s that was about the rudest thing one could say about anyone in politics, but also because he saw, correctly, that the two activities involve making subjective judgements.) Lobby journalism also involves conjecture, which can be done intelligently or recklessly. And, increasingly in the last hundred years, it has been driven by the demand to create news. When MacDonagh worked on *The Times* none of his colleagues was under pressure to provide the paper with a front-page splash, because the paper did not have one. That has changed, and all reporting is probably now more sensational. In lobby journalism this is particularly apparent in the use of dramatic clichés like 'clearest sign yet', 'provoked uproar' or 'faced fresh embarrassment', which are often factually questionable and which are introduced to increase the chances of getting otherwise accurate stories into the paper.[8]

A good example of the lobby's fallibility came in 1995, when John Major stood down and effectively challenged himself for the Tory leadership. John Redwood entered the contest and, before the poll, there was considerable speculation as to how many votes Major would need, not just to win, but to guarantee his long-term survival. Philip Cowley, an academic, later published a study of the coverage pointing out that most political journalists declared in advance that Major would be in serious trouble if more than a hundred Tory MPs either voted against him or abstained. But in the event, when Major won with 111 Tories failing to support him, the same papers by and large declared that his victory was decisive. Cowley describes this as an example of 'pack journalism' going wrong. 'A consensus emerged among the political journalists that a hundred was the danger figure. The only problem was that it was a consensus based on little or no evidence.' Cowley's conclusion is not a flattering one for the lobby: 'When it comes to predicting the future, political journalists – like academics and other "experts" – should be eschewed in favour of Mystic Meg."[9] At the time, journalists were allowed quietly to forget their rash predictions. Under Campbell's regime, it was not always so easy. In 1999, after one government reshuffle that did not live up to media predictions, Campbell celebrated by handing out awards to three papers that got it wrong. To his immense delight, one of the prizes he was able to hand out to his tormentors in the lobby was a CD by the band Garbage.[10]

Although Campbell was entitled to point out that the lobby did not always get it right, the new charge that was levelled after 2001 – that the lobby was contributing to electoral apathy – was a less convincing one. It was claimed that voters were becoming less interested because politics was always presented in a negative way, with an emphasis on 'process' stories that seemed important to the media rather than policy stories relevant to the public at large. If only the media reported politics differently, the argument went, the public would take more interest and show more respect. The televising of Parliament was also supposed to generate interest and respect. But the problem is that these two goals are not necessarily compatible. In fact, the amount of interest the public shows in an institution often appears to be in inverse proportion to the respect in which it is held. It is also odd to accuse political correspondents of making politics boring, given that few people spend more time trying to find things to say about Westminster that might grab the attention of readers and viewers. It is true that in the 1990s (largely as a result of sleaze) coverage became more negative. But newspapers were full of scandal at the time of the Profumo affair, and turnout in the 1964 election was 77 per cent. In recent years voter apathy has been a problem in most Western democracies, including those where the media is much more craven towards politicians than it is in Britain.

The lack of respect shown by modern political journalists towards MPs is, in fact, probably a good thing. On 6 February 1852 *The Times* published a leader setting out what the relationship between government and the press should be. Lord Derby had attacked the paper in Parliament, saying that if it wanted to enjoy the influence of statesmen, it should share the responsibilities of statesmen. In what was to become a definitive statement of a newspaper's duty, *The Times* said that the press had a different function.

> We cannot admit that its purpose is to share the labours of statesmanship, or that it is bound by the same limitations, the same duties, the same liabilities as that of the ministers of the Crown. The purpose and duties of the two powers are constantly separate, generally independent, sometimes diametri-

cally opposed. The dignity and the freedom of the press are trammelled from
the moment it accepts an ancillary position. To perform its duties with entire
independence, and consequently with the utmost public advantage, the press
can enter into no close or binding alliances with the statesmen of the day, nor
can it surrender its permanent interests to the convenience of the ephemeral
power of any government.[11]

One of the most striking changes within the press gallery over the last hundred
years is that journalists have become less willing to share the labours of states-
manship. When Gladstone resigned as Prime Minister in 1894, Henry Lucy sent
him a letter saying that he was 'the most striking personality in the House of
Commons' and declaring: 'I can truly say that there is nothing I have written
during the last 20 years about yourself that I would withhold from your view.'[12]
Lucy was the most prominent political writer of his day. But he was also (and the
two are probably connected) a bit of a creep. It is unlikely that any journalist
would write to a politician in similar terms today. Lobby correspondents were
particularly ingratiating in the years just before and after the Second World War.
Their own rulebook reminded them that they held a 'responsible office'. In
return, politicians were willing to show their gratitude. When R. G. Emery
retired as the *Morning Post*'s political correspondent in the 1930s, shortly before
Bill Deedes took over the post, he received a silver coffee service as a present
from the Cabinet. When political editors retire today, no one would dream of
organising a ministerial whip-round. 'The interests of government and press are
irreconcilable and the healthiest relationship must be one of tension, mutual
suspicion, and constant hostility,' wrote James Margach after retiring from the
Sunday Times.[13] A declaration like that should not necessarily be taken at face
value. Journalists who make these comments are often quite proud of their own
personal relationships with politicians, and Margach was no exception. (*The
Abuse of Power* is full of name-dropping and pictures of the author alongside the
likes of Harold Wilson.) But it is significant that towards the end of the twentieth
century an antagonistic relationship was being seen as desirable.

Political reporting can be said to have improved in other ways. Stories written
by lobby journalists are attributed much more clearly than they were in the days
when reports used to 'lean heavily upon thin air', and the culture of secrecy
surrounding lobby activities has largely disappeared. There is more policy
analysis than there used to be, and the quality of it is better. People know more
about what politicians are really like. What David Butler described as 'informed
atmospheric stories' are more common. The public probably gets reliable

behind-the-scenes information more quickly than in the past, and Whitehall is now covered as an important area in its own right. The standard of writing in news reports, columns and sketches may be better, too (although taste changes, so it is impossible to make an absolute judgement). People can also see for themselves on television what is happening in the chamber, and anyone desperate for a fix of political news can now stay updated twenty-four hours a day. In 1987 Peter Hennessy, the scourge of the old lobby system, declared: 'As a consumer I *know* I am better served by daily written political journalism than at any time since I began to read the papers regularly at the time of Suez.'[14] Now he believes that newspapers have not made the most of the opportunities that arose in the 1990s to expand their political coverage; but he says that the comment he made fifteen years earlier is 'still true to a certain extent'.[15] Butler says that most of the complaints he made when he wrote about the lobby system in the 1960s are no longer relevant.

This is not to say that parliamentary journalism has achieved some state of perfection, as MacDonagh seemed to think it had in 1913. There is still a lot to criticise. Legislation is hardly ever covered in detail. The virtual abolition of gallery reporting means that the old joke about the best way of keeping a secret being to announce it in the chamber has become more true than ever. An enormous amount happens within government that political journalists never find out about. And too many stories that do appear are exaggerated, or misleading, or tendentious or just plain wrong. Yet there is a lot for which the public can be grateful. In 1810, when Sheridan stood in the chamber and came to the defence of the gallery reporters with the words 'Give me but the liberty of the press, and I will give the minister a venal House of peers, I will give him a corrupt and servile House of Commons, I will give him the full swing of the patronage of office . . . And yet, armed with the liberty of the press, I will go forth and meet him undismayed,' he may well have been looking ahead to a future in which all you had was *Today in Parliament*, the political service from the Press Association and Peter Riddell. What he got instead was all that, plus the propaganda, the spin and the nonsense, plus all manner of journalism – from the brilliant to the banal – in between. On balance, he would probably conclude, it was still a good deal.

NOTES

Abbreviations used

HLRO   House of Lords Record Office
PGR   Press Gallery Records
PRO   Public Record Office
LR   Lobby Records

Introduction: The First Press Corps

1 *Parliamentary History*, 31 Dec. 1798, vol. 34, cols 156–66. Like many early parliamentary speeches, Windham's was reported in the third person, rather than the first person.
2 Peter Mandelson on *The Talk Show with Andrew Marr*, BBC Four, 9 April 2002. Transcript from BBC.
3 *Parliamentary History*, 31 Dec. 1798, vol. 34, cols 159–64.
4 See Mitchell Stephens, *A History of News* (Harcourt Brace, 1997), p.227; and Stephens, 'Highlights of Journalism: Inventing Reporting in Eighteenth Century England', *messaGe* (German media magazine), Jan. 2000.
5 See Chapter 4 for further details.
6 Cocks was interviewed in the course of a press gallery inquiry in 1963–4. See Chapter 5 for further details.

Chapter 1: Printers Defy the Ban

1 Simon Schama, *A History of Britain: The British Wars 1603–1776* (BBC Worldwide, 2001), p. 77.
2 Quoted in Hoover, *Samuel Johnson's Parliamentary Reporting*, p. 3.
3 *Commons Journals*, 5 April 1626, vol. 1, pp. 843–4. Quoted in MacDonagh, *The Reporters' Gallery*, p. 82. MacDonagh's book is very thorough and I have drawn on it extensively.
4 *Commons Journals*, 11 April 1628, vol. 1, p. 882.
5 *Commons Journals*, 13 July 1641, vol. 2, p. 209.
6 *Commons Journals*, 2 Feb. 1642, vol. 2, p. 411.

7   Quoted in Black, *The English Press 1621-1861*, p. 6.

8   See MacDonagh, *The Reporters' Gallery*, p. 90.

9   *Commons Journals*, 21 Dec. 1694, pp. 192-3.

10   *Commons Journals*, 3 June 1703, p. 270.

11   Quoted in MacDonagh, *The Reporters' Gallery*, p. 110.

12   Quoted ibid., p. 119.

13   Hawkins, *Life of Dr Samuel Johnson*, p. 95.

14   *History and Proceedings of the House of Commons from the Restoration to the Present Time*, vol. 10, p. 278.

15   Ibid.

16   Ibid., p. 282.

17   Ibid., p. 283.

18   Ibid., pp. 285-7.

19   Ibid., p. 278.

20   Ibid., p. 284.

21   Ibid., pp. 279-80.

22   Ibid., p. 287.

23   Arthur Murphy, *Essay on the Life and Genius of Samuel Johnson* (1792), quoted in Hoover, *Samuel Johnson's Parliamentary Reporting*, p. 33.

24   Murphy, quoted ibid., p. 34.

25   Quoted in MacDonagh, *The Reporters' Gallery*, pp. 135-6.

26   John Almon, *Memoirs of John Almon*, p. 118.

27   Quoted in MacDonagh, *The Reporters' Gallery*, p. 142.

28   For an extended discussion of Johnson's reliability as a reporter, see Hoover, *Samuel Johnson's Parliamentary Reporting*. Hoover finds 'no evidence of intentional bias in the reporting of arguments' in Johnson (p. 130). MacDonagh concludes that Johnson 'deals out with even-handed justice, to Whig and Tory alike, his treasures of eloquence, argument and logic' (*The Reporters' Gallery*, p. 159).

29   Boswell, *Life of Johnson*, p. 110.

30   Quoted ibid., p. 1,386.

31   Sir John Hawkins said 'he was never within the walls of either House of Parliament'. Arthur Murphy quoted Johnson as saying he had been in the gallery of the Commons 'but once'. See Hoover, *Samuel Johnson's Parliamentary Reporting*, p. 28.

32   Almon, *Memoirs*, p. 119.

33   By 1780 a Mr Wall was editor of the *Gazetteer*. He was almost certainly the same man as the one doing the debate reports ten years earlier, and almost certainly the John Henley Wall whose death was recorded in the *Gazetteer* and other papers in 1783. The reports described him as an Irishman, from Tipperary, and a barrister, although he had been called to the Bar only in 1781. See Haig, *The Gazetteer 1735-1797*, pp. 176-7. Haig concludes that Wall 'may be considered the first special parliamentary correspondent employed by an English newspaper' (p. 91).

34   For more detail, see Peter Thomas, 'The Beginning of Parliamentary Reporting in Newspapers 1768-1774', *English Historical Review*, Oct. 1959, vol. 74.

35   Horace Walpole, in *Memoirs of the Reign of George III*, quoted in MacDonagh, *The Reporters' Gallery*, p. 189.

36   Although reporting was banned, Sir Henry Cavendish, a Member and an accomplished shorthand writer, took extensive notes of the debates during this period. His one-man *Hansard* operation was printed only after his death, but it is a good source for what was said in the chamber during the 1771 battle with the printers. *Sir Henry Cavendish's Debates of the House of Commons* (1841), 8 Feb. 1771, p. 257.

37 Ibid., p. 258.
38 See Haig, *The Gazetteer*, p. 105.

Chapter 2: The Gallery Becomes the Fourth Estate of the Realm

1 *Morning Post*, 12 June 1779.
2 Letters from Coleridge to Robert Southey, quoted in MacDonagh, *The Reporters' Gallery*, p. 307. Coleridge does not seem to have been a particularly diligent reporter. According to a story told by one biographer, he fell asleep while listening to William Pitt (the Younger) and had to reconstruct the speech using techniques that would have been familiar to Samuel Johnson. 'It does more credit to the author's head than to his memory,' George Canning is reputed to have said after reading Coleridge's account. Not surprisingly, Coleridge did not stay at the *Morning Post* long. See MacDonagh, *The Reporters' Gallery*, ch. 34.
3 Quoted in A. Aspinall, 'The Reporting and Publishing of the House of Commons' Debates, 1771-1834', in Pares and Taylor (eds), *Essays Presented to Sir Lewis Namier*.
4 Ibid.
5 Quoted in Peter Thomas, 'The Beginning of Parliamentary Reporting in Newspapers, 1768-1774', *English Historical Review*, Oct. 1959, vol. 74.
6 Ibid.
7 Quoted in Hardcastle (ed), *Life of John, Lord Campbell*, p. 108.
8 Stephen, *Memoirs*, p. 293.
9 *Gazetteer*, 11 Nov. 1783, quoted in Haig, *The Gazetteer*, p. 191.
10 William Hazlitt, 'The Periodical Press' (1823), in *The Collected Works of William Hazlitt*, vol. 10.
11 *Parliamentary Debates*, 23 March 1810, col. 34.
12 *Gazetteer*, 20 March 1777. Quoted in Haig, *The Gazetteer*, p. 127.
13 Boswell, *Life of Johnson*, p. 85.
14 *Parliamentary History*, 31 Dec. 1798, vol. 34, col. 163.
15 Woodfall in the *Morning Chronicle* on 12 Feb. 1780. Quoted in Aspinall, 'The Reporting and Publishing of the House of Commons' Debates'.
16 MacDonagh, *The Reporters' Gallery*, p. 309.
17 Quoted ibid., p. 310.
18 *The Times*, 24 May 1803.
19 Quoted in MacDonagh, *The Reporters' Gallery*, p. 311. In fact, a few excerpts were recovered and appear in the *Parliamentary History*.
20 Abbot, *Diary and Correspondence*, p. 421.
21 Stephens, *A History of News*, p. 255.
22 Review of Hallam's *Constitutional History of England*, *Edinburgh Review*, Sept. 1828.
23 For example, under William Pitt's administration, the Civil List secret service accounts record the following payments between 1790 and 1792: the *Diary*, £400; *St James's Evening Chronicle*, £200; *London Evening Post*, £200; *Whitehall Evening Post*, £200; the *Public Ledger*, £100; the *World*, £600; the *Morning Herald*, £600; the *Oracle*, £200; and *The Times*, £300. See *The Times*, *The History of the Times: 'The Thunderer' in the Making*, p. 61. Governments gave up making clandestine grants to newspapers only in the mid-nineteenth century.
24 *Parliamentary Debates*, 6 Feb. 1810, vol. 15, cols 329-31.
25 Ibid., cols 325, 341-3.
26 *Parliamentary Debates*, 23 March 1810, vol. 16, col. 29.
27 Ibid., col. 34.

28 Ibid., col. 27.

29 Quoted in MacDonagh, *The Reporters' Gallery*, p. 316.

30 *Parliamentary Debates*, 6 Feb. 1810, vol. 15, col. 336.

31 *Parliamentary Debates*, 15 June 1819, vol. 40, col. 1,164.

32 Ibid., col. 1,172.

33 *Parliamentary Debates*, 16 June 1819, vol. 40, col. 1,199.

34 Stephen, *Memoirs*, p. 294.

35 The reputation of *The Times* as a paper of record depended upon the accuracy and thoroughness of its debate reports. But not all readers appreciated the service. William Hazlitt offered this assessment: 'It is elaborate, but heavy; full, but not readable: it is stuffed up with official documents, with matter-of-fact details. It seems intended to be deposited in the office of the Keeper of Records, and might be imagined to be composed as well as printed with a steam-engine. It is pompous, dogmatical, and full of pretensions, but neither light, various, nor agreeable. It sells more, and contains more, than any other paper; and when you have said this, you have said it all. It presents a most formidable front to the inexperienced reader. It makes a toil of a pleasure. It is said to be calculated for persons in business, and yet it is the business of a whole morning to get through it.' From his essay 'The Periodical Press' (1823), in *Collected Works of William Hazlitt*, vol. 10.

36 Quoted in MacDonagh, *The Reporters' Gallery*, p. 368.

37 *Parliamentary Debates*, 25 July 1833, vol. 18, col. 1,243. The following day the *Morning Post* commented: 'The general accuracy of the hon and learned gentleman's charges against the reporters and reports may be judged of by the fact that there is *not one* Scotchman connected with the reporting department of this journal.' Quoted in MacDonagh, *The Reporters' Gallery*, p. 369.

38 *The Times*, 26 July 1833.

39 *Parliamentary Debates*, 29 July 1833, vol. 20, col. 86.

40 There is some doubt about when Dickens did start in the House of Commons. In a speech in 1865, he said he started before he was eighteen, which would have meant before 7 February 1830. In the same speech he referred to writing in the 'preposterous pen in the old House of Lords', which suggests that he was there before the Lords opened its gallery with seating in December 1831. John Forster, Dickens's friend and biographer, says he started in 1831, as does Peter Ackroyd in his *Dickens*. But Una Pope-Hennessy, in her biography, says his break came a year later, when he had just turned twenty. See: speech to the Newspaper Press Fund, 20 May 1865, in Fielding (ed.), *The Speeches of Charles Dickens*, p. 347; Forster, *The Life of Charles Dickens*, vol. 1, p. 75; Ackroyd, *Dickens*, p. 140; Pope-Hennessy, *Charles Dickens*, p. 20.

41 Grant, *The Newspaper Press*, vol. 1, p. 298.

42 Quoted in Pope-Hennessy, *Charles Dickens*, p. 28.

43 Forster, *The Life of Charles Dickens*, vol. 1, p. 77.

44 Charles Dickens, *David Copperfield*, (First published 1850; Penguin Classics, 1996), p. 577.

45 Speech to the Newspaper Press Fund, 20 May 1865, in Fielding (ed.), *The Speeches of Charles Dickens*, p. 347.

46 Thomas Clarkson, 'Parliamentary Recollections': a memoir written in 1889 in response to an appeal for contributions to a collection of press gallery reminiscences. It seems that only two reporters bothered to write something for the archive, but the book that contains the material does include a good collection of contemporary newspaper cuttings about the gallery. Clarkson, a former *Daily News* reporter, had retired when he wrote the piece and died shortly afterwards. HLRO PG/Misc/16.

47 Report from the Select Committee on Parliamentary Reporting, 1878, HC 327, evidence from Ross, q. 612.

48 Ibid., evidence from Ross, q. 540.

49 Quoted in Hardcastle, *Life of John, Lord Campbell*, pp. 106–7.

50 Dickens, *David Copperfield*, p. 487.

51 Ibid., pp. 503–4.

52 Ibid., p. 577.

53 See William Maxwell, 'Parliamentary Reporters', *Time*, May 1889. Maxwell was a parliamentary reporter on the *Standard*. In his article he named the different shorthand systems being used by his contemporaries: '60 write Pitman's systems; 12, Taylor's; 6, Gurney's; 3, Lewis'; 1, Gurney-Taylor's; 1, Lowe's; 1, Byrom's; 1, Peachey's; 1, Everett's; 1, Meville-Bell's; 1, Mavor's; 1, Graham's (the American development of Pitman's); and 1, Janes'.' Pitman's went on to become even more popular and within a few decades it was virtually the only system in use in the press gallery. Later, as the intake changed, people arrived using Teeline, a system so basic that even university graduates could master it.

54 Report from the Select Committee on Parliamentary Reporting, 1878, HC 327; evidence from Ross, q. 562.

55 MacDonagh, *The Reporters' Gallery*, pp. 32–3.

56 *The Times*, 11 April 1908.

57 'Parliamentary Reporting', *Contemporary Review*, June 1877.

58 Memoir by Joseph Pullan, a parliamentary reporter on the *Daily News*, entitled 'Wright's Recollections'. (Wright was the long-serving gallery doorkeeper.) Pullan was the other person who responded to the appeal for press gallery reminiscences. He wrote his essay in 1890. HLRO PG/Misc/16.

59 Grant, *The Newspaper Press*, vol. 2, pp. 181–2.

60 Clarkson, 'Parliamentary Recollections'.

61 Clarkson names one perpetrator as Tom A, a reporter on the *Morning Herald*. 'Don't stop me, don't stop me, I'm in a cab,' Tom once told his fellow pedestrians: ibid.

62 MacDonagh, *The Reporters' Gallery*, p. 28.

63 Quoted ibid., p. 54.

64 Cooper, *An Editor's Retrospect*, pp. 80–1.

65 Report from the Select Committee of the House of Lords on Reporting, 1880, HL 66, evidence from Salisbury, q. 2.

66 Ibid., para. 5.

67 Reid, *Memoirs*, pp. 123–4.

68 Cooper, *An Editor's Retrospect*, p. 76.

69 Reid, *Memoirs*, p. 125.

70 Press gallery annual reports 1881 to 1931, HLRO, PG/M/10.

71 Ibid.

72 *Parliamentary Debates*, 4 May 1875, vol. 224, col. 52.

73 Ibid., col. 80.

74 Quoted in MacDonagh, *The Reporters' Gallery*, p. 390.

75 Report from the Select Committee on Parliamentary Reporting, 1878, HC 327, evidence from Gosset, q. 59.

76 Allocated as follows: *Standard*, 17; *The Times*, 16; *Morning Advertiser*, 15; *Daily Telegraph*, 12; *Morning Post*, 11; Press Association, 10; *Daily News*, 10; Central News, 7; *Daily Chronicle*, 7; *Globe*, 6; *Hansard*, 4; Sun and Central Press, 3; *Pall Mall Gazette*, 2; *Echo*, 2; Reuter's, 1. Ibid., evidence from Gosset, q. 43.

77 Report from the Select Committee on House of Commons (Arrangements), 1867, HC 451, evidence from Russell, q. 681.

78 Cooper, *An Editor's Retrospect*, p. 196.

79 In a short history of the press gallery written after the Second World War, William Barkley said that some reporters in the early 1880s were earning £3,000 a year (at least £140,000 today) from their freelance activities and that they owned 'some of the best shoots in Scotland'. Barkley started work in the Commons in the 1920s, when some of his colleagues would have been able to remember the old arrangements. His essay is in *The Press Gallery at Westminster*, a pamphlet produced when Graham Cawthorne was press gallery chairman in 1949/50. It was later revised and reissued.

80 R. G. Emery, 'Fifty Years in Parliament', *Institute of Journalists Journal*, Sept. 1932.

81 *The Times, The History of the Times: The Twentieth Century Test, 1884–1912*, pp. 11–12.

82 Report from the Select Committee on Parliamentary Reporting, 1878, HC 327, evidence from Ross, qs 519–96.

83 Arthur Baker, who was chief of the parliamentary staff on *The Times* from 1934 to 1955. Summaries were much the same then as they were in the nineteenth century. Baker also quotes Wickham Steed: 'A summary should be in the reporter's head, and not in his notebook.' *The House is Sitting* (Blandford Press, 1958), p. 163.

84 Cooper, *An Editor's Retrospect*, pp. 220–1.

85 William Maxwell, 'Parliamentary Reporters', *Time*, May 1889.

86 Report from the Select Committee on Parliamentary Debates, 1907, HC 237, evidence from McCullum, q. 1,028.

87 Lucy, *Sixty Years in the Wilderness*, p. 35.

88 *Daily News*, 3 May 1875.

89 *Parliamentary Debates*, 4 May 1875, vol. 224, col. 65.

Chapter 3: The Lobby Starts to Dominate

1 Centenary Luncheon booklet, 18 Jan. 1984, LR.

2 Margach, *The Anatomy of Power*, p. 125.

3 Entry for 1 March 1870: Denison, *Notes from My Journal*, p. 253.

4 Report from the Select Committee on Parliamentary Reporting, 1878, HC 327, evidence from Gosset, qs 60–4.

5 *Daily News*, 14 Feb. 1885. (One of a series of cuttings on this incident included in the press gallery archive: HLRO PG/Misc/16.)

6 Both quoted in *Pall Mall Gazette*, 14 Feb. 1885.

7 *Dundee Advertiser*, 16 Feb. 1885.

8 *Observer*, 15 Feb. 1885.

9 *Daily News*, 14 Feb. 1885.

10 *Manchester Examiner*, 17 Feb. 1885.

11 *Standard*, 18 Feb. 1885.

12 *Glasgow News*, 18 Feb. 1885.

13 Quoted in MacDonagh, *The Reporters' Gallery*, p. 59.

14 Although there are other places in the building suitable for buttonholing MPs. Paul Einzig, a lobby correspondent during the Second World War and afterwards, used to use the small lobby on the way to the Members' dining room. 'For some inscrutable reason none of my colleagues appreciated the great advantages of this strategic position, so I had it almost always entirely to myself. As a result I secured many an exclusive story through my talks with ministers' (Einzig, *In the Centre of Things*, p. 256). Since the opening of Portcullis House, some journalists have chosen to hang around in the atrium there in the search for stories.

15 Quoted in MacDonagh, *The Reporters' Gallery*, p. 60.

16 William Maxwell, 'Parliamentary Reporters', *Time*, May 1889.

17 Higginbottom, *The Vivid Life*, p. 148.

18 William Maxwell, 'Parliamentary Reporters', *Time*, May 1889.

19 MacDonagh, *The Reporters' Gallery*, p. 61.

20 Ibid., pp. 64–5.

21 Quoted in Masterman, *C. F. G. Masterman*, p. 78.

22 HWM, 'Pictures in Parliament', *Daily News*, 19 Feb. 1901.

23 Masterman, *C. F. G. Masterman*, p. 78.

24 Quoted in Havighurst, *Radical Journalist: H. W. Massingham*, p. 118.

25 Mackintosh, *Echoes of Big Ben*, p. 160.

26 Blumenfeld, *The Press in My Time*, p. 110.

27 See MacDonagh, *The Reporters' Gallery*, p. 10.

28 Quoted ibid., p. 11.

29 Quoted ibid.

30 Quoted ibid., p. 12.

31 Ibid., p. 12.

32 See letter from Walter Erskine, Assistant Serjeant at Arms, to Press Association, 8 Feb. 1916, press gallery minutes book 1915–19, HLRO PG/M/4.

33 *Daily News*, 2 Dec. 1919. (Cody concluded that Astor was wearing 'a simple black tailor-made costume, with a wide silk collar'.)

34 R. G. Emery, 'Fifty Years in Parliament', *Institute of Journalists Journal*, Sept. 1932.

35 Barkley, 'The Press Gallery', in *The Press Gallery at Westminster*.

36 Report from the Select Committee on Parliamentary Reporting, 1878, HC 327, evidence from Ross, q. 552.

37 *Daily Express*, 16 April 1929.

38 Blumenfeld, *The Press in My Time*, p. 112.

39 Ibid., p. 123.

40 See the analysis in Colin Seymour-Ure, 'Parliament and Mass Communications in the Twentieth Century', in Walkland (ed.), *The House of Commons in the Twentieth Century*, p. 564. It shows that parliamentary coverage (measured in the widest sense – including news, sketches, leaders and illustrations, as well as debate reports) filled 7.3 per cent of editorial space in newspapers in 1900, 7 per cent in 1912 and 7.1 per cent in 1924, but just 4.7 per cent in 1936. Seventeen newspapers were analysed.

41 Blumenfeld, *The Press in My Time*, pp. 112–13.

42 Cobbett and Wright fell out spectacularly. Cobbett blamed Wright for mismanaging the money and eight years later denounced him as a 'wretch unequalled in the annals of infamy' by whom he had been 'foully robbed'. Wright successfully sued for libel. See MacDonagh, *The Reporters' Gallery*, pp. 427–8.

43 In 1830 the official title became *Hansard's Parliamentary Debates*. It reverted to *Parliamentary Debates* in 1892.

44 *Daily News*, 8 Aug. 1853. Quoted in H. Donaldson Jordan, 'The Reports of Parliamentary Debates 1803–1908', *Economica*, Nov. 1931.

45 Report from the Select Committee on Parliamentary Debates, 1907, HC 239, evidence from Balfour, q. 2,341.

46 Ibid., evidence from Balfour, q. 2,368.

47 Sales were at their highest immediately at the end of the Second World War, when an average 7,111 copies a day were printed. In 2002 an average 2,387 copies a day were printed. Almost all of these go to official users, like MPs or government departments.

48   Report from the Select Committee on Parliamentary Reporting, 1878, HC 327, evidence from Ross, q. 592.
49   Margach, *The Anatomy of Power*, p. 137
50   Lobby journalists' committee, annual report 1926/27, LR.
51   Lobby journalists' committee, annual report 1929/30, LR.
52   Ibid.
53   Margach, *The Abuse of Power*, pp. 44–8.
54   Lobby journalists' deputation, LR.
55   Lobby journalists' committee, annual report 1930/1, LR.
56   Ibid.
57   Ibid.
58   Lobby journalists' committee, annual report 1931/2, LR.
59   Ibid.
60   Ibid.
61   Ibid.
62   Lobby journalists' committee, annual report 1932/3, LR.
63   Ibid.
64   Lobby journalists' committee, annual report 1935/6, written by Gerard Herlihy, secretary, April 1936, LR.
65   Harris, *Good and Faithful Servant*, p. 73.
66   Margach, *Anatomy of Power*, p. 138.
67   Margach, *Abuse of Power*, pp. 55–6.
68   Margach's phrase: ibid., p. 58.
69   *The Times*, 10 March 1939.
70   Quoted in Cockett, *Twilight of Truth*, p. 105.
71   *King-Hall Newsletter*, 17 March 1939, quoted in Cockett, *Twilight of Truth*, p. 125.
72   Cockett, *Twilight of Truth*, p. 1.
73   This might also be explained by the fact that more people started listening to news on the radio during the war. Before 1939 news was a marginal concern for the BBC.
74   Quoted in Cockett, *Twilight of Truth*, p. 27.
75   McDonald, *Struggles in War and Peace: History of The Times 1939–1966*, p. 20.
76   Quoted ibid., p. 20.
77   Letter from Charles Bateman, press gallery chairman, and Stanley Robinson, press gallery secretary, sent to all MPs, 27 July 1939, HLRO PG/Rob/3.
78   Barkley, *Reporter's Notebook*, p. 74.

Chapter 4: War, Deference and Responsibility

1   Baker, *The House is Sitting*, p. 73.
2   Further details are set out in a lengthy essay called 'The Press Gallery in the War Years' which was written by T. H. O'Donoghue, a member of the *Hansard* staff, for the press gallery's own records (PGR).
3   Letter from Trevor Smith, lobby chairman, to Neville Chamberlain, 21 Sept. 1939, PRO PREM 1/391.
4   Cockett, *Twilight of Truth*, p. 135.
5   Quoted in William Barkley, 'The Press Gallery', in *The Press Gallery at Westminster*.
6   Ibid.

7 Barkley, *Reporter's Notebook*, pp. 79–80.

8 Christiansen, *Headlines All My Life*, p. 114.

9 Report of the Royal Commission on the Press 1947–1949, 1949, Cm 7700, para. 543.

10 A copy of the document survives in the lobby files, dated May 1945.

11 Newcomers were expected to pick it up informally. 'There were no written rules. You just learned as you went along what you did and didn't do,' recalls Bill Deedes, who was in the lobby in 1937 (interview with Bill Deedes, 18 Dec. 2002).

12 For example, it is said that he was the only person outside the Cabinet or the senior ranks of the services who knew in advance about Churchill's visit to the Atlantic conference in 1941. He was also given advance notice of D-Day. See Seymour-Ure, *The Press, Politics and the Public*, p. 205.

13 *The Times*, 14 June 1971.

14 Letter from Norman Robson, acting lobby secretary, to Brig. Sir Charles Howard, Serjeant at Arms, 9 May 1946, LR.

15 Letter from Guy Eden, lobby secretary, to Sir Stafford Cripps, Chancellor, 10 Feb. 1949, LR.

16 Minutes of lobby committee meeting, 4 March 1947, LR.

17 Minutes of lobby committee meeting, 20 Sept. 1946, LR.

18 Report from the Select Committee on the Budget Disclosure, 1947/8, HC 20, memorandum from Guy Eden about the lobby, appendix 3, p. 52.

19 'Mr Eden made some emphatic remarks about the conduct of certain members of the lobby . . . conduct which he did not hesitate to describe as the most outrageous he had witnessed during his twenty-six years' experience of the lobby . . . He had taken such an unfavourable view of so much rudeness shown to those who were guests of the lobby that his first impulse was to resign his office.' Eden was lobby chairman that year. Minutes of lobby committee meeting, 10 Jan. 1951, LR.

20 Report from the Select Committee on the Budget Disclosure, 1947/8, HC 20, memorandum from Guy Eden about the lobby, appendix 3, p. 51.

21 Garry Allighan, 'Labour MP reveals his concept of how party news gets out', *World's Press News*, 3 April 1947.

22 Quoted in report from the committee of privileges, 1946/7, HC 138, para. 2.

23 Garry Allighan, 'Labour MP reveals his concept of how party news gets out', *World's Press News*, 3 April 1947.

24 Report from the committee of privileges, 1946/7, HC 138, para. 7.

25 Ibid., evidence from Allighan, q. 250.

26 Ibid., para. 8.

27 Ibid., para. 16.

28 Ibid., para. 18.

29 Ibid., paras 23–4.

30 *Hansard*, 30 Oct. 1947, vol. 443, cols 1,096–9.

31 Ibid., col. 1,162.

32 Quoted in appendix to report from the committee of privileges, 1946/7, HC 142. Walkden made his statement on 4 August.

33 Ibid., paras 4–5.

34 *Hansard*, 30 Oct. 1947, vol. 443, col. 1,197.

35 The committee argued that although two cases of misconduct by MPs had come to light in the course of its inquiry, there was no evidence to justify 'the general charges made by Mr Allighan' and that those charges were therefore 'wholly unfounded'. Report from the committee of privileges, 1946/7, HC 138, para. 22.

36 *Hansard*, 30 Oct. 1947, vol. 443, col. 1,228.

37 Margach, *The Abuse of Power*, p. 97.

38 *Hansard*, 30 Oct. 1947, vol. 443, cols 1,232–4.
39 Report from the committee of privileges, 1946/7, HC 138, para 10.
40 Oakley, *Inside Track*, p. 87.
41 Or sixty-eight, if you include the headline, the strap and the standfirst.
42 Pimlott, *Hugh Dalton*, p. 524.
43 Report from the Select Committee on the Budget Disclosure, 1947/8, HC 20, para. 7. This sets out Dalton's and Carvel's respective recollections of the conversation. There were minor discrepancies, but broadly they agreed on what was said.
44 Ibid., para. 7.
45 Pimlott, *Hugh Dalton*, p. 526.
46 Report from the Select Committee on the Budget Disclosure, 1947/8, HC 20, para. 16.
47 Ibid., para. 15.
48 Ibid., para. 18.
49 *Hansard*, 13 Nov. 1947, vol. 444, col. 551.
50 Pimlott, *Hugh Dalton*, p. 544.
51 Report from the Select Committee on the Budget Disclosure, 1947/8, HC 20, para. 21.
52 Ibid., para. 17.
53 Ibid., para. 20.
54 'My greatest mistake: Piers Morgan', *Independent*, 16 April 2002.
55 MacDonagh, *The Reporters' Gallery*, p. 298.
56 Report of the Royal Commission on the Press 1947–1949, 1949, Cm 7700, para. 440.
57 Until 1956, when rationing was scrapped, papers were on average one-third the size they were in the 1930s. But no similar reduction was applied to the cover price and profits soared.
58 Report of the Royal Commission on the Press 1947–1949, 1949, Cm 7700, para. 442.
59 The letter appeared on 9 July 1951. Quoted in Barkley, *Reporter's Notebook*, pp. 170–1.
60 *Sunday Express*, 16 Dec. 1956.
61 Second report from the committee of privileges, 1956/7, HC 38, para. 10.
62 Margach, *Abuse of Power*, p. 89.
63 *Hansard*, 23 Feb. 1955, vol. 537, col. 1,277.
64 *Hansard*, 30 Nov. 1955, vol. 546, col. 2,330.
65 *Hansard*, 30 Nov. 1955, vol. 546, cols 2,358–62.
66 Report from the committee of privileges, 1948/9, HC 261.
67 This was particularly unfortunate, for example, for those wanting to cover the select committee on the Obscene Publications Bill in 1957. See '"Ban" on reporting of select committee proceedings", *The Times*, 29 May 1958.
68 MacDonagh, *The Reporters' Gallery*, p. 411. In 1878 the Commons voted to exclude the press when it was debating the murder of the Earl of Leitrim in Donegal. Irish MPs claimed that he was shot not for political reasons, but because he had debauched the wives and daughters of his tenants, and the House decided that in the interests of decency it should discuss the matter in private.
69 Memorandum from Fife Clark to Eden's private office, 28 June 1955, PRO PREM 11/975.
70 Margach, *Abuse of Power*, p. 89.
71 Quoted ibid., p. 69.
72 Memorandum from Fife Clark to Churchill's private office, 29 Oct. 1954, PRO PREM 11/732.
73 Hill, *Both Sides of the Hill*, p. 205.
74 Einzig, *In the Centre of Things*, p. 198.
75 Hill, *Both Sides of the Hill*, p. 204.
76 Evans, *Downing Street Diary*, p. 49.
77 See minutes of lobby committee meeting, 16 Oct. 1941, LR.

78 Quoted in Tunstall, *The Westminster Lobby Correspondents*, p. 125.

79 Quoted ibid, pp. 126–7.

80 Part of the problem was that Wood wrote up what he had learned in a column, but Sir William Haley, *The Times*'s editor, chose to use it on the front page as a story. Ian Aitken used to say when he was the *Guardian*'s political editor that certain stories attract the truth, and that certain stories repel it. Wood's scoop is a classic example of a story that may have been perfectly true when it was written, but which triggered its own cancellation as soon as it appeared in print.

81 Minutes of lobby committee meeting, 22 June 1959.

82 See Barkley, *Reporter's Notebook*, p. 142.

83 In 1955 the lobby committee was reminded at one meeting 'of an occasion on which a phrase used by Lord Swinton at a lobby meeting had been reproduced in quotation marks in a newspaper the next day – although without attribution – and that this had been made the subject of a complaint': minutes of lobby committee meeting, 18 July 1955, LR.

84 Report of the tribunal appointed to inquire into the Vassall case and related matters, 1963, Cm 2009 and 2037 (minutes of evidence), evidence from Waller, q. 2,980.

85 Ibid., evidence from Clark, qs 1,454–5.

86 Ibid., report, para. 273.

87 Ibid., evidence from Clark, q. 1,462.

88 See, for example, John Sergeant's memoirs. 'John Cole used to remind me that the more significant a story, the more important it is to leave in some "weasel words". These can be introduced so as not to interrupt the flow, and when you wake up worrying in the middle of the night you will be glad they were there. Phrases such as "at this stage" or "from what we can gather at the moment" or even the all-purpose "it seems to me"': Sergeant, *Give Me Ten Seconds*, p. 230.

Chapter 5: Secrecy and Openness: The 1960s and 1970s

1   It became a corporation only on 1 January 1927.

2   Quoted in Peter Hill, 'Parliamentary Broadcasting: from TWIW to YIP', *British Journalism Review*, 1993, vol. 4, no. 4.

3   When the BBC was set up, the Newspaper Proprietors Association and the Newspaper Society successfully lobbied for restrictions on its newsgathering activities because they wanted to protect their own industry. As a result, the BBC was not allowed to broadcast bulletins until 7 p.m.

4   Quoted in Peter Hill, 'Parliamentary Broadcasting: from TWIW to YIP', *British Journalism Review*, 1993, vol. 4, no. 4.

5   Ibid.

6   Quoted ibid.

7   *Hansard*, 24 Nov. 1966, vol. 736, col. 1,607.

8   Ibid., col. 1,666.

9   Minutes of lobby committee meeting, 21 Oct. 1969, LR.

10 David Wood, 'The Parliamentary Lobby', *The Political Quarterly*, July–Oct. 1965, vol. 36, no. 3.

11 One reason for the expansion was that in the early 1960s Sunday newspapers acquired full lobby rights. Previously their correspondents had been allowed only limited access to lobby facilities.

12 Ronald Butt, written evidence to the press gallery inquiry 1963/4, HLRO, PG/Misc/4.

13 Transcript of interview with Harold Wilson conducted as part of the press gallery inquiry 1963/4, HLRO PG/Misc/4.

14 Report of the press gallery working party, *Partners in Parliament*, 1964, p. 37.

15 Guy Eden, written evidence to press gallery inquiry, 1963/4, HLRO, PG/Misc/4.

16 Report of the press gallery working party, *Partners in Parliament*, 1964, p. 65.

17 Annie's is the Commons bar reserved exclusively for the use of MPs and lobby correspondents. The original was destroyed by bombing during the war and it was not reopened in 1945 because Attlee's teetotal Chief Whip, William Whiteley, was supposedly worried about his MPs being, as Garry Allighan put it, 'lubricated into loquacity'.

18 Transcript of interview with Sir Barnett Cocks conducted as part of the press gallery inquiry 1963/4, HLRO PG/Misc/4.

19 Robert Carvel, written evidence to press gallery inquiry 1963/4, HLRO, PG/Misc/4.

20 Guy Eden, written evidence to press gallery inquiry 1963/4, HLRO, PG/Misc/4.

21 *Hansard*, 16 July 1971, vol. 821, col. 928.

22 Ibid., col. 994.

23 David Butler, 'Political reporting in Britain', *The Listener*, 15 Aug. 1963.

24 Anthony Howard, 'The role of the lobby correspondent', *The Listener*, 21 Jan. 1965.

25 Ian Waller, 'The "lobby" and beyond', *Encounter*, June 1965.

26 David Wood, 'The Parliamentary Lobby', *The Political Quarterly*, July–Oct. 1965, vol. 36, no. 3.

27 Ibid.

28 Speech at Lloyd memorial home dinner, Odhams, 6 Dec. 1962. Copy included in written evidence to press gallery inquiry, 1963/4, HLRO, PG/Misc/4.

29 Unnamed aide, quoted in Pimlott, *Harold Wilson*, p. 443.

30 'Wilson praises Commons press men', *Daily Mail*, 22 May 1965.

31 Ian Waller, 'The "lobby" and beyond', *Encounter*, June 1965.

32 Quoted in Castle, *The Castle Diaries 1964–1976*, p. 9.

33 Another reason for Howard's departure was that the *Sunday Times* lost its appetite for publishing his Whitehall stories. As part of the Government's attempts to close Howard down, it was suggested that a motion might be tabled in the House of Lords criticising Lord Thomson for the unconstitutional behaviour of his paper. (Whitehall reporting was deemed unconstitutional because civil servants could not answer back.) The threat was never realised, but it may have influenced attitudes at the paper.

34 See Margach, *The Abuse of Power*, p. 145.

35 Originally newspapers did not have political editors. Many of them created the post in the 1960s as a way of getting round the Government's anti-inflation wage controls.

36 Watkins, *A Short Walk Down Fleet Street*, p. 169. When Beloff left the lobby in 1976, Watkins joined the *Observer* to take over writing the political column. Beloff had combined the column with reporting.

37 See Margach, *Abuse of Power*, p. 148.

38 Marcia Williams, *Inside Number 10*, p. 228.

39 Minutes of lobby committee meeting, 22 May 1968, LR.

40 Extract from a speech delivered in Bath. Included in evidence collected by press gallery inquiry 1963/4, HLRO, PG/Misc/4.

41 'The Prime Minister and the press,' *Observer*, 15 May 1969.

42 Minutes of lobby committee meeting, 19 June 1969, LR.

43 Quoted in Margach, *Abuse of Power*, p. 160. Heath said it in 1966.

44 Quoted in Cockerell et al., *Sources Close to the Prime Minister*, p. 125.

45 Letter from Donald Maitland to Keith Renshaw, 24 Nov. 1970, LR.

46 Ibid.

47 Keith Renshaw, 'The Lobby and Attributable Briefings', 10 Nov. 1970, LR.

48 Minutes of meeting of lobby journalists, 2 Dec. 1970, LR.

49 Ibid.

50 Interview with Donald Maitland, 13 Sept. 2002.
51 Minutes of meeting of lobby journalists, 9 Nov. 1971, LR.
52 Gordon Greig, 'The million pound Queen', *Daily Mail*, 21 Oct. 1971.
53 Quoted in second report from the committee of privileges, *Complaint Concerning an Article in the Daily Mail Newspaper of 21st Oct. 1971*, 1971/2, HC 180, para. 1.
54 Ibid., evidence from Greig, q. 214.
55 Ibid., evidence from Greig, q. 225.
56 Ibid., evidence from Greig, q. 235.
57 Ibid., appendix 2, p. xii.
58 Ibid., paras 9–10.
59 Those in favour of suspension were: Hugh Fraser, Patrick Gordon-Walker, Duncan Sandys and Strauss. Those against were Sir Peter Rawlinson (the Attorney General), Bill Deedes, Sir Elwyn Jones and Fred Peart.
60 *Weekly Law Reports*, 2 Nov. 1973.
61 Interview with Frank Johnson, 26 July 2002.
62 First report from the committee of privileges, *Complaint Concerning an Article in The Economist Newspaper of 11th Oct. 1975*, 1975/6, HC 22, para. 5.
63 Ibid., para. 4.
64 *Hansard*, 16 Dec. 1975, vol. 902, cols 1,304–10.
65 Ibid., col. 1,134.
66 Ibid., col. 1,317.
67 Ibid., col. 1,331.
68 Ibid., col. 1,352.
69 Ibid., cols 1,313–14.
70 Marcia Williams, *Inside Number 10*, pp. 223, 229.
71 Minutes of lobby committee meeting, 4 Feb. 1970, LR.
72 Interview with Joe Haines, 13 Dec. 2002.
73 Letter from Joe Haines to John Egan, 19 June 1975, LR.
74 Tom McCaffrey, written evidence to lobby inquiry 1986/7, LR.
75 Interview with Tom McCaffrey, 30 Aug. 2002.
76 Callaghan said that there had been no offensive personal references to Ramsbotham in the official briefing and that it was 'impossible to prove or disprove' what McCaffrey had said afterwards: *Hansard*, 16 May 1977, vol. 932, col. 34.
77 Ibid., col. 40.
78 Minutes of special lobby meeting, 17 May 1977, LR.
79 Minutes of special lobby meeting, 24 May 1977, LR.
80 'No. 10 puts lobby on the record', *The Times*, 19 July 1977.
81 *Hansard*, 19 Oct. 1972, vol. 843, cols 467–8.
82 Ibid., cols 512–18.
83 Ibid., col. 534.
84 Ibid., col. 559.
85 *Hansard*, 24 Feb. 1975, vol. 887, cols 136–7.
86 Ibid., col. 148–9.
87 *Hansard*, 8 March 1976, vol. 907, col. 126.
88 *Hansard*, 16 March 1976, vol. 907, cols 1,132–4.
89 Ibid., cols 1,161–2.
90 Thomas, *George Thomas, Mr Speaker*, p. 185.
91 Sergeant, *Give Me Ten Seconds*, p. 215.

Chapter 6: Secrecy and Openness: The 1980s

1   The grace was delivered by the Revd David Bradford, a lobby journalist on the *Scotsman* in the 1970s who, after leaving journalism for religion, functioned for some years as the press gallery's honorary chaplain.
2   Thatcher's speech was included in a pamphlet printed to commemorate the lunch, LR.
3   Interview with Peter Hennessy, 8 Aug. 2002.
4   Peter Hennessy, 'The Quality of Political Journalism', speech to the Royal Society of Arts, 1 April 1987.
5   Cockerell et al., *Sources Close to the Prime Minister*, p. 33.
6   Ibid.
7   Interview with Peter Hennessy, 8 Aug. 2002.
8   Interview with Ian Aitken, 21 Nov. 2002.
9   Interview with Peter Hennessy, 8 Aug. 2002.
10 Interview with Glyn Mathias, 19 Dec. 2002.
11 *Hansard*, 23 June 1980, vol. 987, col. 22.
12 Will Ellsworth-Jones, 'Let them take note of us, says MP', *Sunday Times*, 29 June 1980.
13 Letter from Peter Jennings, Deputy Serjeant at Arms, to William Russell, press gallery secretary, 21 Dec. 1982, PGR.
14 First report from the committee of privileges, *Report in Times Newspaper Regarding Home Affairs Committee*, 1984/5, HC 308, para. 10.
15 Second report from the committee of privileges, *Premature Disclosure of Proceedings of Select Committees*, 1984/5, HC 555, evidence from Peter Preston and James Naughtie, q. 196.
16 Ibid., para. 43.
17 Ibid., para. 51.
18 Richard Evans, 'Nuclear industry criticised as primitive by MPs', *The Times*, 16 Dec. 1985.
19 Second special report from the environment committee, *Leak of Draft Report on Radioactive Waste*, 1985/6, HC 211, para. 17.
20 First report from the committee of privileges, *Leak of Draft Report of Environment Committee on Radioactive Waste*, 1985/6, HC 376, evidence from Wilson, q. 13.
21 Ibid., para. 19.
22 Ibid., para. 25.
23 *Hansard*, 20 May 1986, vol. 98, cols 297–8.
24 Ibid., col. 318.
25 Ibid., cols 304–5.
26 He was not. Spencer Leigh Hughes was a chairman of the lobby before becoming a Liberal MP in 1910. He was also secretary of the gallery, but was 'hurled from office' for not respecting the gallery's stuffier conventions. Hughes, *Press, Platform and Parliament*, p. 24.
27 *Hansard*, 20 May 1986, vol. 98, col. 315.
28 Ibid., col. 300.
29 Ibid., col. 314.
30 Ibid., col. 302.
31 Interview with Richard Evans, 16 Sept. 2002.
32 Peter Hennessy, 'The case of the visible spokesman: the lobby reforms itself', *New Statesman*, 3 Oct. 1986.
33 In fact Ingham got it wrong. The catchphrase belonged to another character, Mona Lott.

34 Reported in most national newspapers, with glee, 13 May 1986.
35 Ingham gets most indignant about the charge. In *Kill the Messenger*, his autobiography, he says that his accusers have identified no more than half a dozen occasions on which he was supposed to have briefed against ministers and that, given his extensive dealings with the press, this amounts to 'a "rubbishing rate" of little more than one per 6,000 briefings': Ingham, *Kill the Messenger*, p. 320.
36 Ibid., p. 335.
37 See Harris, *Good and Faithful Servant*, p. 151.
38 Ingham, *Kill the Messenger*, p. 196.
39 Peter Preston, *Guardian* evidence to lobby inquiry, 20 Nov. 1986, LR.
40 Joe Haines, evidence to lobby inquiry, LR.
41 Quoted in Harris, *Good and Faithful Servant*, p. 92.
42 Ibid., p. 92.
43 Jones, *Soundbites and Spin Doctors*, p. 87.
44 Tom Utley, 'Number 10 may rue the day they made the press do its job', *Daily Telegraph*, 4 May 2002.
45 Robert Harris, 'Confessions of a lobby correspondent', *Sunday Times*, 14 Jan. 1990.
46 Jon Hibbs, submission to lobby inquiry, 18 Nov. 1986, LR.
47 Ian Aitken, submission to lobby inquiry, LR.
48 Letter from Bernard Ingham to David Hughes, 24 Nov. 1986, LR.
49 Letter from Bernard Ingham to David Hughes, 28 Nov. 1986, LR.
50 Letter from Bernard Ingham to David Hughes, 5 Dec. 1986, LR.
51 Letter from Bernard Ingham to David Hughes, 6 Nov. 1987, LR.
52 Ingham, *Kill the Messenger*, p. 201.
53 Ingham's response might have had something to do with the fact that the author of the report was one Anthony Bevins. Letter from Bernard Ingham to John Fisher, lobby secretary, 22 Nov. 1982, LR.
54 Nicholas Comfort, 'Kinnock faces snub over ban on reporters', *Daily Telegraph*, 30 Jan. 1986.
55 The lobby's decision to act collectively for the sake of its members but not for print workers did not go down well with the Labour leader. 'It would appear that solidarity in the profession is not dead, merely selective,' he wrote back to Moncrieff, 29 Jan. 1986, LR.
56 That is not to say that individuals in the press gallery were necessarily biased against Labour, because reporters do not always share the views of their newspapers. When Jeremy Tunstall investigated the political allegiances of journalists in the late 1960s, he concluded: 'A general predisposition toward "moderate" and centre political views is noticeable among most – but not all – lobby correspondents': *The Westminster Lobby Correspondents*, p. 36. William Maxwell probably got it about right when he was writing on this subject in 1889. 'The truth seems to be that reporters acquire a distaste for active politics without losing any of the keen interest with which they watch the movement of parties. The Conservatism and Radicalism of the gallery have an unmistakable flavour of cynicism,' he said: William Maxwell, 'Parliamentary Reporters', *Time*, May 1889.
57 After Kinnock's meeting with the President, Reagan's press secretary, Marlin Fitzwater, gave a briefing rubbishing Labour's defence policy. Fitzwater's account of the Reagan–Kinnock meeting made it sound more frosty than it really was, and even though the outcome was the same – public denunciation of Labour – Campbell (one reporter who did not acquire a distaste for active politics) thought that his colleagues should have done more to expose the White House's apparent duplicity. These days he would probably criticise any journalist focusing on such detail instead of the big picture for being obsessed with 'processology'. *New Statesman*, 3 April 1987.
58 Oborne, *Alastair Campbell*, pp. 112–19.
59 Watkins, *A Short Walk Down Fleet Street*, p. 66.

60 Obituary by Colin Welch, *Daily Telegraph*, 28 Dec. 1971.
61 Watkins, *A Short Walk Down Fleet Street*, p. 66.
62 *Hansard*, 9 Feb. 1988, vol. 127, col. 183.
63 The Lords voted in favour of a public television experiment on 8 December 1983. When the chamber was first televised for the public on 23 January 1985, the Earl of Stockton (the former Prime Minister, Harold Macmillan) stole the limelight with a virtuoso demolition of the Government's monetarist economic policies.
64 Memorandum from John Deans, press gallery secretary, to the Commons accommodation and administration subcommittee, 17 July 1989, PGR.
65 *Hansard*, 21 Nov. 1989, vol. 162, col. 7.
66 Andrew Rawnsley, 'History, kilts and an implausible leading lady', *Guardian*, 22 Nov. 1989.
67 Interview with Adam Boulton, 19 Dec. 2002.
68 His speech, 'Beyond Spin: Government and the Media', is printed in *Broadcasting Politics*, a Fabian Society pamphlet published in March 1999.
69 Steve Richards, *Soundbite Politics*, Reuter Foundation Paper 14 (Green College, Oxford), 1995.
70 Oakley, *Inside Track*, p. 195.
71 Marr, *Ruling Britannia*, p. 298.
72 *Hansard* Society annual lecture, 22 May 2002.
73 Speech to press gallery lunch, 12 June 2002.

Chapter 7: Sleaze, Spin and Cynicism

1 Speech to press gallery lunch, 23 April 1945, HLRO PG/Rob/2.
2 Jack Straw, 'Ask no questions, hear more lies', *Independent*, 24 Oct. 1993.
3 Bob Franklin, 'Keeping It "Bright, Light and Trite": Changing Newspaper Reporting of Parliament', *Parliamentary Affairs*, April 1996, vol. 49, no. 2. His conclusions specifically relate to changes between 1990 and 1994, and are based on an analysis of coverage in the *Guardian*, *The Times* and the *Daily Mirror*.
4 Committee on Standards in Public Life, *Standards in Public Life*, 1995, Cm 2850–1 and 2, evidence from Simon Jenkins, q. 24.
5 See Hastings, *Editor*, p. 179.
6 The rule originated not because ministers were so stupid that they needed a full two weeks to come up with answers to tabled questions, but because questions were originally taken in the order in which they were tabled, and if MPs put them down far in advance, they could guarantee being at the top of the list on a particular day. The system was eventually changed so that questions were taken in a random order. But by then the practice of tabling them early had stuck.
7 Blumenfeld, *The Press in My Time*, p. 124.
8 Bagehot, *The English Constitution*, pp. 100–1.
9 Ibid., p. 125.
10 MPs have a much broader range of geographical and professional experience than London journalists, and they probably have more contact with the public. Often they have greater specialist knowledge. In these respects they are much better qualified to interrogate ministers. The big advantage journalists have is that when they hold the Government to account, they can do so very publicly, with an audience or readership of millions. If being accountable means being made to look stupid if you get something wrong, the front page of the *Sun* has more clout than an opposition politician at the despatch box (although there is, of course, nothing to stop the two working in tandem).
11 Interview with David Hencke, 1 Aug. 2002.

12 Interview with John Deans, 2 July 2002.
13 Jill Sherman, 'Meal that left a nasty aftertaste for Labour', *The Times*, 14 Sept. 1996. Sherman was also at Luigi's, sitting next to Kinnock.
14 Abdela, *A Strange Old Mother*.
15 *Hansard*, 23 Oct. 2000, vol. 355, col. 10.
16 See e.g. Quentin Letts, 'How fares Parliament's answer to Rab C. Nesbitt?' (15 Feb. 2001), 'An astonished silence and a Speaker out of his depth' (7 Feb. 2002) or 'Class hatred and a second rate speaker' (12 Feb. 2002), all in the *Daily Mail*.
17 Simon Carr, 'Braddocks gassed and the Speaker slumped in the Commons necropolis', *Independent*, 12 June 2002.
18 Except Martin himself, who sent a flunkey to reprimand Carr. Carr made fun of the episode in his sketch the following day.
19 Quoted in Peter Hennessy, 'The Quality of Political Journalism', speech to the Royal Society of Arts, 1 April 1987.
20 Bill Hagerty, 'Cap'n Spin Does Lose his Rag!', *British Journalism Review*, vol. 11, no. 2, 2000.
21 Report of the working group on the Government Information Service, Nov. 1997, paras 26–7.
22 Ibid., para. 27.
23 Michael White, 'Inside story of a Campbell briefing', *Guardian*, 15 March 2000.
24 Quoted in Jones, *The Control Freaks*, p. 193.
25 Alastair Campbell, letter to the editor, *Daily Telegraph*, 15 March 2000.
26 Alan Rusbridger, 'Spin-doctors: no more ghostly voices', *Guardian*, 15 July 2000.
27 Quoted in Jones, *Sultans of Spin*, pp. 129–30.
28 Quoted in Raymond Snoddy, 'Brown's advisers tell how they manipulated the media', *The Times*, 26 Sept. 1997. The programme was shown after Labour came to power, but Whelan made the comment to the cameras in January, before the election. Brown was delivering an important economic speech and Whelan was explaining why, to preserve the element of surprise, he persuaded reporters in advance not to expect an announcement about tax policy, when in fact that was exactly what they got.
29 For details see Jones, *Control Freaks*, pp. 133–8.
30 *Hansard*, 26 July 2000, vol. 354, col. 1,114.
31 Even though one of the journalists gave him a copy (it was Michael Heseltine's statement on coal on 15 July 1992), Benn still blamed the press for the arrangement. 'The media just think they run the place, and if I had time I would make an issue of it in the House, because I really do not see why journalists should get a statement to be made to the House before Members do': Benn, *Free At Last!*, p. 122.
32 Interview with Charles Moore, 20 Nov. 2002.
33 In its report, the modernisation committee said the procedure was useful to MPs who wanted to call a snap vote but it recommended that, instead of spying strangers, MPs should be able to call an immediate division by moving that the House proceed to the next business. When MPs debated the report, Ann Taylor, Leader of the Commons, said there were unforeseen problems with the committee's recommendation: it could result in business being lost, and it could not be used when there was no next business. Instead she settled on the 'sitting in private' solution.
34 Select Committee on Modernisation of the House of Commons, *Modernisation of the House of Commons: A Reform Programme*, 2001/2, HC 1168-I, para. 5.
35 *Hansard*, 29 Oct. 2002, vol. 391, col. 700.
36 Barrie Clement and Andrew Grice, 'Use attack to bury bad news', *Independent*, 9 Oct. 2001.
37 Quoted in Paul Eastham, 'For 118 years, ministers have faced scrutiny by the lobby system. Yesterday, at barely a moment's notice, Blair axed it', *Daily Mail*, 3 May 2002.

38 Quoted in Tom Baldwin, 'No. 10 plans curbs on media pack', *The Times*, 1 June 2002.
39 Quoted in Claire Cozens, 'Labour trying to hijack news agenda, warns Sky chief', Guardian Unlimited website, 16 Oct. 2002.

Conclusion: 'Mutual Suspicion and Constant Hostility'

1 'What a Member of Parliament says is now faithfully reproduced in the Official Report as he said it . . . That being so, may it not now be said that the evolution of the Reporter's Gallery is completed?' his book concluded. MacDonagh, *The Reporters' Gallery* , p. 445.
2 Ibid., p. viii.
3 Peter Mandelson on *The Talk Show with Andrew Marr*, BBC Four, 9 April 2002. Transcript from BBC.
4 Quoted in Harris, *Good and Faithful Servant* , p. 176.
5 Livery lecture, 5 Feb. 1986. Quoted in Ingham, *Kill the Messenger*, p. 366.
6 Bill Hagerty, 'Cap'n Spin Does Lose his Rag!', *British Journalism Review*, vol. 11, no. 2, 2000.
7 Ibid.
8 To save hostile reviewers the bother, an electronic cuttings search will show that all of these phrases have appeared in stories that also include the words 'by Andrew Sparrow'. There are worse embarrassments, too. I would not for a moment claim to be exempt from the shortcomings of lobby journalism.
9 Philip Cowley, '111 Not Out: The Press and the 1995 Conservative Leadership Contest', *Talking Politics*, Spring 1996, vol. 8, no. 3.
10 'Won' by the *Daily Telegraph*, for a story suggesting that Paddy Ashdown could become Northern Ireland Secretary. The first prize went to the *Independent*, for calling for John Reid to become a member of the Cabinet when he was already in it, and the second prize went to the *Financial Times*, for tipping Frank Dobson to become Leader of the Commons.
11 The following section of the editorial is better known: 'The first duty of the press is to obtain the earliest and most correct intelligence of the events of the time, and instantly, by disclosing them, to make them the common property of the nation. The statesman collects his information secretly and by secret means; he keeps back even the current intelligence of the day with ludicrous precautions, until diplomacy is beaten in the race with publicity. The press lives by disclosures; whatever passes into its keeping becomes a part of the knowledge and the history of our times.' *The Times*, 6 Feb. 1852.
12 Quoted in Matthew (ed.), *The Gladstone Diaries*, vol. 13, p. 394.
13 Margach, *The Anatomy of Power*, p. 129.
14 Peter Hennessy, 'The Quality of Political Journalism', speech to the Royal Society of Arts, 1 April 1987.
15 Interview with Peter Hennessy, 8 Aug. 2002.

BIBLIOGRAPHY

Abbot, Charles (Lord Colchester), *The Diary and Correspondence of Charles Abbot, Lord Colchester* (John Murray, 1861)

Abdela, Lesley, *A Strange Old Mother* (Charter 88, 1994)

Ackroyd, Peter, *Dickens* (Minerva, 1991)

Almon, John, *Memoirs of John Almon* (1790)

Bagehot, Walter, *The English Constitution* (Oxford University Press, 2001; first publ. 1867)

Baker, Arthur, *The House is Sitting* (Blandford Press, 1958)

Barkley, William, *Reporter's Notebook* (Oldbourne, 1959)

Benn, Tony, *Free At Last!* (Hutchinson, 2002)

Black, Jeremy, *The English Press, 1621–1861* (Sutton Publishing, 2001)

Blumenfeld, R. D., *The Press in My Time* (Rich & Cowan, 1933)

Bond, Maurice, *Guide to the Records of Parliament* (HMSO, 1971)

Boswell, James, *Life of Johnson* (Oxford University Press, 1980; first publ. 1791)

Butt, Ronald, *The Power of Parliament* (Constable, 1967)

Castle, Barbara, *The Castle Diaries, 1964–1976* (Papermac, 1990)

Cavendish, Henry, *Sir Henry Cavendish's Debates of the House of Commons* (1841)

Christiansen, Arthur, *Headlines All My Life* (Heinemann, 1961)

Cockerell, Michael, *Live from Number 10* (Faber & Faber, 1988)

Cockerell, Michael, Hennessy, Peter and Walker, David, *Sources Close to the Prime Minister* (Papermac, 1985; first publ. 1984)

Cockett, Richard, *Twilight of Truth* (Weidenfeld & Nicolson, 1989)

Cole, John, *As It Seemed To Me* (Weidenfeld & Nicolson, 1995)

Cooper, Charles, *An Editor's Retrospect* (Macmillan, 1896)

Curran, James, and Seaton, Jean, *Power without Responsibility* (Routledge, 1997)

Deedes, W. F., *Dear Bill* (Macmillan, 1997)

Denison, John Evelyn (Viscount Ossington), *Notes from My Journal* (John Murray, 1900)

Dickens, Charles, *David Copperfield* (Penguin, 1996; first publ. 1850)

Einzig, Paul, *In the Centre of Things* (Hutchinson, 1960)

Engel, Matthew, *Tickle the Public* (Indigo, 1997)

Evans, Harold, *Downing Street Diary* (Hodder & Stoughton, 1981)

Fielding, K. J. (ed.), *The Speeches of Charles Dickens* (Oxford University Press, 1960)

Forster, John, *The Life of Charles Dickens* (Chapman & Hall, 1872)

Frank, Joseph, *The Beginnings of the English Newspaper* (Harvard University Press, 1961)

Gardiner, George, *A Bastard's Tale* (Aurum, 1999)

Goldie, Grace Wyndham, *Facing the Nation* (Bodley Head, 1977)

Grant, James, *The Newspaper Press* (Tinsley Brothers, 1871)

Haig, Robert, *The Gazetteer, 1735–1797* (Southern Illinois University Press, 1960)

Hall, Samuel Carter, *Retrospect of a Long Life* (Richard Bentley & Son, 1883)

Hardcastle, the Hon. Mrs (ed.), *Life of John, Lord Campbell* (John Murray, 1881)

Harris, Robert, *Good and Faithful Servant* (Faber & Faber, 1990)

Hastings, Max, *Editor* (Macmillan, 2002)

Havighurst, Alfred F., *Radical Journalist: H. W. Massingham* (Cambridge University Press, 1974)

Hawkins, Sir John, *Life of Dr Samuel Johnson* (1787)

Hazlitt, William, *Collected Works of William Hazlitt*, vol. 10 (J. M. Dent, 1904)

Higginbottom, Frederick, *The Vivid Life* (Simpkin Marshall, 1934)

Hill, Charles (Lord Hill of Luton), *Both Sides of the Hill* (Heinemann, 1964)

History and Proceedings of the House of Commons from the Restoration to the Present Time, vol. 10 (Richard Chandler, 1742)

Hoover, Benjamin Beard, *Samuel Johnson's Parliamentary Reporting* (University of California Press, 1953)

Hughes, Spencer Leigh, *Press, Platform and Parliament* (Nisbet, 1918)

Ingham, Bernard, *Kill the Messenger* (HarperCollins, 1991)

Jones, Nicholas, *The Control Freaks* (Politico's, 2002)

Jones, Nicholas, *Soundbites and Spin Doctors* (Cassell, 1995)

Jones, Nicholas, *Sultans of Spin* (Orion, 2000)

Jones, Stanley, *Hazlitt: A Life* (Oxford University Press, 1989)

Law, William, *Our Hansard* (Sir Isaac Pitman & Sons, 1950)

Leigh, David and Vulliamy, Ed, *Sleaze* (Fourth Estate, 1997)

Lindsay, T. F., *Parliament from the Press Gallery* (Macmillan, 1967)

Lucy, Henry, *Sixty Years in the Wilderness* (Smith, Elder, 1909)

McDonald, Iverach, *Struggles in War and Peace: History of The Times 1939–1966* (*Times* Books, 1984)

MacDonagh, Michael, *The Reporters' Gallery* (Hodder and Stoughton, 1920; first publ. 1913)

Mackintosh, Sir Alexander, *Echoes of Big Ben* (Jarrolds, 1945)

Maitland, Donald, *Diverse Times, Sundry Places* (Alpha Press, 1996)

Margach, James, *The Abuse of Power* (W. H. Allen, 1978)

Margach, James, *The Anatomy of Power* (W. H. Allen, 1979)

Marr, Andrew, *Ruling Britannia* (Michael Joseph, 1995)

Masterman, Lucy, *C. F. G. Masterman* (Nicholson & Watson, 1939)

Matthew, H. C. G. (ed.), *The Gladstone Diaries*, vol. 13 (Oxford University Press, 1994)

Oakley, Robin, *Inside Track* (Corgi, 2002; first publ. 2001)

Oborne, Peter, *Alastair Campbell* (Aurum, 1999)

Ogilvy-Webb, Marjorie, *The Government Explains* (Allen & Unwin, 1965)

Pares, Richard and Taylor, A. J. P. (eds), *Essays Presented to Sir Lewis Namier* (Macmillan, 1956)

Pimlott, Ben, *Harold Wilson* (HarperCollins, 1993)

Pimlott, Ben, *Hugh Dalton* (HarperCollins, 1995)

Pope-Hennessy, Una, *Charles Dickens* (Chatto & Windus, 1945)

Raymond, Joad (ed.), *Making the News: An Anthology of Newsbooks of Revolutionary England, 1642–1660* (Windrush Press, 1993)

Reid, Sir Wemyss, *Memoirs of Sir Wemyss Reid* (Cassell, 1905)

Riddell, Peter, *Parliament under Blair* (Politico's, 2000)

Safire, William, *Safire's New Political Dictionary* (Random House, 1993)

Schama, Simon, *A History of Britain: The British Wars 1603–1776* (BBC Worldwide, 2001)

Scotsman, The, *The Glorious Privilege* (Nelson, 1967)

Seaton, Jean (ed.), *Politics and the Media: Harlots and Prerogatives at the Turn of the Millennium* (Political Quarterly/Blackwell, 1998)

Sergeant, John, *Give Me Ten Seconds* (Pan, 2002)

Seymour-Ure, Colin, *The Political Impact of Mass Media* (Constable, 1974)

Seymour-Ure, Colin, *The Press, Politics and the Public* (Methuen, 1968)

Sidebotham, Herbert, *Pillars of the State* (Nisbet, 1921)

Silvester, Christopher, *The Pimlico Companion to Parliament* (Pimlico, 1997)

Stephen, James, *The Memoirs of James Stephen*, ed. Merle Bevington (Hogarth Press, 1954)

Stephens, Mitchell, *A History of News* (Harcourt Brace, 1997)

Thomas, George, *George Thomas, Mr Speaker* (Guild Publishing, 1985)

Times, The, *The History of the Times: 'The Thunderer' in the Making, 1785–1841* (*The Times*, 1935)

Times, The, *The History of the Times: The Twentieth Century Test, 1884–1912* (*The Times*, 1947)

Trethowan, Ian, *Split Screen* (Hamish Hamilton, 1984)

Tunstall, Jeremy, *Newspaper Power* (Oxford University Press, 1996)

Tunstall, Jeremy, *The Westminster Lobby Correspondents* (Routledge & Kegan Paul, 1970)

Walkland, S. A. (ed.), *The House of Commons in the Twentieth Century* (Oxford University Press, 1979)

Watkins, Alan, *A Short Walk Down Fleet Street* (Duckbacks, 2001)

Whale, John, *The Half-Shut Eye* (Macmillan, 1970)

Whale, John, *Journalism and Government* (Macmillan, 1972)

Wilding, Norman, and Laundy, Philip, *An Encyclopaedia of Parliament* (Cassell, 1958)

Williams, Francis, *Press, Parliament and People* (Heinemann, 1946)

Williams, Kevin, *Get Me a Murder a Day!* (Arnold, 1998)

Williams, Marcia, *Inside Number 10* (Weidenfeld & Nicolson, 1972

INDEX

Abbot, Charles 30
Abdela, Lesley 186
Aberdeen Free Post 171
Abuse of Power 202
Aitken, Jonathan 142, 153, 165, 184
Alexander, Andrew 140, 187
Alison, Willie 100
Allighan, Garry 95–97, 98, 99, 100, 159
Almon, John 7, 16, 18, 20
     memoirs 18–19
Anatomy of Power 58, 72
Ashton, Joe 148
Astley, Thomas 11, 19
Astor, Lady Nancy 66, 131
Attlee, Clement 83, 88, 93, 95, 103, 153, 171
     attitude to media 107, 110

Baines, Edward 47
Baker, Kenneth 141
Baldwin, Henry 21
Baldwin, Stanley 78
Balfour, Arthur 57, 71
Bagehot, Walter 181–2
Barber, Anthony 139
Barkley, William 67, 68, 86–7, 105, 115
Barnes, Thomas 35
Barrow, John Henry 37
Barry, Charles 5, 40,

Batsford, Brian 147
BBC (see British Broadcasting Corporation)
Beard, Tom 38
Belfast Evening Telegraph 66
Bellamy, John 27
Beloff, Nora 131
Benn, Tony 151, 159, 193
Bevins, Anthony 128, 160, 162, 163, 168, 182, 186, 187
Bevins, Reginald 160, 162
Biffen, John 5, 158, 159–160, 163
Blair, Cherie 197
Blair, Tony 189, 190, 193
     becoming Prime Minister 187–188
     monthly press conferences 196
     Queen Mother's Lying-in-state 195
Blumenfeld, Ralph 65, 68–9, 181
Boardman, Harry 171
Boothby, Sir Robert 108
Boothroyd, Betty 192
Boswell, James 7, 28
Boulton, Adam 173, 196
Bowe, Colette 161
Boyd, Francis 171
Boyer, Abel 10
Boyne, Harry 171
Bradlaugh, Charles 66
Bright, Timothy 41
British Broadcasting Corporation (BBC) 172, 186

24-hour news 174, 180
broadcasting Parliament 120, 173
competition from ITV 108, 173–4
coverage of general elections 122
first parliamentary correspondents 121
formation 120
fourteen day rule 105–108
radio coverage 80, 148–150
Brown, Gordon 176, 192
Burke, Edmund 21
Butler, David 128–9, 152, 202, 203
Byers, Stephen 186, 195

Callaghan, James 144, 145, 146
Campbell, Alastair 59, 75, 93, 128, 174, 178,
    189–190
        as press secretary 188, 189
        complaints about press 169, 190, 195,
            199–200
        director of communications and strategy
            195
Campbell, Lord 26, 41–2
Canning, George 35
Carr, Robert 147
Carr, Simon 187
Carrington, Lord 116–7
Carter, President Jimmy 145
Carvel, John 90, 100
        budget story scandal 100–104, 118, 145
Carvel, Robert 127, 132, 145
Cater, Percy 115
Cave, Edward (see also *Gentleman's Magazine*) 11,
    12, 16, 19
        print embargo 12
Cavendish, Sir Henry 26
        use of shorthand 41
Central News Agency 50, 66
Chamberlain, Neville 46, 78–79, 87
Chandler, Richard 12, 14
Channon, Paul 142, 168
Charles I 8–9
Charles, Prince of Wales 145
Christiansen, Arthur 86
Churchill, Sir Winston 87, 97, 103, 105, 171, 178,
    182
        as Chancellor of the Exchequer 68
        attitude to press 111

becoming Prime Minister 84, 87
Budget 68
maiden speech 63, 64–5
Clark, Douglas 83, 117–8
Clark, Fife 109
Clarke, Kenneth 104, 186
Clarkson, Thomas 40
Clifton-Brown, Douglas 105
Clynes, John 74
Cobbett, William 34, 69
Cobbett's Parliamentary Debates 70
Cobbett's Weekly Political Register 69
Cockerell, Michael 128, 151, 152, 168, 190–191
Cockett, Richard 79
Cocks, Sir Barnett 120, 126
Cocks, Michael 159
Cody, Marguerite 66, 85
Coe, Jim 166
Coldrick, William 105
Coleridge, Samuel Taylor 25, 29
Commons Journal 9, 59
Contemporary Review 24
Cook, Ivor 139–140
Cook, Robin 176, 195
Cooper, Charles 46, 51, 55,
Cooper, Thompson 48
Cosgrave, Patrick 145
Cosmopolitan 186
Courthope, Sir George 77
Cowley, Philip 200
Cranfield, Arthur 101, 103
Crawford, Douglas 141
Cripps, Sir Stafford 92, 171
Crosby, Brass 22–23
Crossman, Richard 122

Daily Advertiser 19
Daily Chronicle 64
Daily Express 53, 65, 68, 86, 92, 100, 105, 116,
    132
Daily Mail 53, 65, 115, 128, 132, 160, 187, 193,
    197
Daily Mirror 53, 95, 104, 188
Daily News 48, 54, 56, 60, 64, 66
Daily Sketch 74
Daily Telegraph 74, 80, 139–140, 162, 171, 180,
    190, 193

Daily Worker 108
Dalton, Hugh 100, 145–6
    Budget leak 100–102
    resignation 102
David Copperfield 39, 42
Davies, Haydn 99
Dawson, Geoffrey 80
Deans, John 173, 185
Deedes, Bill 77, 202
de Gaulle, General Charles 136
Denison, John Evelyn 58
Denning, Lord 140, 187
Derby, Lord 201
Dering, Sir Edward 9
    expulsion from House of Commons 9
Diary 27
Dickens, Charles 24
    skill as parliamentary reporter 38–9
    view of political life 39
    view of shorthand 42
Dickinson, John 145
Digby, Lord 9
Disraeli, Benjamin 48
Dobson, Frank 186, 190
Dobson, Stanley 97, 98
Downing Street press office 88
Duff Cooper, Alfred 80, 87
Dundee Advertiser 60
Dunphy, Henry 44
Dyer, John 10

Economist 140–1
Ede, Chuter 105
Eden, Anthony 108, 109
    attending lobby briefings 109–110
    resignation 128
Eden, Guy 4, 87, 94, 101, 118, 125, 127
    career 92
    co-author of lobby rules 90–91
Edinburgh Review 24
Egan, John 143
Einzig, Paul 111
Elizabeth, the Queen Mother 138, 195
Elizabeth II 138
Emery, R. G 67, 202
English Civil War 9
English Constitution 181

Erskine, David 66
Evans, Richard 157–8, 159–160, 183
Evans, Thomas 21
Evening News 102, 145
Evening Standard 96, 98, 100, 102, 133, 145, 167

Fairlie, Henry 170–1
Farquharson, George 33
Financial Times 124–5, 153, 165, 171, 183
Finnerty, Peter 35
FitzRoy, Edward 86
Foot, Michael 147, 159, 168
Foote, Samuel 15
Foster Fraser, John 46
Foreign Press Association 196, 197
Forster, John 38
Francis, Dr Philip 15
Franklin, Bob 179

Galbraith, Thomas 116
Gallery reporting (see press gallery, lobby jour-
    nalism, political journalism)
Gandhi, Mahatma 74
Gardiner, George 135
Gazetteer 19, 21, 27, 28
General Evening Post 21
General Strike 72–3
Gentleman's Magazine 11, 12
    camouflaged reports 16, 19
    reporting breach 19
    writers 16, 17
George III 3
Gilmour, Sir Ian 159
Gladstone, William 51, 62, 164, 202
Glasgow Herald 68
Good and Faithful Servant 163
Gosset, Ralph Allen 51, 58
Gow, Ian 173
Grant, James 38
Greig, Gordon 138–9, 141, 156, 157
Grocott, Bruce 149
Guardian 58, 153, 156, 161, 162, 165, 166–7, 171,
    182, 188, 190
    boycotting lobby briefings 163, 168
    investigation into Jonanthan Aitken 184
Gunn, Herbert 87, 96

Gurney, Joseph 41
Gurney, Thomas 41
Gurney, W. B. 41
Guthrie, William 17

Haines, Joe 59, 120, 143, 148, 163, 191
    as press secretary 132, 142
Haldane, Lord 67
Haley, Sir William 121
Hamilton, Neil 184
Hamilton, Willie 138
Hansard 8, 37, 109, 155, 179, 198
    as independent publication 34
    comprehensive debate record 69, 70
    relationship with press 71–2
Hansard, Thomas Curson 70
Hansard, Luke 70
Harcourt, Sir William 63, 116
Hardy, James 196
Harris, David 147, 159
Harris, Robert 163, 165
Harris, Wilson 99
Hartington, Lord 49, 55, 127
Hazlitt, William 28
Heath, Edward 133, 136, 142
Hebden Bridge Times 199
Heighway, Arthur 98, 99
Hencke, David 182–3
Henderson, Arthur 73
Henderson, William 73, 74
Hennessy, Peter 128, 151, 152, 153, 160, 162, 168,
    183, 203
Henry, Mitchell 56
Heseltine, Michael 161–2, 168
Hibbs, Jon 165
Higginbottom, Frederick 62
Hitler, Adolph 79, 90
Hogg, Douglas 159, 160
Hogg, Quintin 96, 97, 123
Hogg, Sarah 159
Hooker, John 8
Hounam, Peter 104
House of Commons
    1738 reporting ban debate 12–15
    1738 reporting ban resolution 48
    1771 debate on press conduct 5
    1986 move to ban journalists 5, 158–160

19th century fire 40,
19th century reporters reprimanded 35,
19th century sitting times 29,
accoustics in new building 40, 46
attempts to stop publications 3
censorship review 156
change of hours 194–5
debate into select committee leaks
    157–160
debates on televising Commons 122–3,
    172–4
enforcing printing ban 12, 16, 20, 22–23
excluding reporters from House 141, 158–9
first woman MP 66
Home Rule 49
inquiry into bribery allegations 95–7, 99
installation of microphones 89
Maastricht Bill 181, 185
modernisation committee 193
printers defying arrest 21–22
printing vote results 9
problems with new building 40–1
radio broadcasting debate 148–9
reaction to first political newsletters 9,
refusing entry to the gallery 30,
reporters' telephone system 125
St Stephen's Chapel 24,
standing order debate 31–33
standing order revision 49
summoning reporters to the bar 11, 21,
    105
temporary chambers during war 88
use of standing order 25, 86, 108–109
using newsletters against Charles I 9,
Vassall Inquiry 116–8
House of Lords
    accoustic problems 46, 81– 2
    confrontation with printers 23
    exclusive space for reporters 39
    installation of microphones 67
    note-taking ban 25
    printers punished under libel laws 12
    radio coverage 149
    recommendation for gallery 39–40
    televising 122, 173
    use of side galleries 47
Houses of Parliament
    1885 terrorist attack 59

fire 5, 40
  post war reconstruction 89
  war damage 5, 88
  war evacuation procedures 84
Howard, Anthony 120, 129, 130, 152, 183–4
Howard, Sir Charles 92
Hughes, David 165
Hughes, Spencer Leigh 61
Hume, Joseph 35
Hunt, John 155

Independent 128, 161, 162, 165, 166–7, 168, 182, 187, 193
Independent Television Network (ITN) 122, 181
Ingham, Bernard 75, 89, 151, 153, 168, 182, 188, 190
  as press secretary 161, 162–3, 166–167, 199
  role in Westland affair 161

Jackson, Gordon 165
Jay, Peter 145
Jenkins, Hugh 132
Jenkins, Simon 178, 179
Johnson, Frank 140
Johnson, Samuel 7
  as parliamentary reporter 15–16, 17, 18
  visit to house of Commons 18
Jones, Christopher 150
Jones, George 190
Jones, Nicholas 164
Jowitt, Sir William 74
Junor, John 105, 187

Kavanagh, Trevor 190
Kelly, Tom 195
King-Hall Newsletter 79
Kinnock, Neil 152, 154, 163, 166, 168–9, 172, 185
Kirk, Jack 74
Kisbey, R 44
Knight, Andrew 140–1, 157

Lawson, Nigel 154, 167
Leeds Mercury 47, 50

Letts, Quentin 187
Levin, Bernard 140
Lewis, Charles 48
Licensing Act 1662 9
Life of Johnson 7, 28
Liverpool Daily Post 132, 160, 171
Liverpool Echo 164
Lloyd George, David 46, 64, 171
Lloyd, Selwyn 114–5
Lloyd-Hughes, Trevor 132
Lobby briefings 75, 109–110, 135, 161
Lobby exclusivity 85
Lobby internal inquiry 163–5, 167
Lobby journalism (see also press gallery, political journalism)
  1885 entry rules 59–61
  1945 rulebook 4, 90–91
  20th century relations with government 73
  access for foreign lobby journalists 77, 92, 196
  access for provincial press 58–9
  access to ministers 76
  accused of breaking Official Secret Act 74
  admission to Commons terrace 125–6, 185
  anti-lobby newspapers 161–3, 166–7, 168
  beginnings of 58, 62,
  'Black Book' 112–4
  blacklisting MPs 78
  caricature of 164
  centenary 57–8, 151–2
  Chamberlain's pre-war statement to 78–80
  confidentiality 92, 112–113, 114
  Downing Street briefings 137
  entertaining MPs 99–100, 186
  first lobby correspondents 61
  Government liaison officer 74–75
  message board code 94
  non-attribution 76–77, 111–112, 115–6, 146
  'on the record' briefings 135, 146–7, 154, 188–9
  public questioning of lobby system 128
  status 63, 114
  Wilson's 'White Commonwealth' 132

Lobby membership 115
Lobby reforms 143–4, 154, 165–166, 167, 188, 197
Lobby secrecy 93–4,
Lobby system 72
London Chronicle 19
London Evening Post 18
London Magazine 11, 12, 16, 19
London Packet 21
Lovat, Lord 19
Lucy, Henry 171, 202
    'London letter' 55
    sketch-writing pioneer 54, 61, 64
Lyttelton, Lord 23

Maastricht Bil 181, 185
McCaffrey, Tom 144, 145–6, 147
Macaulay,Thomas Babington 24
McCullum, John Fisher 55
MacDonagh, Michael 4, 30, 31, 45, 63, 104, 164, 194, 198, 200, 203
MacDonald, Ramsay 73, 74, 78
McKie, David 179
Mackintosh, Alexander 171
Macmillan, Harold 114–5, 160, 169
Mail on Sunday 195, 197
Maitland, Donald 134–6
Major, John 181, 183
    as Prime Minister 168
    leadership crisis 174–5, 200
Manchester Evening News 171
Manchester Examiner 60
Manchester Guardian 121, 171
Mandelson, Peter 184, 191, 199
    opinion of press 1, 2, 3
    use of 'spin' 191
Manners-Sutton, Charles 35
Margach, James 58, 72, 78, 99, 202
Marr, Andrew 176
Martin, Michael 186–7
Massingham, Henry 63–5, 69, 170
Massingham, Hugh 170–1
Masterman, Charles 64
Mathias, Glyn 154
Maxwell, Robert 126
Maxwell, William 55, 57, 62
Memoirs of John Almon 7

Meredith, Sir William 25, 28
Middlesex Journal 20, 21
Mikardo, Ian 158
Miller, John 21 - 22
Ministry of Information 84, 85, 112
    employment numbers 88
Mirror of Parliament 37–38
Mittal, Lakshmi 195
Moncrieff, Chris 93, 161, 165, 169
Moore, Charles 193
Moore, Jo 195
Morgan, Piers 104
Morning Chronicle 20, 26, 27, 35, 41
    boycott on certain MPs 37
    Charles Dickens on staff 38–9
    complaints to the House 30
    influence 28
Morning Post 25, 29, 34, 36, 77, 202
Morning Star 46, 50
Morrison, Herbert 97, 99
Morrison, Peter 148
Mountfield, Robin 188–9
Murdoch, Rupert 168, 173, 179
Murphy, Arthur 15

Nally, William 95
National Association of Journalists 60
National Audit Office 183
Naughtie, James 156
Newspaper Press Fund 24
News Chronicle 74
News of the World 168
New Statesman 129, 169
Nichols, John 18
North Briton 20
North, Lord 21, 22–23
Northcliffe, Lord 68
Northcote, Sir Stafford 70

Oakley, Robin 172, 175
Oborne, Peter 169, 188
Observer 60, 131, 133, 165, 170
    breach of privilege 86
O'Connell, Daniel 35
    attack on honesty of the press 36
    coverage of speeches 36–37

O' Donnell, Gus 168
Office of Public Service 188
O' Hennessey, 'General' 44
Oliver, Richard 22–23
Onslow, Arthur 12, 20
Onslow, Colonel George 20, 21, 23, 128, 154
Orwell, George 88
Owen, David 152, 154, 163

Panorama 152
Pardoe, John 141
Partners in Parliament 127
Payne Collier, John 35
Peel, Arthur 66
Peel, Sir Robert 37
Perry, James 27–28, 179
Phipps, Captain Constantine 21
Pimlott, Ben 100, 103
Pitt, Ernest 61
Pitt, William (the Elder) 15
        speech as reported by Johnson 17
Pitt, William (the Younger) 30, 33
        speech on war with Napoleon 30
Poliltical journalism (see also press gallery, lobby
    journalism)
        1738 reporting ban 12–15, 126
        17th century press freedom 9
        18th century growth 10
        18th century printers avoiding arrest 21
        18th century reporting technique 20, 28
        1947 Budget leak scandal 100–102
        19th century conflicts with Commons
            35–37
        19th century facilities 47–8
        19th century reporters' respectability
            33–34
        19th century reporting styles 53–4
        20th century changes in journalism 69
        a 'fourth estate of the realm' 31
        acquiring legal status 50
        blame for electoral apathy 199
        boycotting MPs speeches 34–35
        camouflaged reporting 16
        class intake 43
        collective reporting 27
        Commons reporting concessions 127–8
        development of sketch writers 54–56, 71

        emergence of broadcast media 88
        entry for women reporters 65–6
        first press corp 3
        foreign newspaper reporters 65–6, 77
        forms of 4
        fourteen day rule 105–108, 182
        'great abuses' 12
        inclusions on honours lists 171–2
        initial relations with press officers 89
        modern political column 170–171
        MPs in favour of press 49, 99
        'new journalism' 53, 112
        parliamentary reporting established 23
        paying for stories 96, 97
        political bias 105, 182
        positive role acknowledged by House 31
        press freedom 14
        press responsibility 2
        printing speeches outlawed 12
        provinicial reporters 47, 50–1
        reporting select committee leaks 138,
            156–7, 159–160
        shorthand 41, 43
        'sleaze' 183–4
        'spin' 191–2
        tabloidisation 176–7
        Televising Parliament debate 120,
            147–8
        television's effect on newspaper jour-
            nalism 123–4, 150, 173, 176, 180
        the effect of the public relations officer
            78
        'tidying up' speeches 43
Poole, Oliver 169–170
Press Association 50, 55, 66, 92, 93, 161, 165, 203
Press Complaints Commission 195
press gallery (see also lobby journalism, political
    journalism)
        18th century gallery conditions 24 -25
        19th century reporting 29–30, 44–5,
            53–54
        20th century facilities 65, 124–5
        accoustic problems 40–1
        admittance to public gallery 4
        as an institution 44
        assistance in gaining seats 30–31
        collaboration between reporters 45–6
        committee room 18 45

complaints due to non-entry 30–31
expenses 38–39, 45
first women reporters 131
foundation of press gallery 70
increasing reporters' gallery space 51
note-taking ban 25, 27, 155
post-fire galleries 40
post-war accomodation 89
press gallery anniversaries 5–6,
seat allocation 50–1, 65
use of tape recorders 155–6
war censorship 85–6
Preston, Peter 162–3, 182–3
Private Eye 61
Public Advertiser 19, 26
Public Ledger 23
Pugin, Augustus 40
Pulteney, William 7, 13, 15, 16,
Punch 61
Pym, Francis 161, 163

Radcliffe, Lord 116
Radio Times 120, 121
Raikes, Robert 11, 102
Ramsbottom, Sir Peter 145–6
Ratner, Gerald 192
Rawnsley, Andrew 173
Reagan, Ronald 169
Redfern, John 87
Redwood, John 200
Reid, Wemyss 47, 50,
Reith, John 121
Renshaw, Keith 134–5
Reporters' Gallery 4, 45, 63
Restoration 9
Reuters 66
Richards, Steve 174, 175
Riddell, Peter 165, 203
Ridley, Nicholas 183
Robinson, Geoffrey 184
Robson, Norman 92
Rooker, Jeff 141
Ross, Charles 41–2, 52–3, 67, 71
Rossi, Sir Hugh 157
Royal Commission on the Press 105
Rule Britannia 176
Rusbridger, Alan 191
Russell, Lord Charles James Fox 51

Russell, Lord John 40
Russell, William 155

St James's Chronicle 19, 21
St John-Stevas, Norman 154, 155
St Stephen's Chapel 24
Salisbury, Lord 46–7
Schofield, Guy 97
Schreiber, Mark 140–1, 157
Scotsman 46, 55, 65, 68, 161, 168
select committee leaks 156–8
Sergeant, John 150
Sheridan, Richard Brinsley 31, 203
    speaking in favour of free press 32–33
Shrewsbury Chronicle 54
Shore, Peter 5, 158
shorthand 41–43
    Brachygraphy, or an Easy and
        Compendious System of Shorthand 41
Short, Edward 148
Simon, Sir John 85
Sixsmith, Martin 195
Sky News 173–4, 181
Smollet, Tobias 18
Smith, Godric 195
Smith, Tim 184
Smith, Trevor 85
Snape, Peter 187
Sopel, Jon 186
Sources Close to the Prime Minister 151–2, 153,
    168, 190
–*Spectator* 99, 140, 145, 171, 195
'spin' 191–2
Standard 61, 63
Stanley, Lord 38
standing order regarding strangers 25, 86,
    108–9
Star 100, 102
Steel, David 152, 154, 163
Stephen, James 26, 28, 34,
Stephens, Mitchell 31
Steward, George 73, 78, 88, 134
    as press liaison officer 75–76
Strauss, George 139, 141
Straw, Jack 179, 180
Sullivan, Alexander 49
Suez crisis 108, 190
Sun 145, 160, 168

Sunday Express 160, 164
Sunday Mirror 169
Sunday Telegraph 58, 117, 129
Sunday Times 129, 131, 155, 165, 168, 183, 202
    'cash for questions' affair 184
Swinton, Lord 111

Taylor, Sir Charles 105
televising Parliament 120, 122, 123–4, 147– 8,
    150, 173, 176, 180
Terry, Walter 132, 138
Thatcher, Margaret 140, 141, 152, 160, 161, 168,
    199
Thomas, George 150
Thompson, Roger 21, 22
Thompson, Teddy 121
Thorpe, Jeremy 141
Thomson Regional Newspapers 165
Tierney, George 34–35
Times, The 34, 56, 63, 67, 70, 79, 92, 114–5, 121,
    131, 147
    152, 162, 168, 172, 176, 183, 193, 200, 201
        accused of misrepresentation 35–37
        boycotting MPs speeches 36–37
        breach of privilege 48
        complaints to the house 30
        debate coverage decline 179–180
        libel case 50
        lobby correspondents 61, 160, 167
        privileges 115
        select committee leaks 156–8
        support for appeasement 80
Today 107, 175, 192
Today in Parliament 121, 203
True Sun 38
Truelove, Frederick 74
Tunstall, Jeremy 113
Turner, Charles 20
Twilight of Truth 80, 85

Uncensored British News Bulletin 86
Usher, Herbert 74
Utley, Tom 164

Vansittart, Sir Robert 79
Vassall, John 116–9

Vassell Inquiry 116–8
Votes and Proceedings 9

Walkden, Evelyn 97, 98, 99
Walker, David 128, 151, 152, 168
Walker-Smith, Sir Derek 139
Wall, Mr 19
Waller, Ian 58, 117, 129
Walpole, Horatio 17
Walpole, Sir Robert 13, 15, 16
Walter, John 50
Walters, Simon 195
Wason, Rigby 50
Watkins, Alan 170
Way, Leslie 110, 136
Weatherill, Bernard 152
Wedderburn, Alexander 15
Western Morning News 110, 136
Westminster Lobby Correspondents 113
Wheble, John 21–22
Whelan, Charlie 178, 192
White, Michael 58
Whitehall Evening Post 21
Whitelaw, William 127
Whittam Smith, Andreas 161
Wigg, George 109
Wilkes, John
        as Alderman 22
        as Lord Mayor 23
        expulsion from Commons 22
        Middlesex election 18
        support for printers 22, 23
William III 9
Williams, Francis 93, 110
Williams, Marcia 132, 142
Wilson, Charles 157, 160
Wilson, Harold 123, 133, 141, 174–5, 191, 202
        praise for lobby correspondents 130
        press paranoia 131–2
        re-election 142
Wimbledon Gazette 92
Windham, William 78
        as Secretary of War 28
        attack on press 1, 2, 3, 29, 31–32
        hypocrisy 34
Winn, Anthony 80
Winnington, Thomas 12
Women's Penny Paper 66, 186

Wood, David 115, 124, 129–130
Woodfall, Henry 26
Woodfall, William 20, 21, 26, 28, 31
    reporting technique 26–27
    set up the *Diary* 27
    unable to get in the gallery 29–30
World at One 186
World War II 78–80, 83, 94, 178

World's Press News 95, 98
Wright, Peter 166
Wright, Thompson 48
Wyndham, Sir William 14–15, 23

Yesterday in Parliament 43, 121–2, 149
Yonge, Sir William 12, 14